Lecture Notes in Artificial Intel

Edited by J. G. Carbonell and J. Siekmann

Subseries of Lecture Notes in Computer Science

Leonard Bolc   Zbigniew Michalewicz
Toyoaki Nishida (Eds.)

Intelligent Media Technology for Communicative Intelligence

Second International Workshop, IMTCI 2004
Warsaw, Poland, September 13-14, 2004
Revised Selected Papers

 Springer

Series Editors

Jaime G. Carbonell, Carnegie Mellon University, Pittsburgh, PA, USA
Jörg Siekmann, University of Saarland, Saarbrücken, Germany

Volume Editors

Leonard Bolc
Polish-Japanese Institute of Information Technology
Koszykowa 86, 02-008 Warsaw, Poland
and
Polish Academy of Science, Institute of Computer Science
Ordona 21, 01-237 Warsaw, Poland
E-mail: Leonard.Bolc@ipipan.waw.pl

Zbigniew Michalewicz
Polish-Japanese Institute of Information Technology
Koszykowa 86, 02-008 Warsaw, Poland
and
University of Adelaide, School of Computer Science
South Australia 5005, Australia
E-mail: zbyszek@cs.adelaide.edu.au

Toyoaki Nishida
Kyoto University, Graduate School of Informatics
Department of Intelligence Science and Technology
Yoshida-Honmachi, Sakyo-ku, Kyoto 606-8501, Japan
E-mail: nishida@i.kyoto-u.ac.jp

Library of Congress Control Number: 2005933039

CR Subject Classification (1998): I.2, H.5.2-3, H.3, H.4

ISSN   0302-9743
ISBN-10   3-540-29035-4 Springer Berlin Heidelberg New York
ISBN-13   978-3-540-29035-3 Springer Berlin Heidelberg New York

Springer is a part of Springer Science+Business Media

springeronline.com

© Springer-Verlag Berlin Heidelberg 2005

Typesetting: Camera-ready by author, data conversion by Scientific Publishing Services, Chennai, India
Printed on acid-free paper   SPIN: 11558637   06/3142   5 4 3 2 1 0

Preface

The 2nd Workshop on Intelligent Media Technology for Communicative Intelligence commemorating the 10th anniversary of the Polish-Japanese Institute of Information Technology in Warsaw aimed to explore the current research topics in the field of intelligent media technologies for communicative intelligence.

Communicative intelligence represents a new challenge towards building a super-intelligence on the ubiquitous global network by accumulating a huge amount of human and knowledge resources. The term "communicative intelligence" reflects the view that communication is at the very core of intelligence and its creation. Communication permits novel ideas to emerge from intimate interactions by multiple agents, ranging from collaboration to competition. The recent advance of information and communication technologies has established an information infrastructure that allows humans and artifacts to communicate with each other beyond space and time. It enables us to advance a step further to realize a communicative intelligence with many fruitful applications.

Intelligent media technologies attempt to capture and augment people's communicative activities by embedding computers into the environment to enhance interactions in an unobtrusive manner. The introduction of embodied conversational agents that might mediate conversations among people in a social context is the next step in the process. The scope of intelligent media technologies includes design and development of intelligent supports for content production, distribution, and utilization, since rich content is crucial for communication in many applications. The promising applications of intelligence media technologies include e-learning, knowledge management systems, e-democracy, and other communication-intensive subject domains.

The first workshop was held in Tokyo, Japan in August 2002, as PRICAI 2002 (7th Pacific Rim International Conference on Artificial Intelligence) WS-5: International Workshop on Intelligent Media Technology for Communicative Reality. As indicated by the title, the role of reality was emphasized at that time. We considered that communication plays the central role not only in interpreting existing objects but also in attributing information to physical objects. The physical substances in the real world make sense to us only if they are associated with a meaning in the conceptual world. Typical examples are historical objects displayed in a museum. They make sense only if their historical facts and stories are well presented to the visitor. The sense of reality comes from the way in which physical and information features of those objects interact with each other.

The first workshop consisted of three invited talks and nine presentations. The invited talks covered key dimensions of the communicative reality, including computer-mediated interaction in the real world, situated conversations, and conversational agents. The presentations addressed additional topics such as video-based interactive media, a personalized navigation system, immersive distance learning, shared understanding by ontology building, analysis of facial expression for estimating the conversation mood, embodied communication of information and atmosphere by a team of robots, conversational contents for knowledgeable conversational agents, meaning acquisition from communications, and cognitive linguistic modelling of understanding irony.

The scope of this workshop covered much wider areas than the previous one. The topics involved media technologies from areas of artificial intelligence, Web intelligence, human-computer interaction, and other intelligent and cognitive technologies that may lead to the development of individual or collective intelligence.

This volume consists of two keynote papers, six plenary papers, and 38 regular papers. The topics include the following:

1. Perceptual technologies for capturing semantic information
2. Smart environments that support communicative activities
3. Embodied conversational agents that create and mediate knowledge in a social context
4. Sociable agents that cohabit with people in the real world
5. Intelligent content production and management for communicating intellectual assets
6. Automatic media annotation generation
7. Intelligent grids built as overlays on grid technologies
8. Measurement and evaluation of communicative intelligence
9. E-learning and multimedia technologies in education
10. Applications of communicative intelligence

We hope this workshop contributed to further advancing the state of the art in intelligent media technologies.

Finally, we would like to thank the members of the Program and Organizing Committees for their hard work in making this workshop happen.

March 2005   Leonard Bolc
                                            Zbigniew Michalewicz
                                               Toyoaki Nishida

Organization

Conference Chairs

Toyoaki Nishida (Kyoto University, Japan)
Jerzy Paweł Nowacki (PJIIT, Poland)

Program Committee

Leonard Bolc (PJIIT, and IPI PAN, Poland)
Witold Kosiński (PJIIT, Poland)
Sadao Kurohashi (University of Tokyo, Japan)
Krzysztof Marasek (PJIIT, Poland)
Zbigniew Michalewicz (PJIIT, Poland, and University of Adelaide, Australia)
Michihiko Minoh (Kyoto University, Japan)
Lech Polkowski (PJIIT, Poland)
Zbigniew Raś (PJIIT, Poland, and University of North Carolina at Charlotte, USA)
Franciszek Seredyński (PJIIT, and IPI PAN, Poland)
Kazimierz Subieta (PJIIT, and IPI PAN, Poland)
Yasuyuki Sumi (Kyoto University, Japan)
Rin-ichiro Taniguchi (Kyushu University, Japan)
Wolfgang Wahlster (German Research Center for AI, Germany)

Organizing Committee

Tomasz Rutkowski
Paweł Wiemann

Table of Contents

Design Intelligent Web Applications Using Web Modelling Language (WebML)

Włodzimierz Dąbrowski, Tomasz Czwarno, and Szymon Merklejn

Polish-Japanese Institute of Information Technology,
ul. Koszykowa 86, 02-008 Warsaw, Poland
{wlodek, tomasz.czwarno, szymon.merklejn}@pjwstk.edu.pl

Abstract. This article will describe the Web Modelling Language (WebML), a notation for visually designing intelligent Web application at the conceptual level. All the concepts of WebML are specified both graphically and in the XML standard. WebML defines four orthogonal dimensions: structural model, hypertext model (splits on composition model and navigational model), presentation model and personalisation model. All models enable a high-level intelligent approach to designing and maintaining Web site.

1 Introduction

Designing and development of Web applications could be seen as an easy job. This is a good approach for small (home written) Web sites, which are based on simply static language like HTML. Nowadays there are a lot of technologies like JSP, PHP or ASP for a dynamic Web site development. Each of these technologies makes a designing process more complex. This also causes problems with later maintenance of the applications. The best solution for this complexity is to put into practice appropriate designing methodology. From early nineties, many Web designing methodologies were formed. Most of them are not adequate to nowadays. WebML is the most recent methodology, that considers all aspects of a designing process and allows a designer to involve all available technologies in an intelligent way.

2 What Is WebML

Web Modelling Language (WebML) is a conceptual language for high-level designing, which divides the whole designing process into few orthogonal dimensions. Each dimension describes a specific aspect of Web application designing by WebML concepts and semantics. WebML is an integrated set of models, that covers all aspects of a designing process. WebML is also a language for data-intensive Web sites, closely connected with database systems, which become much more popular nowadays. WebML is easy to learn and use in designing and also later in the maintaining phase in the whole software life cycle. Due to XML, WebML is a methodology independent on publishing language and database system, which makes this methodology more flexible and intelligent.

L. Bolc et al. (Eds.): IMTCI 2004, LNAI 3490, pp. 1–11, 2005.

3   XML in WebML

All information in WebML can be stored in an XML format. Each model in WebML has an XML representation and each step of the designing process ends with a proper XML document. This approach simplifies the whole designing process. The designer can start or finish his work on any step, for example: it is possible to create a proper XML document from an existing database structure and use it as input for WebML.

Due to an XML document, Web pages can by generated using XML transformation. This can by done automatically, in the end of the designing process. Also publishing language can be easily changed. Even at the end of the designing process, the designer can still choose the database system and implementation language.

4   WebML Models

The conceptual model of Web application, specified by WebML, forms five orthogonal perspectives, that cover all aspects of Web applications: structure model, composition model, navigation model, presentation model and personalisation model. Each of these perspectives considers a different aspect of a Web application, but concerns the same application domain. The structure model expresses the data content of the Web site. The composition model specifies which elements compose hypertext and make up pages. The navigation model specifies links between composition elements. The presentation model specifies the layout and graphic appearance of pages, independently of the publishing language. The personalisation model considers user or group of users requirements. Because of close connection of composition and navigation model, both of them form a hypertext model of a Web application.

4.1   Structural Model

The structural model includes the data content of the Web site. Data is modelled in terms of entities and relationships like in a database design process. It is possible to set generalisation hierarchies between entities. WebML does not specify yet any other notation to represent data model. It is up to a designer which notation (E/R model, ODMG object-oriented model, UML class diagram) will be used.

4.1.1   Entities

Entities represent an object in the real word. An individual object is an instance of entity. All the instances of an entity form the population of the entity. Entities have named properties – called attributes – with type associated. An attribute is a property common to the instances of an entity. It can be also called scalar attribute or mono-valued attribute. Some objects may have not a meaningful value for an attribute (e.g., total sale). An attribute, which has a set of values, is called multi-valued attribute and can be represented by means of an entity plus a relationship. An attribute, which has an internal structure (e.g., an address may consist of several fields), is called structured attribute and is represented by means of an entity plus relationship.

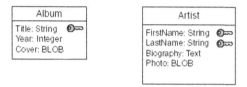

Fig. 1. Example of WebML entities

```
<ENTITY id="Album">
    <ATTRIBUTE id="Title" type="String"/>
    <ATTRIBUTE id="Year" type="Integer"/>
    <ATTRIBUTE id="Cover" type="BLOB"/>
</ENTITY>

<ENTITY id="Artist">
    <ATTRIBUTE id="FirstName" type="String"/>
    <ATTRIBUTE id="LastName" type="String"/>
    <ATTRIBUTE id="Biografy" type="Text"/>
    <ATTRIBUTE id="Photo" type="BLOB"/>
</ENTITY>
```

Code 1. Example of XML representation of a WebML entities

4.1.2 Relationships

Relationship represents semantic connections between entities. Relationship between two entities can be also called binary relationship. There are also N-ary relationships, which involve more than two entities. N-ary relationships are represented by an entity plus N binary relationships. Relationships may be given role names and cardinality constraints. The relationship role is a one of two directions under which relationship can be regarded (e.g., Figure 2 – relationship Publication may have two roles: Published_By and Publishes). For each direction of the relationship the maximum and minimum cardinality constraints can be specified (e.g., Figure 2 – for role Publishes, an Artist may produce zero or more Albums and for role Published_By, an Album has with one and only one Artist). Relationship can also has attributes that refer to pairs of entities. These attributes are represented by entity and two relationships.

Fig. 2. Example of a WebML relationship between entities

```
<ENTITY id="Album">
    <ATTRIBUTE id="Title" type="String"/>
    <ATTRIBUTE id="Year" type="Integer"/>
    <ATTRIBUTE id="Cover" type="BLOB"/>
    <RELATIONSHIP id="Published_By" to="Artist"
inverse="Publishes"
    minCard="1" maxCard="1"/>
</ENTITY>

<ENTITY id="Artist">
    <ATTRIBUTE id="FirstName" type="String"/>
    <ATTRIBUTE id="LastName" type="String"/>
    <ATTRIBUTE id="Biografy" type="Text"/>
    <ATTRIBUTE id="Photo" type="BLOB"/>
    <RELATIONSHIP id="Publishes" to="Album"
inverse="Published_By"
    minCard="0" maxCard="N"/>
</ENTITY>
```

Code 2. Example of XML representation of WebML relationship between entities

4.1.3 IS-A Hierarchy

An IS-A hierarchy represents a special connection between two entities. One of entities (sub-entity) is a special case of the other one (super-entity). The sub-entity inherits the properties of the super-entity. The IS-A hierarchies may have several levels.

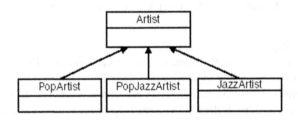

Fig. 3. Example of WebML IS-A hierarchy

```
<ENTITY id="PopArtist">
    <ISA-HIERARCHY id="isa-popartist" to="Artist"/>
</ENTITY>
```

Code 3. Example of XML representation of a WebML IS-A hierarchy

4.2 Composition Model

Composition model specifies which nodes compose the hypertext contained in the Web site. Elements can be specified as content units, i.e., the atomic information elements that can appear in the Web site, or pages, i.e., containers of content units that can be delivered to the end user. In a concrete HTML implementation of these elements, content units can form HTML files whereas pages can form HTML frames that organised such files on the screen.

4.2.1 Content Units

Content units are atomic content elements that publish information designed in the data model. Simple content unit can treat to whole population of a given entity. Population can be decreased by selection condition called selector, i.e., the specification of a set of restrictions that determine the actual population of entity to be used as the content of the unit at runtime, this is similar to "WHERE" clause in SQL language. The selector is associated with specific input and output parameters. Input parameters are used by a selector to compute a population of the current unit and output parameters compute other unit or units depending on the current unit.

In WebML there are five specified primary types of content units: data units, multi-data units, index units, scroller units and entry units.

4.2.1.1   Data Units

Data units represent a single object of a given entity.

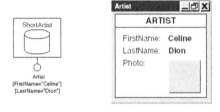

Fig. 4. Example of a WebML data unit, and rendition in HTML

```
<DATAUNIT id=''SchortArtist'' entity=''Artist''>
    <INCLUDE attribute=''FirstName'' />
    <INCLUDE attribute=''LastName'' />
    <INCLUDE attribute=''Photo'' />
</DATAUNIT>
```

Code 4. Example of XML representation of WebML data unit

4.2.1.2   Multi-data Units

A multi-data unit represents several objects of an entity together, by repeating the presentation of several data units.

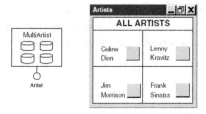

Fig. 5. Example of a WebML multi-data unit, and rendition in HTM

```
<MULTIDATAUNIT id=''MultiArtist'' entity=''Artist''>
    <DATAUNIT id=''SchortArtist'' entity=''Artist''>
        <INCLUDEALL />
    </DATAUNIT>
</MULTIDATAUNIT>
```

Code 5. Example of XML representation of WebML multi-data unit

4.2.1.3   Index Units
An index unit represents multiple objects of an entity as a list.

Fig. 6. Example of a WebML index unit, and rendition in HTML

```
<INDEXUNIT id=''AlbumIndex'' entity=''Album'' >
    <DESCRIPTION Key=''Title''>
</INDEXUNIT>
\vspace{3mm}
```

Code 6. Example of XML representation of WebML index unit

4.2.1.4   Scroller Units
A scroller unit provides commands to scroll through the objects in a set.

4.2.1.5   Entry Units
An entry unit supports form-based data entry.

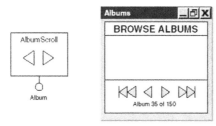

Fig. 7. Example of a WebML scroller unit, and rendition in HTM

```
<SCROLLERUNIT id=''AlbumSrcoll'' entity=''Album''
first=''yes'' last=''yes'' previous=''yes'' next=''yes'' />
```

Code 7. Example of XML representation of WebML scroller unit

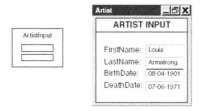

Fig. 8. Example of a WebML entry unit, and rendition in HTML

```
<ENTRYUNIT id=''ArtistInput''>
    <FIELD id=''FirstName'' type=''text''>
    <FIELD id=''LastName'' type=''text''>
    <FIELD id=''BirthDate'' type=''date''>
    <FIELD id=''DeathDate'' type=''date''>
</ENTRYUNIT>
```

Code 8. Example of XML representation of WebML entry unit

4.2.2 Pages

Pages are elements of a Web site delivered to the end user as a container of hypertext. Typical pages consist of a content unit or several content units. Pages with the same homogeneous content can be set in areas. Pages and areas can form groups called site views. Because of the separation between the structure model and the hypertext model, it is possible to define multiple views on the same data for different users or a group of users. In this context, a page can be declared as the home page of a site view, which means that page is presented by default when entering the whole site view. A page can also be declared as a landmark page, which means that a page can be reached from all the other pages of the same area as well as site views. It can be also reached as a default page, which means that a page is presented by default when entering the enclosing area.

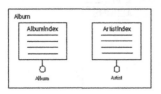 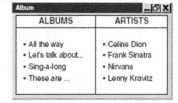

Fig. 9. Example of a WebML page, and rendition in HTM

```
<PAGE id=''Album''>
    <UNIT id=''AlbumIndex''>
    <UNIT id=''ArtistIndex''>
</PAGE>
```

Code 9. Example of XML representation of WebML page

4.3 Navigation Model

The navigation model specifies how pages and content units form a hypertext structure in terms of links. Links represent relationships between entities from the structural model. In the WebML terminology, links which are crossing boundaries of pages are called inter-page links, whereas links where source and destination are inside the same page are called intra-page links. Links are also divided into contextual and non-contextual links, contextual when a link transports some information from source to destination element, and non-contextual when a link does not transport information.

4.3.1 Inter-page Links
Inter-pages links cross boundaries of pages.

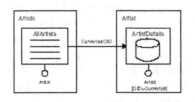  

Fig. 10. Example of a WebML inter-page, contextual link, and rendition in HTML

```
<INDEXUNIT id=''AllArtists'' entity=''Artist''>
    <DESCRIPTION key=''Name'' />
</INDEXUNIT>
<DATAUNIT id=''ArtistDetail'' entity=''Artist''>
    <INCLUDE attribute=''FirstName'' />
    <INCLUDE attribute=''LastName'' />
    <INCLUDE attribute=''Photo'' />
</DATAUNIT>
<PAGE id=''Artists''>
    <UNIT id=''AllArtists''>
    <HYPERLINK id=''inter'' to=''Artist'' />
</PAGE>
<PAGE id=''Artist''>
    <UNIT id=''ArtistDetail''>
</PAGE>
```

Code 10. Example of XML representation of WebML inter-page, contextual link

4.3.2 Intra-page Links

Intra-page links do not cross boundaries of pages.

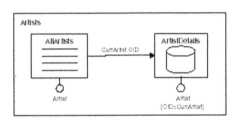

Fig. 11. Example of a WebML intra-page, contextual link, and rendition in HTML

```
<INDEXUNIT id=''AllArtists'' entity=''Artist''>
    <DESCRIPTION key=''Name'' />
    <INFOLINK id=''intra'' to=''ArtistDetails'' />
</INDEXUNIT>
<DATAUNIT id=''ArtistDetails'' entity=''Artist''>
    <INCLUDEALL />
</DATAUNIT>
<PAGE id=''Artists''>
    <UNIT id=''AllArtists''>
    <UNIT id=''ArtistDetails''>
</PAGE>
```

Code 11. Example of XML representation of intra-page, contextual link

4.4   Presentation Model

The presentation model is concerned with the actual look and feel of the designing application (pages). It is an independent graphic definition of the page content identified by the composition model. WebML pages are rendered according to a style sheet. The style sheet defines the layout of pages and content units into such a layout. A style sheet is also independent of the actual language used for page rendition. XSL style sheets take as input WebML specifications, which is coded as XML documents conforming to the WebML Document Type Definition, and gives on output page templates embodying the required mark-up code and data access queries.

There are two categories of style sheets provided by WebML: untyped style sheet (also called models) and typed style sheet. The untyped style sheet describes the page layout independently from its content, whereas the typed style sheet describes the pages, which have specific content. Presentation in WebML is a powerful option. Pages can be generated in any time and language (HTML, XHTML), also look and feel of whole system can be quickly and easily changed. This gives a designer time for decisions which language should be used.

4.5   Personalisation Model

The personalisation model describes the content or presentation style, dependent on the user or group of users with the same characteristics. WebML includes explicit notation of group and user. The personalisation model is connected with the special entities from the structure model representing user and group. Each user or group is described by means of specific properties which are modelled as special type of entities in the structure schema. Typically the user's or group's profile contains data which is a result of user's or group's actions (e.g., the most frequently visited pages in an application). Personalisation is also connected with the site views from the composition model. Each user or group (with specific characteristic) is represented by site views. There are two types of personalisation: declarative personalisation and procedural personalisation. The declarative personalisation defines content, which depends on the properties that are associated with the user or group. In declarative personalisation, system fills in the information relative to each user when computing the content of units. In the procedural personalisation content depends on user or group activity. WebML includes an XML syntax for writing business rules that compute and store user-specific information. Typical tasks performed by business rules are the assignment of users to user groups based on dynamically collected information (e.g., the purchase history in e-shop), the logging of user actions into user-specific data structures (user tracking) and more.

5   Role of WebML in Intelligent Web Applications Design

The intelligent application is an application which can control certain processes without a help of application's administrator or someone who is responsible for this application. This makes easier the whole maintaining process of this application. WebML has built in processes, assumptions and conceptions to design the application in this way. The main thing in WebML, which provides intelligent maintaining, is the personalisation model. It describes the content of pages for specific user profile or group of users. It is possible to define in this model, what user will see on his screen precisely. As mentioned above, there are two categories of personalisation. The first one, declarative personalisation, is used to define static properties for each user or group (e.g., there is a normal user which can see some part of the application and a super user which has a larger view on the application). These properties are set by the designer (or, for example, administrator of the application) and an application follows by these rules. The second type of personalisation is procedural personalisation which is used to define dynamic changes in the application (e.g., it can pop up a page with appropriate advertisement for a user). All information about user's behaviours, habits or tastes can be stored for later processing or other use.

The intelligent application is also an application where pages can be quickly modified and the publishing language or database system can be easily changed. To do this, the special software was developed called WebRatio Site Development Studio. Also all aspects mentioned earlier are fully supported by WebRatio tool. Implementation process is not supported by WebML. To generate a Web site, appropriate transformation can be done by applying XSL transformations on an XML document, which represents each modelled element on the Web site. WebRatio makes possible designing structural models, hypertext models and structure mapping onto a datasource. Due to XML, implementation can be done on independent platform like JSP or ASP.NET and the database system can be easily changedd (MySql, SQL Server, PostgreSQL and more). All of this gives a designer a powerful tool to managing and designing application. The designer just uses a WebML methodology to design an application (structure, hypertext, presentation, personalisation) in WebRatio, and application (templates) is generated by few clicks at the end of the design process. The last big advantage of WebML is that WebML (as a methodology) is more friendly for a user than some publishing or query language. This enables a designer to produce templates quicker and in any publishing language or database system without knowing them.

6   Conclusion

In this paper, we have presented Web Modelling Language (WebML) as a high-level designing language for modelling complex data-intensive Web sites. We have shown how separation between data model, composition model and navigational model influences the designing process, in terms of presentation and personalisation. We have described that presentation is independent on the data presented on the Web site. We also have described how the same information can be structured in different site views, in terms of user and group profiles and personalisation.

References

1. www.webml.org: The Web Modelling Language home site
2. Kaufmann, M.: Designing Data-Intensive Web Applications – Fig. [1–11]
3. Cerio, S., Fraternali, P., Bongio A.: Web Modelling (WebML): a modeling language for designing Web sites
4. Brombilla, M., Comai, S., Fraternali, P.: Hypertext Semantics for Web Applications Cimai, S., Fraternali, P.: A semantic model for specifying data-intensive Web applications using WebML
5. www.webratio.com: WebRatio – Site Development Studio home site

Text Understanding for Conversational Agent

Daisuke Kawahara, Ryohei Sasano, and Sadao Kurohashi

University of Tokyo, 7-3-1 Hongo Bunkyo-ku, Tokyo, 113-8656, Japan
{kawahara, sasano, kuro}@kc.t.u-tokyo.ac.jp

Abstract. This paper describes a text understanding system for conversational agents. The system resolves zero, direct and indirect anaphors in Japanese texts by integrating two sorts of linguistic resources: a hand-annotated corpus with various relations and automatically constructed case frames. The corpus has relevance tags which consist of predicate-argument relations, relations between nouns and coreferences, and is utilised for learning parameters of the system and testing it. The case frames are indispensable knowledge both for detecting zero/indirect anaphors and estimating appropriate antecedents. Our preliminary experiments showed promising results.

1   Introduction

Many contents-based conversational agents have been proposed so far (e.g. Rea [1], EgoChat [2]). In EgoChat; "knowledge card" is used as a unit of the contents; "knowledge card" is a small piece of text that is semantically coherent. To evolve such a conversational agent, it is necessary to understand the knowledge cards by structuring them automatically. This structuring enables sophisticated natural language processing technologies such as accurate question answering and automatic summarisation. Furthermore, these technologies bring natural communication between the agent and human.

The first step for structuring a knowledge card is to grasp various explicit / implicit relations in texts, such as syntactic relations, coreferences, and antecedents of indirect anaphora. Syntactic relation analysis, i.e. parsing, has achieved great success both in English and Japanese. Anaphora resolution, i.e. direct anaphora (coreference) resolution and indirect anaphora (bridging reference) resolution, in English is different from that in Japanese as shown in Table 1.

In English, direct anaphors consist mainly of pronouns and definite noun phrases, and have achieved some success by machine learning techniques based on linguistic clues, such as definiteness, number, and gender [3]. On the other hand, an indirect anaphora resolution is much more difficult, and a part of this phenomenon has been studied [4].

In Japanese, both direct and indirect anaphora resolutions are difficult. Direct anaphors are rarely expressed as pronouns, and become zero anaphors. This induces a big problem of detecting zero anaphors. To address this problem, elaborate knowledge for each verb is required. This observation applies to an indirect anaphora resolution. That is, indirect anaphors are cast as zero anaphors of nouns, and can be detected by knowledge for each noun.

L. Bolc et al. (Eds.): IMTCI 2004, LNAI 3490, pp. 12–20, 2005.

Table 1. Anaphora resolution in English and Japanese

	direct anaphora	indirect anaphora
E	ANT $\cdots$ V pronoun the NP	ANT $\cdots$ the NP
J	ANT $\cdots$ V ϕ	ANT $\cdots$ N (of ϕ)

As for such knowledge, case frames can be employed. They describe what kinds of relations (case slots) each verb/noun has and what kinds of words can fill each case slot. The case frames can be utilised to detect zero/indirect anaphors and furthermore find their appropriate antecedents. In addition, a corpus in which many relations in texts are annotated is utilised for learning parameters of the system, testing and evaluating it.

This paper proposes a text understanding system, which can resolve zero, direct and indirect anaphora in Japanese texts, based on the two kinds of resources: "Relevance-tagged corpus" and automatically constructed case frames. "Relevance-tagged corpus" is a handmade corpus with relevance tags that consist of predicate-argument relations, coreferences, and relations between nouns [5]. The case frames, which are constructed from large corpora, describe relations between words and what kinds of words each word is related to [6].

2   Relevance-Tagged Corpus

"Relevance-tagged corpus" currently consists of about 5,000 sentences of 400 Japanese newspaper articles. Its annotation has three classes of relations: predicate-argument relations, coreferences, and relations between nouns.

2.1   Predicate-Argument Relations

In Japanese, postpositions function as case markers such as *ga* (nominative), *wo* (accusative), and *ni* (dative)[1]. To annotate predicate-argument relations, we give the predicate a tag that consists of an argument word and a case-marking relation (postposition itself).

For example, in Figure 1, *Ichiro* and *shimbun* 'newspaper' modify *yonde* 'read', and are arguments of *yonde*. The relation between *shimbun* and *yonde* is *wo* (accusative), which is indicated by the postposition following *shimbun*. Accordingly, the tag "*wo:shimbun*" is given to *yonde*.

In addition, *Ichiro* modifies *yonde*, but the relation between them is hidden by a topic marker (TM) *wa*. Since this *wa* functions as nominative, "*ga:Ichiro*" is given to *yonde*.

---

[1] In the examples of this paper, we use the abbreviations of the cases: nom (nominative), acc (accusative), dat (dative).

```
(1) Ichiro-wa    shimbun-wo    yonde    suteta.
    Ichiro-nom   newspaper-acc read     throw away
                                  ↑         ↑
                               ga:Ichiro   ga:Ichiro
                               wo:shimbun  wo:shimbun
        (Ichiro read a newspaper and threw (it) away.)

(2) Shikashi  imouto-wa   sore-wo   yomi-takatta.
    but       sister-TM   it-acc    want to read
                  ↑          ↑          ↑
              no:Ichiro   =:shimbun  ga:imouto
                                     wo:sore
        (But (his) sister wanted to read it.)
```

Fig. 1. Tagging example

For *suteta* 'throw away', its nominative and accusative are zero anaphors. Since their antecedents are *Ichiro* and *shimbun*, respectively, the tags "*ga:Ichiro*" and "*wo:shimbun*" are given to *suteta*.

2.2   Relations Between Nouns

Not only predicates but also nouns have some intrinsic relations with other nouns in a text. When two nouns in a text are related to each other, a tag is given to the latter noun.

In the second sentence of Figure 1, since *imouto* 'sister' means "*Ichiro no imouto*" '*Ichiro's* sister', the tag "*no:Ichiro*" is given to *imouto*, though "*Ichiro no*" does not appear in the sentence. In this example, *imouto* requires intrinsic relations to other nouns. This is a so-called relational noun.

Not only relational nouns but also almost all nouns have some intrinsic relations: *kuruma* 'car' and *handle*, *mado* 'window' and *curtain*. We also handle these relations.

2.3   Coreferences

When two nouns refer to the same entity, these two nouns are coreferential. To mark a coreference relation, "=" is used. A tag of this relation is given to the latter noun of two coreferential nouns.

In Figure 1, *sore* 'it' refers to *shimbun* 'newspaper', and the tag "*=:shimbun*" is given to *sore*.

3   Automatic Case Frame Construction

To realise text understanding, knowledge of the world is indispensable. As to this knowledge, we exploit case frames, which describe relations between words and what kinds of words each word is related to. We construct the case frames for verbs and for nouns using the following two methods.

3.1 Verbal Case Frames

The biggest problem in the automatic construction of verbal case frames is a verb sense ambiguity. Verbs which have different meanings should have different case frames, but it is hard to disambiguate verb senses precisely. To deal with this problem, predicate-argument examples which are collected from a large corpus are distinguished by coupling a verb and its closest case component. That is, examples are not distinguished by verbs such as *naru* 'make/become' and *tsumu* 'load/accumulate', but by couples such as "*tomodachi ni naru*" 'make a friend', "*byouki ni naru*" 'become sick', "*nimotsu wo tsumu*" 'load baggage', and "*keiken wo tsumu*" 'accumulate experience'.

This process makes separate case frames which have almost the same meaning or usage. For example, "*nimotsu wo tsumu*" 'load baggage' and "*busshi wo tsumu*" 'load supply' are separate case frames. To merge these similar case frames and increase coverage of the case frame, the case frames are clustered.

To sum up, the procedure for the automatic construction of verbal case frames is as follows.

1. A large raw corpus is parsed by the Japanese parser, KNP, and reliable predicate-argument examples are extracted from the parse results.
2. The extracted examples are bundled according to the verb and its closest case component.
3. The case frames are clustered using a similarity measure function, resulting in the final case frames. The similarity is calculated using a Japanese thesaurus [7], and its maximum score is 1.0. The details of the similarity measure function are described in [6].

We constructed verbal case frames by this procedure from newspaper articles of 25 years (about 25,000,000 sentences). The result consists of 23,000 predicates, and the average number of case frames for a predicate is 14.5. In Table 2, some examples of the resulting case frames are shown.

Table 2. Verbal case frame examples

	CM	examples
youritsu (1) 'support'	ga	\<agent\>, group, party, $\cdots$
	wo	\<agent\>, candidate, applicant
	ni	\<agent\>, district, election, $\cdots$
youritsu (2) 'support'	ga	\<agent\>
	wo	\<agent\>, assemblyman, minister, $\cdots$
	ni	\<agent\>, candidate, successor, $\cdots$
$\vdots$	$\vdots$	$\vdots$

3.2 Nominal Case Frames

In the case of verbs, syntactic structures such as subject/object/PP in English or case markers such as *ga*, *wo*, *ni* in Japanese can be utilised as a strong clue to distinguish several obligatory cases and adjuncts (and adverbs), which makes it feasible to construct the case frames automatically as above.

On the other hand, in the case of nouns, obligatory cases of noun N_h appear, in most cases, in the single form of noun phrase "N_h of N_m" in English, or "N_m *no* N_h" in Japanese. This single form can express several obligatory cases, and furthermore optional cases, for example, "*rugby no coach*" (obligatory case concerning what sport), "*club no coach*" (obligatory case concerning which institution), and "*kyonen* 'last year' *no coach*" (optional case). Therefore, the key issue to construct nominal case frames is to analyse "N_h of N_m" or "N_m *no* N_h" phrases to distinguish obligatory case examples and others.

Nominal case frames are constructed from large corpora based on an accurate analysis of "N_m *no* N_h" phrases using an ordinary dictionary and a thesaurus [8]. First, syntactically unambiguous noun phrases "N_m *no* N_h" are collected from the automatic parse results used for the verbal case frames. The extracted noun phrases are analysed using two methods: dictionary-based analysis (DBA) and semantic feature-based analysis (SBA).

DBA utilises an ordinary dictionary, because it has obligatory case information of nouns in its definition sentences. For example, "*rugby no coach*" can be interpreted by the definition of *coach* ("a person who teaches the technique in some sport") as follows: the dictionary describes that the noun *coach* has an obligatory case of *sport*, and the phrase "*rugby no coach*" specifies that the *sport* is *rugby*. That is, the interpretation of the phrase can be regarded as matching *rugby* in the phrase to *some sport* in the *coach* definition.

Since diverse relations in "N_m *no* N_h" are handled by DBA, the remaining relations can be detected by SBA, that is, simple rules which check the semantic features (in the thesaurus [7]) of N_m and/or N_h. For example, a rule "N_m:ORGANIZATION, N_h:HUMAN → ⟨belonging⟩" analyzes a phrase "*team no coach*", and we can see that *team* has ⟨belonging⟩ relation to *coach*.

Table 3. Nominal case frame examples

	case slot	examples
hyoujou 'expression'	[one] [feelings]	people, partner, · · · relief, margin, · · ·
hisashi (1)	[house, window]	parking, store, hall, · · ·
hisashi (2)	[cap]	cap, helmet, · · ·
hikidashi (1)	[desk, chest]	desk, chest, dresser, · · ·
hikidashi (2)	⟨other⟩	credit, fund, saving, · · ·
coach	[sport] ⟨belonging⟩	baseball, swimming, · · · team, club, · · ·

† *hisashi* means 'eaves/visor', and *hikidashi* means 'drawer'.

We constructed nominal case frames by this procedure from newspaper articles of 25 years. The result consists of 17,000 nouns, and the average number of case frames for a noun is 1.06. Some examples of the resulting case frames are shown in Table 3. In this table, "[···]" denotes an analysis result by DBA, and "⟨···⟩" denotes an analysis result by SBA.

4   Text Understanding System

We build a Japanese text understanding system using the "Relevance-tagged corpus" and the case frames. This system simultaneously resolves various anaphora, such as zero, direct, and indirect anaphora. So far, previous researches have tackled each resolution task independently. However, these anaphora should be solved together, because various kinds of relations are related interactively.

For the anaphora resolution, the following two clues can be considered:

– Anaphors and their context have syntactic and semantic constraints to their antecedents.
– Anaphors are likely to have their antecedents in their close position.

As for the first clue, we employ the automatically constructed case frames, which provide wide-coverage and fine-grained selectional restriction.

The second clue, namely the distance tendency, has been tried to capture by previous researches. However, they used only flat distance, such as the number of words or sentences. To model the distance tendency more precisely, we classify locational relations between anaphors and their possible antecedents by considering structures in texts, such as subordinate/main clauses and embedded sentences. Using the "Relevance-tagged corpus", we calculate how likely each location has antecedents, and acquire the order of an antecedent location preference [9].

In addition to these two devices, we exploit a machine learning technique to consider various features related to the determination of an antecedent, including syntactic constraints, and make a Japanese anaphora resolution system. This system examines candidates in the order of an antecedent location preference, and selects as its antecedent the first candidate which is labelled as positive by a machine learner and satisfies the selectional restriction based on the case frames.

The outline of our algorithm is as follows.

1. Parse an input sentence using the Japanese parser, KNP.
2. Process each verb and noun in the sentence from left to right by the following steps.
   2.1. Perform the following processes for each case frame of the target verb/noun.
      i. Match a word which has syntactic relation to the target word with an appropriate case slot of the case frame. Regard case slots that have no correspondence as zero/indirect anaphors.
      ii. Estimate an antecedent of each anaphor detected.
   2.2. Select a case frame which has the highest total score, and output the analysis result for the case frame.

The rest of this section describes the steps (i) and (ii) in detail.

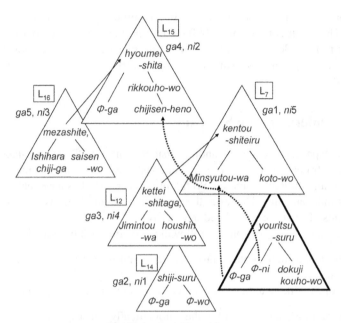

Fig. 2. Analysis Example

4.1 Matching Syntactically Related Elements with Case Slots

A word that has a syntactic relation to the target word is matched with an appropriate case slot in the case frame.

If the target word is a verb, its syntactically related words are its case components. They are matched against the case frame according to their case markers [10].

If the target word is a noun, its syntactically related words are not always case components, but are obligatory or optional elements. To distinguish them, a similarity threshold is employed. That is, a syntactically related word whose similarity to a case slot exceeds a threshold is considered as an obligatory element, namely a case component, and can be assigned to the case slot. The case component is assigned to the most similar case slot among the case slots in the case frame.

The result of the above matching process tells if the zero/indirect anaphors exist. That is, vacant case slots in the case frame, which have no correspondence with the input case components, mean zero/indirect anaphors.

For example, in the case of *youritsu* 'support' in Figure 2, *wo* case slot has a corresponding case component, but *ga* and *ni* case slots are vacant. Accordingly, two zero anaphors are identified in *ga* and *ni* case of *youritsu*.

4.2 Antecedent Estimation

We estimate antecedents of zero, direct and indirect anaphors based on examples in the case frames and the classifier. We examine possible antecedents in order of the antecedent location preference, and label them positive/negative using the binary classifier. If a possible antecedent is classified as positive and its similarity to examples in its case slot exceeds a threshold, it is determined as the antecedent. At this moment, the procedure finishes, and further candidates are not tested.

For example, *youritsu* 'support' in Figure 2 has zero anaphors in *ga* and *ni*. The ordered possible antecedents for *ga* are L_7:*Minsyutou*, L_{14}:*Jimintou*(ϕ *ga*), L_{14}:*"Ishihara chiji"*(ϕ *wo*), $\cdots$. The first candidate *Minsyutou* (similarity:0.73), which is labelled as positive by the classifier, and whose similarity to the case frame examples exceeds the threshold (0.60), is determined as the antecedent.

5   Experimental Results

We conducted two experiments to evaluate the zero anaphora resolution and the indirect anaphora resolution.

5.1   Experimental Result of Zero Anaphora Resolution

We ran an experiment on 100 newspaper articles in the "Relevance-tagged corpus" to evaluate the zero anaphora resolution. The antecedent location preference and the classifier are learned from 279 newspaper articles. Table 4 shows the experimental result.

5.2   Experimental Result of Indirect Anaphora Resolution

We ran an experiment on 10 newspaper articles in the "Relevance-tagged corpus" to evaluate the indirect anaphora resolution. The experimental setting is the same as the zero anaphora resolution. Table 5 shows the experimental result.

Table 4. Experimental result of zero anaphora resolution

precision	recall	F
515/924 (0.557)	515/1087 (0.474)	0.512

Table 5. Experimental result of indirect anaphora resolution

precision	recall	F
25/45 (0.556)	25/41 (0.610)	0.581

6   Discussion and Conclusion

We have proposed a text understanding system that resolves zero, direct, and indirect anaphora in Japanese texts. For a zero anaphora resolution, the precision and recall were 55.7% and 47.4%. For an indirect anaphora resolution, the precision and recall were 55.6% and 61.0%. Major errors are caused by a context sensitivity of obligatory cases, multiple candidates with the same semantic feature, and a word sense ambiguity in example matching. We plan to improve the accuracy by investigating resolution errors, and furthermore incorporate the text understanding system into a conversational agent.

References

1. Cassell, J., Bickmore, T., Billinghurst, M., Campbell, L., Chang, K., Vilhjálmsson, H., Yan, H.: Embodiment in conversational interfaces: Rea. In: Proceedings of the CHI99. (1999) 520–527
2. Kubota, H., Kurohashi, S., Nishida, T.: Virtualized-egos using knowledge cards. In: Proceedings of the 7th Pacific Rim International Conference on Artificial Intelligence WS-5 International Workshop on Intelligent Media Technology for Communicative Reality. (2002) 51–54
3. Yang, X., Zhou, G., Su, J., Tan, C.L.: Coreference resolution using competition learning approach. In: Proceedings of the 41st Annual Meeting of the Association for Computational Linguistics. (2003) 176–183
4. Poesio, M., Ishikawa, T., im Walde, S.S., Vieira, R.: Acquiring lexical knowledge for anaphora resolution. In: Proceedings of the 3rd International Conference on Language Resources and Evaluation. (2002) 1220–1224
5. Kawahara, D., Kurohashi, S., Hasida, K.: Construction of a Japanese relevance-tagged corpus. In: Proceedings of the 3rd International Conference on Language Resources and Evaluation. (2002) 2008–2013
6. Kawahara, D., Kurohashi, S.: Fertilization of case frame dictionary for robust Japanese case analysis. In: Proceedings of the 19th International Conference on Computational Linguistics. (2002) 425–431
7. Ikehara, S., Miyazaki, M., Shirai, S., Yokoo, A., Nakaiwa, H., Ogura, K., Hayashi, Y.O.Y., eds.: Japanese Lexicon. Iwanami Publishing (1997)
8. Kurohashi, S., Sakai, Y.: Semantic analysis of Japanese noun phrases: A new approach to dictionary-based understanding. In: Proceedings of the 37th Annual Meeting of the Association for Computational Linguistics. (1999) 481–488
9. Kawahara, D., Kurohashi, S.: Zero pronoun resolution based on automatically constructed case frames and structural preference of antecedents. In: Proceedings of the 1st International Joint Conference on Natural Language Processing. (2004)
10. Kurohashi, S., Nagao, M.: A method of case structure analysis for Japanese sentences based on examples in case frame dictionary. In: IEICE Transactions on Information and Systems. Volume E77-D No.2. (1994)

Calculus with Fuzzy Numbers

Witold Kosiński[1], Piotr Prokopowicz[2,3], and Dominik Ślęzak[4,1]

[1] Polish-Japanese Institute of Information Technology,
Research Center, ul. Koszykowa 86, 02-008 Warsaw, Poland
wkos@pjwstk.edu.pl
[2] Institute of Fundamental Technological Research, PAS (IPPT PAN),
PSWiP, ul.Świętokrzyska 21, 00-049 Warsaw, Poland
[3] University of Bydgoszcz Institute of Environmental Mechanics
and Applied Computer Science,
ul. Chodkiewicza 30, 85-064 Bydgoszcz, Poland
reiden10@wp.pl
[4] The University of Regina, Department of Computer Science,
Regina, SK, S4S 0A2 Canada
slezak@uregina.ca

Abstract. Algebra of ordered fuzzy numbers (OFN) is defined to handle with fuzzy inputs in a quantitative way, exactly in the same way as with real numbers. Additional two structures: algebraic and normed (topological) are introduced to define a general form of defuzzyfication operators. A useful implementation of a Fuzzy Calculator allows counting with the general type membership relations.

1   Introduction

Nowadays, fuzzy approach is helpful while dealing with non-exact data involving human vagueness in large multimedia databases. In real-life problems both parameters and data used in mathematical modelling are vague. The vagueness can be described by fuzzy numbers and sets.

Communication, data mining, pattern recognition, system modelling, diagnosis, image analysis, fault detection and others are fields where clustering plays an important role. However, in practice constructed clusters overlap, and some data vectors belong to several clusters with different degrees of membership. A natural way to describe this situation results in implementing the fuzzy set theory [18,21], where the membership of a vector $\mathbf{x}_k$ to the i-th cluster U_i is a value from the unit interval $[0, 1]$. Approximate reasoning, on the other hand, by means of compositional fuzzy rules of inference can help in dealing with uncertainty inherent in the processed knowledge, especially when building a fuzzy decision support system for decision making tasks in different domains of applications [25,27,28].

All those situations require well known fuzzy logic and even more – arithmetics of fuzzy numbers, in order to perform operations on fuzzy observations. Fuzzy concepts have been introduced in order to model such vague terms as observed values of some physical or economic terms, like pressure values or stock market rates, that can be inaccurate, can be noisy or can be difficult to measure with an appropriate precision

L. Bolc et al. (Eds.): IMTCI 2004, LNAI 3490, pp. 21–28, 2005.

because of technical reasons. In our daily life there are many cases where observations of objects in a population are fuzzy. In modern complex and large-scale systems it is difficult to adopt the systems using only exact data. Also in this case, it is inevitable to adopt non-exact data involving human vagueness. In this way we are approaching the concept of the fuzzy observation.

The commonly accepted theory of fuzzy numbers [1] is that set up in [4] by Dubois and Prade in 1978, who proposed a restricted class of membership functions, called (L, R)–numbers with two so-called shape functions: L and R. (L, R)–numbers can be used for the formalisation of basic vague terms. However, approximations of fuzzy functions and operations are needed if one wants to follow the Zadeh's extension principle [26,27]. It leads to some drawbacks that concern properties of fuzzy algebraic operations, as well as to unexpected and uncontrollable results of repeatedly applied operations [23,24].

Classical fuzzy numbers (sets) are convenient as far as a simple interpretation in the set-theoretical language is concerned. However, we could ask: How can we imagine fuzzy information, say X, in such a way that by adding it to the fuzzy number A the fuzzy number C will be obtained? In our previous papers (see [14] for references) we tried to answer that question in terms of so-called *improper parts* of fuzzy numbers. In this paper we consider the algebra of ordered fuzzy numbers that leads to an efficient tool in dealing with unprecise, fuzzy quantitative terms.

2 Motivations

One of the goals of our paper is to construct a revised concept of a fuzzy number, and at the same time to have the algebra of crisp (non-fuzzy) numbers inside the concept. The other goal is to preserve as much of the properties of the classical so-called *crisp reals R* as possible, in order to facilitate real world applications as e.g. in fuzzy control systems. The new concept allows for utilising the fuzzy arithmetic and constructing an algebra of fuzzy numbers. By doing this, the new model of fuzzy numbers has obtained an extra feature which was not present in the previous ones: neither in the classical Zadeh's model, nor in the more recent model of so-called convex fuzzy numbers. This feature, called in [12,14] the orientation, requires a new interpretation as well as a special care in dealing with ordered fuzzy numbers. To avoid confusion at this stage of development, let us stress that any fuzzy number, either classical (crisp or convex fuzzy) or ordered (new type), has its *opposite number* which is obtained from the given number by multiplication with minus one. For the new type of fuzzy numbers, multiplication by a negative real not only affects the support, but also the orientation swaps. It is important that to a given ordered fuzzy number two kinds of opposite elements are defined: the classical, one can say an algebraic opposite number (element) obtained by its multiplication with a negative crisp one, and the complementary number which differs from the opposite one by the orientation. Relating to an ordered fuzzy number, its opposite and complementary elements make the calculation more complex, however with new features. On the one hand a sum of an ordered fuzzy number and its algebraic opposite gives a crisp zero, like in the standard algebra of real number. On the other hand the complementary number can play the role of the opposite number in the sense of the Zadeh's model, since the sum of the both – the (ordered fuzzy) number and its complementary one – gives a fuzzy zero, non-crisp, in general.

We have to admit that the application of the new type of fuzzy numbers is restricted to such real-life situations where also the modelled circumstances provide information about orientation. In particular, in majority of existing approaches, for a fuzzy number A the difference $A - A$ gives a fuzzy zero. However, this leads to unbounded growth of the support of fuzziness if a sequence of arithmetic operations is performed between two (classical) fuzzy numbers. To overcome this unpleasant circumstance the concept of the orientation of a fuzzy number has been introduced as well as simple operations between those new objects, called here ordered fuzzy numbers, which are represented by pairs of continuous functions defined on the unit interval [0,1]. Those pairs are the counterparts of the inverses of the increasing and decreasing parts of convex fuzzy numbers. In a particular case, for the pairs (f, g) where $f, g \in C^0([0, 1])$ which satisfy: 1)$f \leq g$ and 2)f and g are invertible, with f increasing and g decreasing, one can recover the class of fuzzy numbers called convex ones [3,20]. Then as long as multiplication by negative numbers is not performed, classical fuzzy calculus is equivalent to the present operations defined for ordered fuzzy numbers (with negative orientation).

Doing the present development, we would like to refer to one of the very first representations of a fuzzy set defined on a universe X (the real axis $\boldsymbol{R}$, say) of discourse. In that representation (cf. [6,26]) a fuzzy set (read here: a fuzzy number) A is defined as a set of ordered pairs $\{(x, \mu_x); x \in X\}$, where $\mu_x \in [0, 1]$ has been called the grade (or level) of membership of x in A. At that stage, no other assumptions concerning μ_x have been made. Later on, one assumed that μ_x is (or must be) a function of x. However, originally, A was just a relation in a product space $X \times [0, 1]$.

3   Attempts

A number of attempts to introduce non-standard operations on fuzzy numbers have been made [1,3,7,22,23]. It was noticed that in order to construct operations more suitable for their algorithmisation a kind of invertibility of their membership functions is required. In [10,16,17,20] the idea of modelling fuzzy numbers by means of convex or quasi-convex functions (cf. [19]) is discussed. We continue this work by defining quasi-convex functions related to fuzzy numbers in a more general fashion (called a fuzzy observation, compare its definition in [14]) enabling modelling both dynamics of changes of fuzzy membership levels and the domain of fuzzy real itself. It is worthwhile to mention here that even starting from the most popular trapezoidal membership functions, algebraic operations can lead outside this family, towards such generalised quasi-convex functions.

That more general definition enables to cope with several drawbacks. Moreover, it seems to provide a solution for other problems, like, e.g., the problem of defining an ordering over fuzzy numbers (cf.[12]). Here we should mention that Klir was the first who in [7] has revised fuzzy arithmetic to take relevant requisite constraint (the equality constraint, exactly) into account and obtained $A - A = 0$, with crisp 0, as well as the existence of inverse fuzzy numbers for the arithmetic operations. Some partial results of similar importance were obtained by Sanchez in [22] by introducing an extended operation of a very complex structure. Our approach, however, is much simpler from mathematical point of view, since it does not use the extension principle but refers to the functional representation of fuzzy numbers in a more direct way.

In the classical approach the **extension principle** gives a formal apparatus to carry over operations (e.g. arithmetic or algebraic) from sets to fuzzy sets. Then in the case of the so-called convex fuzzy numbers (cf. [3]) the arithmetic operations are algorithmised with the help of the so-called α-sections of membership functions. It leads to the operations on intervals. The local invertibility of quasi-concave membership functions, on the other hand, enables to define operations in terms of the inverses of the corresponding monotonic parts, as was pointed out in our previous papers [11,13]. In our last paper [14] we went further and have defined a more general class of fuzzy number, called **ordered fuzzy number**, just as a pair of continuous functions defined on the interval [0, 1]. Those pairs are counterparts of the mentioned inverses.

4   Ordered Fuzzy Numbers

Here the concept of membership functions [1] is weakened by requiring a mere *membership relation* and a fuzzy number is identified with an ordered pair of continuous real functions defined on the interval [0, 1].

Definition 1. *By an ordered fuzzy number A we mean an ordered pair $A = (f, g)$ of continuous functions $f, g : [0, 1] \to \mathbf{R}$.*

We call the corresponding elements: f – the **up-part** and g – the **down-part** of the fuzzy number A. The continuity of both parts implies their images are bounded intervals, say

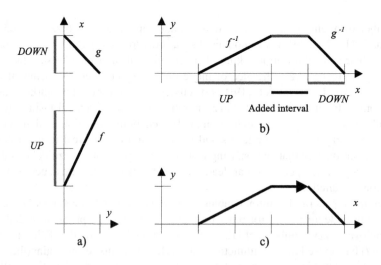

Fig. 1. a) Ordered fuzzy number, b) Ordered fuzzy number presented as fuzzy number in classical meaning, c) Simplified mark denotes the order of inverted functions

UP and $DOWN$, respectively (Fig. 1a). Let us use symbols to mark boundaries for $UP = (l_A, 1_A^+)$ and for $DOWN = (1_A^-, p_A)$.

In general, functions f, g need not be invertible, only continuity is required; they give the real variable $x \in \mathbf{R}$ in terms of $y \in [0, 1]$, if one refers to the classical membership function denotation. If we add a function of x on the interval $[1_A^+, 1_A^-]$ with constant value equal to 1, we may define a kind of membership function (relation) of a fuzzy set. When $f \leq g$ are both invertible, f is increasing, and g is decreasing, we get a mathematical object which presents a convex fuzzy number in the classical sense [7,23].

We can appoint an extra feature, named an **orientation** (marked by an arrow in Fig. 1c), to underline that we are dealing with an ordered pair of functions.

Definition 2. *Let* $A = (f_A, g_A), B = (f_B, g_B)$ *and* $C = (f_C, g_C)$ *be mathematical objects called ordered fuzzy numbers. The sum* $C = A + B$, *subtraction* $C = A - B$, *product* $C = A \cdot B$, *and division* $C = A/B$ *are defined by formula*

$$f_C(y) = f_A(y) \star f_B(y) \qquad \wedge \qquad g_C(y) = g_A(y) \star g_B(y) \tag{1}$$

where "$\star$" *works for* "$+$", "$-$", "$\cdot$", *and* "$/$", *respectively, and where* A/B *is defined, iff zero does not belong to intervals* UP *and* $DOWN$ *of* B.

Subtraction of B is the same as addition of the opposite of B, i.e. the number $(-1) \cdot B$. If for $A = (f, g)$ we define its **complement** $\bar{A} = (-g, -f)$ (please note that $\bar{A} \neq (-1) \cdot A$), then the sum $A + \bar{A}$ gives a fuzzy zero $0 = (f - g, -(f - g))$ in the sense of the classical fuzzy number calculus.

Definition 3. *Let* $A = (f_A, g_A), B = (f_B, g_B)$ *and* $C = (f_C, g_C)$ *be mathematical objects called ordered fuzzy numbers. The maximum* $C = \max(A, B) = A \vee B$ *and the minimum* $C = \min(A, B) = A \wedge B$ *are defined by formula*

$$f_C(y) = func\{f_A(y), f_B(y)\} \qquad \wedge \qquad g_C(y) = func\{g_A(y), g_B(y)\} \tag{2}$$

where "$func$" *works for* "max" *and* "min", *respectively.*

Many operations can be defined in this way, suitable for the pairs of functions. The **Fuzzy Calculator** has been already created as a calculation tool by our co-worker Mr. Roman Koleśnik [9]. It lets an easy future use of all mathematical objects described as ordered fuzzy numbers.

5   Further Extensions

Banach Algebra. The pointwise multiplication by a scalar (crisp) number, together with the operation addition lead to a *linear structure* $\mathcal{R}$ the set of all OFN's, which is isomorphic to the linear space of real 2D vector-valued functions defined on the unit interval $I = [0, 1]$. Further, one can introduce the norm over $\mathcal{R}$ as follows:

$$||x|| = \max(\sup_{s \in I} |x_{up}(s)|, \sup_{s \in I} |x_{down}(s)|) \tag{3}$$

Hence $\mathcal{R}$ can be identified with $C([0,1]) \times C([0,1])$. Finally, $\mathcal{R}$ is a Banach algebra with the unity $(1^{\dagger}, 1^{\dagger})$– a pair of constant functions $1^{\dagger}(y) = 1$, for $y \in [0,1]$. Previously, a Banach structure of an extension of convex fuzzy numbers was introduced by Goetschel and Voxman [5]. However, they were only interested in the linear structure of this extension.

Order Relation and Ideals. On the space $\mathcal{R}$ we can introduce a pre–order [15] by defining a function W with the help of the relation

$$W(A) = (x_{up} + x_{down}), \qquad (4)$$

its value $W(A)$ is a variation of the number $A = (x_{up}, x_{down})$. Then we say that the ordered fuzzy number A is not smaller than the number B, and write $A \succ B$, if

$$W(A) \geq W(B) \Leftrightarrow W(A - B) \geq 0 \qquad (5)$$

i.e. when the function $W(A - B)$ is non–negative. We say that the number C is non-negative if its variation is not smaller than zero, i.e. when $W(C) \geq 0$. Notice that there are ordered fuzzy numbers that are not comparable with zero. We say that a number D is around zero if its variation is the constant function equal to zero, i.e. $W(D) = 0^{\dagger}$. Thanks to this relation in the Banach algebra $\mathcal{R}$ we may define two ideals: the left and the right ones, which are non-trivial and possess proper divisors of zero [15].

Defuzzyfication. This is the main operation in fuzzy inference systems and fuzzy controllers [1,17,25]. The problem arises what can be done for the generalisation of classical fuzzy numbers onto ordered fuzzy numbers? In the case of the product space $\mathcal{R}$, according to the Banach-Kakutami-Riesz representation theorem, each bounded linear functional ϕ is given by a sum of two bounded, linear functionals defined on the factor space $C([0,1])$, i.e.

$$\phi(x_{up}, x_{down}) = \int_0^1 x_{up}(s)\mu_1(ds) + \int_0^1 x_{down}(s)\mu_2(ds) \qquad (6)$$

where the pair of continuous functions $(x_{up}, x_{down}) \in \mathcal{R}$ represents an ordered fuzzy number, and μ_1, μ_2 are two Radon measures on $[0,1]$.

From this formula an infinite number of defuzzyfication methods can be defined. In particular, the standard procedure given in terms of the area under membership function can be generalised. It is realised by the pair of linear combinations of the Lebesgue measure of $[0,1]$. Moreover, a number of non-linear defuzzyfication operators can be defined as compositions of multivariant nonlinear functions defined on the Cartesian products of $\boldsymbol{R}$ and linear continuous functionals on the Banach space $\mathcal{R}$ [15].

It is worthwhile to mention that some further generalisations of ordered fuzzy numbers to ordered fuzzy sets (defined on a different universe than reals $\boldsymbol{R}$) can be introduced (cf. [15]). Moreover, one can think about weakening of the continuity assumption made in our fundamental definition of ordered fuzzy numbers and to consider pairs of real valued functions of the interval $[0,1]$ that are of bounded variation. Then all algebraic properties of new objects will be preserved with a small change of the norm. However, it will the subject of the next publication.

Acknowledgement. The research work on the paper was partially done in the framework of the KBN Project (State Committee for Scientific Research) No. 4 T11C 038 25. The third author was partially supported by the research grant of the Natural Sciences and Engineering Research Council of Canada.

References

1. Czogała, E., Pedrycz, W.: *Elements and Methods of Fuzzy Set Theory* (in Polish), PWN, Warszawa, Poland (1985)
2. Czogała E., Kowalczyk R.: Towards an application of a fuzzy decision support system in cheesemaking process control. In: *Zbiory rozmyte i ich zastosowania – Fuzzy Sets and their Applications*, J. Chojcan, J. Łęski (eds), WPŚ, Gliwice, Poland (2001) pp. 421–430
3. Drewniak, J.: Fuzzy numbers (in Polish), in: *Zbiory rozmyte i ich zastosowania – Fuzzy Sets and their Applications* , J. Chojcan, J. Łęski (eds), WPŚ, Gliwice, Poland (2001) pp. 103–129
4. Dubois, D., Prade, H.: Operations on fuzzy numbers, *Int. J. System Science*, **9** (1978) 576–578.
5. Goetschel, R. Jr., Voxman, W.: (1986), Elementary fuzzy calculus, *Fuzzy Sets and Systems*, **18**, 31–43
6. Kacprzyk, J.: *Fuzzy Sets in System Analysis* (in Polish) PWN, Warszawa, Poland (1986)
7. Klir, G.J.: Fuzzy arithmetic with requisite constraints, *Fuzzy Sets and Systems*, **91** (1997) 165–175
8. Kosiński, W.: On defuzzyfication of ordered fuzzy numbers, in: *ICAISC 2004, 7th Int. Conference, Zakopane, Poland, June 2004*, L. Rutkowski, Jörg Siekmann, R. Tadeusiewicz, Lofti A. Zadeh (Eds.) LNAI, vol. 3070, pp. 326–331, Springer-Verlag, Berlin, Heidelberg, 2004
9. Kosiński, W., Koleśnik, R., Prokopowicz, P., Frischmuth, K.: On algebra of ordered fuzzy numbers, in: *Soft Computing – Foundations and Theoretical Aspects*, K. T. Atanassov, O. Hryniewicz, J. Kacprzyk (eds.) Akademicka Oficyna Wydawnicza EXIT, Warszawa 2004, pp. 291–302
10. Kosiński, W., Piechór, K., Prokopowicz, P., Tyburek, K.: On algorithmic approach to operations on fuzzy numbers, in: *Methods of Artificial Intelligence in Mechanics and Mechanical Engineering*, T. Burczyński, W. Cholewa (eds.), PACM, Gliwice, Poland (2001) 95–98
11. Kosiński, W., Prokopowicz, P., Ślęzak D.: Fuzzy numbers with algebraic operations: algorithmic approach, in: *Intelligent Information Systems 2002*, M. Kłopotek, S.T. Wierzchoń, M. Michalewicz(eds.) Proc.IIS'2002, Sopot, June 3-6, 2002, Poland, Physica Verlag, 2002, pp. 311–320
12. Kosiński, W., Prokopowicz, P., Ślęzak, D.: Drawback of fuzzy arthmetics - new intutions and propositions, in: *Proc. Methods of Aritificial Intelligence*, T. Burczyński, W. Cholewa, W. Moczulski(eds.), PACM,Gliwice, Poland (2002), pp. 231–237
13. Kosiński, W., Prokopowicz, P., Ślęzak D.: On algebraic operations on fuzzy numbers, in *Intelligent Information Processing and Web Mining*, Proc. of the International IIS: IIPWM'03 Conference held in Zakopane, Poland, June 2-5,2003, M. Kłopotek, S.T. Wierzchoń, K. Trojanowski(eds.), Physica Verlag, 2003, pp. 353–362
14. Kosiński, W., Prokopowicz, P., Ślęzak D.: Ordered fuzzy numbers, *Bulletin of the Polish Academy of Sciences, Ser. Sci. Math.*, **51** (3), (2003), 327–339
15. Kosiński, W., Prokopowicz, P.: Algebra of fuzzy numbers (in Polish), *Matematyka Stosowana. Matematyka dla Społeczeństwa*, **5 (46)**(2004), 37–63
16. Kosiński, W., Słysz, P.: Fuzzy reals and their quotient space with algebraic operations, *Bull. Pol. Acad. Sci., Sér. Techn. Scien.*, **41** (30) (1993), 285-295

17. Kosiński, W., Weigl, M .: General mapping approximation problems solving by neural networks and fuzzy inference systems, *Systems Analysis Modelling Simulation*, **30** (1), (1998), 11–28

18. Łęski, J.: Ordered weighted generalized conditional possibilistic clustering, in: *Zbiory rozmyte i ich zastosowania – Fuzzy Sets and their Applications, Prace dedykowane Profesorowi Ernestowi Czogale*, J. Chojcan, J. Łęski (eds.), WPŚ, Gliwice, Poland (2001), pp. 469–479

19. Martos B.: *Nonlinear Programming – Theory and methods*, PWN, Warszawa, Poland (1983) (Polish translation of the English original published by Akadémiai Kiadó, Budapest, 1975)

20. Nguyen, H.T.: A note on the extension principle for fuzzy sets, *J. Math. Anal. Appl.* **64**, (1978), 369–380

21. Pedrycz, W.: Conditional fuzzy clustering in the design of radial basic function neural networks, *IEEE Trans. Neural Networks* **9** 4, (1998) 601–612

22. Sanchez, E.: (1984), Solutions of fuzzy equations with extended operations, *Fuzzy Sets and Systems*, **12**, 237–248

23. Wagenknecht, M.: (2001), On the approximate treatment of fuzzy arithmetics by inclusion, linear regression and information content estimation, in: *Zbiory rozmyte i ich zastosowania – Fuzzy sets and their applications*, J. Chojcan, J. Łęski (eds.), Wydawnictwo Politechniki Śląskiej, Gliwice, 291–310

24. Wagenknecht, M., Hampel, R., Schneider, V.: Computational aspects of fuzzy arithmetic based on Archimedean t-norms, *Fuzzy Sets and Systems*, **123/1** (2001) 49–62

25. Yager, R.R., Filev, D.P.: *Essentials of Fuzzy Modeling and Control*, John Wiley & Sons, Inc., 1994

26. Zadeh, L.A.: Fuzzy sets, *Information and Control*, **8** (1965) 338–353

27. Zadeh, L.A.: The concept of a linguistic variable and its application to approximate reasoning, Part I, *Information Sciences*, **8** (1975) 199–249

28. Zadeh, L.A.: The role of fuzzy logic in the management of uncertainty in expert systems, *Fuzzy Sets and Systems*, **11** (1983) 199–227.

Intelligent Data Integration Middleware Based on Updateable Views

Hanna Kozankiewicz[1], Krzysztof Stencel[2], and Kazimierz Subieta[1,3]

[1] Institute of Computer Sciences of the Polish Academy of Sciences, Warsaw, Poland
{hanka, subieta}@ipipan.waw.pl
[2] Institute of Informatics Warsaw University, Warsaw, Poland
stencel@mimuw.edu.pl
[3] Polish-Japanese Institute of Information Technology,
ul. Koszykowa 86, 02-008 Warsaw, Poland

Abstract. We present a new approach to the grid technology which is based on updateable views. Views are used in two ways: (1) as wrappers of local servers which adopt local schemata to the federated database requirements; (2) as a facility for intelligent data integration and transformation into a canonical form according to the federated database schema. Views deliver virtual updatable objects to global clients. Objects can be associated with methods which present the procedural part of remote services, like e.g., in Web Services. The fundamental quality of the approach is transparency of servers: the user perceives the distributed data/service environment as an integrated virtual whole. Such a quality is achieved by applications based on CORBA. We attempt to achieve a higher level of transparency by providing means for integrating horizontal and vertical fragmentations of data and by taking into account various forms of data redundancy. The approach is based on a very simple and universal architecture and on the stack-based approach (SBA) to object-oriented query languages.

1 Introduction

The grid technology provides a new information processing culture which integrates many local services into a big virtual service, summing all the resources belonging to particular services. The grid user is interested in services rather than in service providers thus local service providers should be transparent for applications. Such transparency has to be supported by many technical solutions concerning the network infrastructure and distributed data/service environment.

In this paper we focus on data-intensive applications where distribution of bulk data implies distributed and parallel computation. From this point of view, the grid technology can be perceived as continuation of federated databases, the topic which has been developed for many years in the database domain. It worked out many concepts which are close to the current grid research, such as various forms of transparency, heterogeneity, canonical data models, distributed transactions, metamodels, etc.

The key issue behind such integration is *transparency*, which means abstraction from secondary features of distributed resources. There are many forms of transparency, in particular location, access, concurrency, implementation, scaling, fragmentation,

L. Bolc et al. (Eds.): IMTCI 2004, LNAI 3490, pp. 29–39, 2005.

replication, indexing and failure transparency. Due to transparency (implemented on the middleware level) some complex technical details of the distributed data/service environment need not to be taken into account in the application code. Thus transparency much amplifies programmers' productivity and greatly supports flexibility and maintainability of software products.

In this paper we present the architecture of an intelligent middleware which allows integrating data and services stored at remote sites. Similarly to CORBA in our mechanism we assume autonomy of local data/service providers. Autonomy means that to a big extent service providers do not need to change their current information systems in order to be connected to the grid. Data and services of a particular server are made visible for global applications through a *wrapper* which virtually maps the data/services to some assumed *canonical object model*. Then, all contributing services are integrated into the virtual whole by means of a *updateable views*. They create a virtual object/service store available for global applications. Integration is based on some protocol which makes transparent data transport issues, server locations, object and collection fragmentations, redundancies, replications, etc. An important element of our grid architecture can be a resource registry – a database which keeps information on location of data and services. The registry is a counterpart of UDDI or CORBA Trading Service which enables businesses to discover each other on the Web. To some extent it is also our approach to capabilities that recently referred to in the Web context as Semantic Web.

The novelty of our approach to the grid technology is that we propose to use updateable object-oriented views with full computational power. Such views (defined in a very high-level query language) much facilitate the development of intelligent mappings between heterogeneous data/service ontologies. The approach allows the designers to reduce the time required for development and maintenance of database federations. Views are defined in the query language SBQL which is integrated with imperative constructs (e.g. updating) and abstractions (functions, methods, procedures). While the idea of using views for integration of distributed/federated databases is not new (see e.g. [1, 8, 13]), to the best of our knowledge implementation of this feature is still a challenge because of the updateability of virtual views and the practical universality of view definitions. In our recent research [3, 4, 6] we have developed and implemented object-oriented virtual views which have full algorithmic power and are updateable with no anomalies and limitations. Our views support full transparency of virtual objects, i.e. the programmer is unable to distinguish stored and virtual objects by any programming option. Due to this feature views can be considered as a general facility for integrating distributed and heterogeneous resources, including methods acting on virtual objects. The advantage of our approach is that it offers a very simple architecture which is much more flexible and universal than the currently known integration technologies for distributed heterogeneous data/service environments.

The rest of this paper is structured as follows. The next section sketches the main ideas of the Stack-Based Approach. Section 3 introduces a mechanism of updateable views which is the basis of our middleware. In Section 4 we present the architecture of intelligent middleware. In Section 5 we show an example which illustrates how data integration is described and performed within our approach. Section 6 introduces resource registry where the information on the location of data and services are kept. In Section 7 we presented an example of the registry usage. Section 8 concludes.

2   Stack-Based Approach

Our grid mechanism is based on the Stack-Based Approach (*SBA*) to query languages [7, 9]. *SBA* treats a query language as a kind of a programming language. Therefore, queries are evaluated using mechanisms which are common in programming languages. The approach is based on the *naming-scoping-binding* principle which means that each name in the query is bound to the proper run-time entity depending on the scope for the name. The mechanism of name binding and scopes are managed by means of environment stack (*ENVS*). The stack consists of sections and each of these sections describes a different environment e.g., environment of the databases, or of the user session. *ENVS'* sections consist of entities called *binders* whose role is to relate a name with a run-time entity (object, procedure, view, etc). Binding of the name n means that the query interpreter looks through the consecutive sections of the *ENVS* to find the closest (to *ENVS* top) binder with name n. The result of binding is a proper run-time entity (an object identifier, a physical memory address, etc.) *SBA* defines an abstract formal framework that is known as the Stack-Based Query Language (*SBQL*). In *SBQL* queries can be defined in the following way:

(a) a literal or a name (of the variable, procedure, view, etc) is an atomic query
(b) more complex queries can be built form the simpler ones using unary operators (like *not, factorial, sin*) and binary operators (like **where**, *max*, +, ∀).

In *SBQL* all operators are orthogonal (with exception of typing constraints). In this way in *SBQL* can be assembled complex queries. Example *SBQL* queries are: *1, 2+2, Book, Book* **where** *author* = "Lem", *Book.(title, author)*. *SBQL* also supports procedures and functional procedures with no restrictions on their computational complexity. Procedures can be defined with or without parameters, can have local environment, can call other procedures, and can have side-effects. Procedures are key elements of the *SBQL* view mechanism.

3   Updateable Views in SBA

A view is a mapping of stored data into virtual ones. In the classical approach (SQL) a view is a function, similar to programming languages' functions. View updating means that a function result is treated as an l-value in updating statements. Such an approach, however, appeared to be inconsistent due to problems with finding unequivocal mapping of updates on virtual data into updates on stored data. In our approach to view updates [3, 4] a view definer can extend a view definition by the information on update intents. The information allows the programmer to eliminate ambiguities connected with multiple ways of performing a view update and the risk of warping user intention, which is the well-known problem related to view updates [3]. In our approach a view definition consists of two main parts:

(1) A mapping between stored and virtual objects. This part of the view definition has a form of a functional procedure that returns entities called *seeds*. They are used as parameters for the re-defining procedures. This part of the view definition is identified by the clause *virtual objects*.

(2) Re-definitions of generic operations that can be performed on virtual objects. We have identified four such operations on virtual objects, i.e., *dereference* returning the value of a given virtual object, *insertion* of an object into a given virtual object, *deletion* of a given virtual object, and *update* the value of a given virtual object. The view definer has freedom to decide which of them and how these operations should be re-defined. (If an operation is not defined for virtual objects, it is forbidden). Description of these operations also has a form of functional procedures with arbitrary complexity. To distinguish operations we use fixed names *on_retrieve*, *on_insert*, *on_delete*, *on_update*.

View definitions can contain other elements such as definition of subviews, internal state variables, etc.

Below we present an example of a view definition. The view contains information on books that are categorised as books on databases (i.e. in the list of categories they have, among others, a keyword "database"). The view should define the following operations: the dereference that returns the title of a given book, the protected operation of deletion, and the protected operation of update that changes title of the book to the new value. The view definition can look as follows:

---

create view *DatabaseBookDef* {

    /* definition of the mapping between stored and virtual objects */

    virtual objects *DatabaseBook* {
        return (*Book* **where** *category* **contains** "database") **as** *b*;}

    /* redefinition of operations for virtual objects */

    on_retrieve do { **return** *b.title*; }

    on_update *new_titile* **do** { **if** *hasUpdatePermission*() **then** *b.title* := *new_title*; }

    on_delete do { **if** *hasDeletePermission*() **then delete** *b*;}

  /* further elements of the view definition */

}

Note, that the operation *on_insert* is not defined thus it is not permitted. We can call this view in the following query:

(*DatabaseBook* **as** *db* **where** *db* = "An Introduction to Databases")
:= "An Introduction to Database Systems"

In this invocation there is an implicit call of *on_retrieve* when the interpreter performs dereference of *db* before comparison "=", and *on_update* when it performs ":=". The example illustrates the most important feature of our view mechanism i.e. transparency. The users operate on virtual objects in the same manner as they operate on stored objects and in fact, they do not have to be aware that a given object does not really exist and is only generated by the view.

View Update Process. A query interpreter must distinguish updates of virtual data and updates of stored data. Thus we have introduced the notion of a virtual identifier. It is a counterpart of an identifier of a stored object. A virtual identifier, besides information on the seed of a virtual object, contains information on the definition of view that has generated the given virtual object.

When the user performs an update operation on a virtual object, a query interpreter detects that it deals with a virtual object due to its virtual identifier. Thus, instead of the generic update operation the interpreter calls the corresponding procedure defined within the view definition. The interpreter knows which operation is to be called due to view definition identifier included into the virtual identifier.

4   Architecture of the Intelligent Middleware

In this section we present the architecture of our intelligent middleware. The heart of our approach is *the global virtual object and service store* (shortly: *global virtual store*) [2, 5]. The store keeps information about relationships between virtual objects/services and local servers. The store is defined through the query language *SBQL* and updateable views defined in *SBQL*.

On the top of the architecture we have *global clients*, i.e. applications that send requests to the global virtual store. Global clients use *global schema* – a collection of definitions of data/services provided by the global virtual store. The global schema is agreed upon by a consortium agreement, by a standard or by a law that establishes business and technical requirements for the grid, and rights and limitations of the grid participants.

The grid offers data/services supplied by *local servers*. Each of these local servers shares data/services according to its *local schema*. The syntax and semantics of these schemata as well as the business features of the data and services can be very distinct at each local server. The schemata can be written in, e.g. OMG IDL, WSDL and ODL and they are invisible to the grid users.

The first step of integration of a local server into the grid is done by the administrators of local servers who define the *contributory schemata*. Such schema is the description of the data and services contributed by the local server to the grid. The local servers' administrators also define *contributory views* that constitute the mapping of the local data/services to the canonical data/service model assumed by the grid. The second step of the integration of local servers into the grid is the creation of *global views*. These views are stored inside the global virtual store. Their interface is defined by the global schema. They map the data and services provided by the local servers to the data and services available to the global clients.

The global views are defined by the *grid designer*, which is a person, a team or software that generates global views upon the contributory schemata, the global schema and the integration schema. The *integration schema* contains additional information how particular data and services of local servers contribute to the global canonical model of the grid. Note that the integration schema does not duplicate the definitions from the contributory schemata. It holds only the items that cannot be included in the contributory schemata, e.g. the way to integrate pieces of a fragmented object the relationships among local servers that they are not aware of. The integration schema is used during the creation of views of the global virtual store.

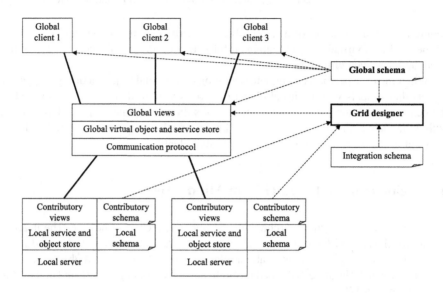

Fig. 1. Architecture of the GRID illustrating creation of the view definition

Local servers and our middleware communicate using the *communication proto-col* – a collection of routines which can be used in the definition of global views. These routines not only allow the grid developer to determine operations on objects stored at local servers (like update, delete), but also contain some routines that allow the developer to check the state (up or down) of a local server, access time to a local server and other dynamic features of the distributed resources.

The architecture of our middleware is presented in the Fig. 1. Solid lines represent run-time relationships (queries, requests and answers). Global clients request services of the global virtual store. The global virtual store requests services of the local servers. These are the only run-time relationships. The association with the grid designer is not run-time, but it is in force only during creation (definition) of global views. Dashed arrows stand for the definition relationships, i.e. associations that are employed during creation of software (development and compilation) and the global views. The programmers of global applications (global clients) use the global schema. The global views conform to the global schema. The grid designer uses the contributory schemata, the global schema and the integration schema to develop global virtual object and service store.

A key concept of our architecture is that users of the grid see data and services as if they were stored in the single place. The global clients can query the virtual store as well as update it. We underline that such a grid would be much more difficult to develop if we would not have updateable views. In SBA views are just complex objects, thus they can contain methods and procedures as well as the local variables that store the state of these views. Therefore, our views can offer at least the same robustness as CORBA objects or Web Services, due to the fact that the expressive power of SBQL and its views is the power of a universal programming language.

5   Data Integration Example

Assume a database that contains *Book* objects with attributes *ISBN*, *title*, *author* and *price*. Below, we present an example of integration of horizontally fragmented data with a replication. Assume there are three local servers located in Cracow, Gdansk, and Warsaw (we call these servers by their locations). Each server keeps data of the books. All contributory schemata are the same. In the considered case the integration schema contains the following information:

- The local servers in Cracow and Warsaw contain the same data.
- Data should be retrieved from a replica with shorter access time.
- Data in Cracow cannot be modified.
- Data in Warsaw can be modified, and the changes are immediately and automatically reflected in Cracow.
- Each book is uniquely identified by *ISBN*.
- Updating from a global application may change only the *title* of a book.

The global database is the virtual union of the databases in Warsaw and Gdansk or (alternatively) in Cracow and Gdansk. The access timeout for users is 300 seconds. The definition of the global view might look as shown below:

```
create view MyBookDef {
    virtual objects MyBook {
        int accessTimeout := 300;
        int accessTimeCracow := accessTimeout;
        int accessTimeWarsaw := accessTimeout;

        if alive(Cracow) then accessTimeCracow := checkAccessTime(Cracow);
        if alive( Warsaw ) then accessTimeWarsaw := checkAccessTime(Warsaw);
        if min(accessTimeCracow, accessTimeWarsaw) ≥ accessTimeout then {
                                    throw exception(accessTooSlow); return ∅; }
        return (Gdansk.Book ∪
                    if accessTimeCracow < accessTimeWarsaw then Cracow.Book
                    else Warsaw.Book) as b /* returning seeds */
    }
    on_retrieve do {
        return b.(deref(title) as title, deref(author) as author,
                    deref(price) as price, deref(ISBN) as ISBN ) }
    on_delete do {
        delete ( if server(b) = Cracow then
                    (Warsaw.Book where ISBN = b.ISBN) else b) }
    on_update newBook do {
        ( if server(b) = Cracow then (Warsaw.Book where ISBN = b.ISBN)
                    else b).title := newBook.title; }
    .../* further elements of the view definition */
}
```

Note that the view refers to objects from a particular server using the name of its location (e.g. *Warsaw . Book*). The view delegates the updates to appropriate servers. The view definer can use implicitly several routines of the communication protocol, for instance, the navigation ("**.**"), **insert**, **delete**, update ("**:=**"). These remote operations are called as if they were local. There are also auxiliary routines of the communication protocol. In the example their calls are underlined. Functions *alive* and *checkAccessTime* are used to determine, which of the two local servers (Warsaw or Cracow) should be used when constructing the virtual objects. Function *server* determines which server is the origin for the given virtual object. This routine makes it possible to distinguish proper updating site, for instance, because objects in Cracow cannot be updated one must make appropriate updates in Warsaw.

We would like to emphasise that the global clients of the view cannot see the origin of particular virtual objects. The seeds of virtual objects are encapsulated and global clients just refer to the name of the view and attribute names, like in the following query that returns the titles of all books by Lem:

$$(MyBook \textbf{ where } author = \text{“Lem”}) . title$$

or in an updating statement (*change title "Salaris" into "Solaris"*):

$$(MyBook \textbf{ where } title = \text{“Salaris”}) := (\text{“Solaris” } \textbf{as } title);$$

6   Registration of Data and Services

In a more advanced architectural variant we assume that local servers can dynamically submit and revoke data and services to other grid participants. To this end we introduce a resource registry in the spirit of UDDI [10] or CORBA Trading Service [11]. The registry is a database which allows finding a provider of the needed resource. Resources stored at local servers can be described, for instance, using WSDL [12].

The scenario of the registry usage would look similar as in case of CORBA Trading Service or UDDI. An middleware sends the request to the registry to find the location of the given resource. As a response it receives information on resource location, possibly together with a detailed description of the given resource (e.g. in WSDL). After discovering the required service the middleware communicates directly to the provider to ask for the given service or data. (Note, that in our architecture the registry is not visible for the applications working on the top of the middleware; we assume that only the middleware communicates with the registry.)

From the other side the service/data providers can submit resources to the registry. In order to do it, the provider sends a registering message (with resource description) to the server that manages the registry. If the registration is accepted, the corresponding record will be added to the registry. Of course later, at any time the provider can revoke a resource from the registry.

Our middleware can use information stored in the registry during user requests processing, i.e. within a definition of global views there can be included calls to the registry. Technically, it means that the virtual object store has to keep information on location of the server that manages the registry (this information is stored in the same form as the information on the local servers, i.e. as a special object, so called server object, in the global object store).

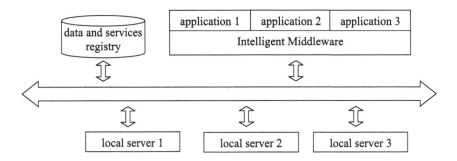

Fig. 2. Architecture of the middleware with data and services registry

The logical architecture of our middleware with resource registry is presented in the Fig. 2. Note that the architecture reminds the CORBA architecture with ORB (*Object Request Broker*). This similarity is true only to some extent – the role of CORBA's bus and our communication layer is to transport objects. However, there are significant differences between CORBA and our intelligent middleware. First of all, we define the middleware using a query language what increases level of abstraction and in this way speed up middleware development and facilitate its maintenance. Secondly, in CORBA it is assumed that resources are only horizontally partitioned, not replicated and not redundant, whereas our approach supports horizontal and vertical fragmentation, can resolve replications and can make a choice from redundant or repeating data/services.

We can imagine that the resource registry might also be a part of the virtual object store (or be kept as a part of a view state). Although such a solution would lower the communication overhead, it would be less universal and modular. In our architecture a separate registry can be reused by multiple middlewares.

7   Example of Resource Registry Usage

In this section we present an example usage of the resource registry. Let us assume that we have two local servers in Gdansk and in Warsaw as in the previous example and each of them keeps information on books. The global view should deliver data integrated from both servers. Additionally, the prices of books from both servers should be converted from USD to EUR according to the up-to-date exchange rates. We assume that the location of the server which provides a service of currency exchange should not be hard-coded into a view definition. Instead, the view should ask the resource registry for a location of such service. The example view definition might look as below:

```
create view MyBook2Def {
    virtual objects MyBook2 {
        return (Gdansk.Book Warsaw.Book) as b;
    }
    on_retrieve do {
            /* get a service that provides a currency calculator (for simplicity we as-
            sumed that the resource registry returns only one such a resource) */
            create (resRegistry.Service
                    where name = "CurrencyExchangeCalculator") as serviceServer;
            /* ask for performing currency conversion */
            create ( serviceServer . CurrencyExchangeCalculator .
                                    convertUSD2EUR( b.price )) as priceEUR;
            /* return result to the user */
            return b.(deref(title) as title, deref(author) as author,
                    priceEUR as price, deref(ISBN) as ISBN )
    }
    .../* further elements of the view definition */
}
```

This example shows that within our middleware we can query the resource registry in the same manner as we can query local servers. In comparison to classical solution known, e.g. from CORBA an advantage relies in the fact that we do not need any additional mechanisms or any specific protocol routines to support the registry.

In our example when the client calls the view *MyBook2* the query interpreter asks the resource registry *resRegistry* for the service with a name *CurrencyExchangeCalculator*. When the registry returns information on the needed service there is created a new server object with a name *serviceServer*. Now, the query interpreter can send directly to this server a request to convert a price of the given book from USD to EUR. Finally, the information on book with price in EUR is returned to a client.

In our assumptions there should be also transparency of connecting/disconnecting a server. In particular, the view should deal with the newly found server in the same manner as it deals with the local server that are already present in the grid.

The resource registry can also keep the information on the location of data. For instance, a server may register itself as a replica of the other server. In such manner we can significantly increase reliability of our intelligent middleware. In case of the failure of a server, an alternative source for given data/service can be found.

8   Conclusion

We have presented a novel approach to implementation of grid databases that is based on updateable views. The approach fulfills some fundamental requirements for grid applications such as transparency, interoperability, and computational universality. The approach is based on a powerful query language SBQL which ensures high abstraction level. The advantage is decreasing development time of a new grid application and simpler adaptation to changing requirements. The presented view mechanism is flexible and allows one to describe any mapping between local databases and a federated database. Because our views can also map methods, we offer facilities as powerful as CORBA or Web Services. In this paper we have also proposed the usage of resource registry within our middleware which we believe highly increases the middleware universality and reliability.

We have implemented SBQL and virtual updateable views for XML repositories based on the DOM model. After this experience our nearest plans assume implementation of our approach to the grid technology within the prototype ODRA, an object-oriented database platform build from scratch by our team (ca. 20 researchers) under .NET. Currently in ODRA we have finished implementation of SBQL and are advanced in implementation of other functionalities (imperative constructs, procedures, methods, views, distribution protocols, etc.) that are necessary to make our idea sufficiently ready for testing and prototype applications.

References

1. Bellahsene, Z.: *Extending a View Mechanism to Support Schema Evolution in Federated Database Systems.* Proc. of DEXA 1997, 573–582
2. Kaczmarski, K., Habela, P., Subieta, K.: *Metadata in a Data Grid Construction.* Workshop on Emerging Technologies for Next generation GRID (ETNGRID-2004), June 2004, Proc. published by IEEE
3. Kozankiewicz, H., Leszczyłoski, J., Płodzień, J., Subieta K.: *Updateable Object Views.* Institute of Computer Science Polish Ac. Sci. Report 950, October 2002
4. Kozankiewicz, H., Leszczyłowski, J., Subieta, K.: *Updateable XML Views.* Proc. of ADBIS'03, Springer LNCS 2798, 2003, 385–399
5. Kozankiewicz, H., Stencel, K., Subieta, K.: *Integration of Heterogeneous Resources through Updatable Views.* Workshop on Emerging Technologies for Next Generation GRID (ETNGRID-2004), June 2004, Proc. published by IEEE
6. Kozankiewicz, H., Subieta, K.: *SBQL Views – Prototype of Updateable Views.* Proc. 8th ADBIS Conf., September 2004, Budapest, Hungary
7. Subieta, K., Kambayashi, Y., Leszczyłowski, J.: *Procedures in Object-Oriented Query Languages.* Proc. of 21-st VLDB Conf., 1995, 182–193
8. Subieta, K.: *Mapping Heterogeneous Ontologies through Object Views.* Proc. 3-rd Workshop on Engineering Federated Information Systems (EFIS 2000), IOS Press, 1–10, 2000
9. Subieta, K.: *Theory and Construction of Object-Oriented Query Languages.* Editors of the Polish-Japanese Institute of Information Technology, 2004, 522 pages
10. Atkinson, B., Bellwood, T. et al.: *UDDI Spec Technical Committee Specification.* http://www.uddi.org/
11. *Object Management Group: OMG CORBA^{TM}/IIOP^{TM} Specifications.* http://www.omg.org/technology/documents/corba_spec_catalog.htm, 2002
12. Christensen, E., Curbera, F., Meredith, G., Weerawarana, S.: *Web Services Description Language (WSDL) 1.1.* W3C Note 15 March 2001, http://www.w3.org /TR/wsdl
13. Halevy, A. Y.: *Answering queries using views.* A survey. VLDB J. 10(4): 270–294 (2001)

Real Terrain Visualisation on the Basis of GIS Data*

Jacek Lebiedź and Krzysztof Mieloszyk

Gdańsk University of Technology,
Faculty of Electronics, Telecommunications and Informatics,
ul. G. Narutowicza 11/12, 80-952 Gdańsk, Poland
jacekl@eti.pg.gda.pl, krzymi@due.mech.pg.gda.pl

Abstract. The paper presents a concept of interactive system Vis3D for realistic real terrain visualisation based on Geographical Information Systems (GIS) data. Taking account of complexity and inaccuracy of geographical data this system has to work in two phases: off-line and on-line. The former off-line phase should convert data from GIS format to a form adapted for rendering algorithms (the intermediate form of data is called Terrain Model for Visualisation TMV). Using this form the latter on-line phase can generate a realistic image efficiently. This paper describes both phases, indicates difficulties in their realisation and shows the ways for overcoming them.

1 Introduction

Visualisation of real terrain seems to be very useful. Particularly it may be helpful for training of rescue teams during their way towards disaster areas (e.g. after an earthquake). Virtual inspection of cataclysm place just before rescue operation can improve efficiency and safety of the action [7]. Another example of real terrain visualisation serviceability is virtual sightseeing. Tourists planning an excursion could wander through visualised towns and choose the route for a real outing.

For its usefulness visualisation of real terrain should fulfil two conditions: *fidelity* and *realism*. A user of the visualisation system will expect that all visually important details of displayed objects will be present in a picture (*fidelity*). Unfortunately, these details are rather absent in existing Geographical Information Systems (GIS) databases. We do not find the information about chimneys and windows of buildings, about branches and leaves of trees, about zebra crossings and surface of roads, etc. Another problem is a demand for photorealism of generated image (*realism*), which clashes with complexity of scene. A human cannot accept identical oval trees, motionless rivers, and box-like buildings.

In order to attain to efficiency of interactive system for real terrain visualisation a process of preparing of data for visualisation should be separated from a process of generating an actual view. The former process does not depend on an observer position and can be performed only once before proper visualisation. The latter process should create an image each time, when the next animation frame is needed. Therefore interactive system for real terrain visualisation should be decomposed into two subsystems: terrain modelling and image generating (Fig. 1).

---
* Funded in part by the State Committee for Scientific Research (KBN) grant 4-T11C-004-22.

L. Bolc et al. (Eds.): IMTCI 2004, LNAI 3490, pp. 40–49, 2005.

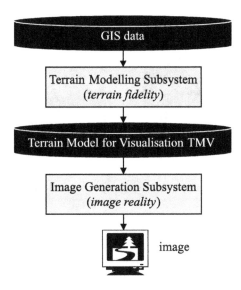

Fig. 1. Scheme of interactive system for real terrain visualisation Vis3D

A basic task of the terrain modelling subsystem is the conversion of GIS data into a form convenient for rendering algorithms. This form of data may be called Terrain Model for Visualisation (TMV). In order to increase fidelity of the image the conversion should be connected with complementing of lacking information about terrain and objects that are on it. The image generating subsystem should only create an image on the base of information stored in TMV optimised from the point of view of rendering functions. Unfortunately, execution time of the image generation process is limited by requirement of animation smoothness. Therefore for achieving maximal possible realism this process must use adequate methods for simplification of far parts of scene.

Below, both of the subsystems are described in separated parts with an emphasis on presentation of methods for increasing of terrain fidelity and image realism. In the last part of the paper there is shown TMV that is particularly prepared for our interactive system for real terrain visualisation Vis3D.

2   Terrain Fidelity

GIS data are not very detailed (Fig. 2). Of course an assumption that lacking information could be completed by a human, is rather credulous. Wanting information must be obtained automatically on the basis of existing data. Only the use of heuristics can help us to acquire missing information.

A tree is an example of an object which is represented in GIS data only by terrestrial coordinates. Usually neither height nor species is given. However we can try to predict these tree features by an analysis of geographical and biological environment influence: other trees, roads, rivers in neighborhood, height above the sea level, terrain configuration, kind of soil, etc. Lonely trees look different from these in groups. Some

Fig. 2. An example of visualisation system based on GIS data [5]

varieties of trees grow along the roads (lindens), other along the rivers (willows), other in the fields (maples). Pines are satisfied with sandy soil, whereas oaks need rich soil. Kind of soil and geographical region determine not only species of trees but also their forms. Trees growing in mountains differ in height and shape from these that occur on the sea coast. Additional differentiation of shapes of identically described trees in some neighbourhood is also very important for image perception (Fig. 3).

Fig. 3. An example of trees and buildings visualisation [4]

Buildings are described in GIS data by outline of their foundations. There is no information about shape of roof and colour of walls. Often the height of building is unknown, too. Fortunately, the lacking description of building can be estimated on the basis of shape and area of foundations (e.g. building height) and the geographical and cultural environment. The building parallel with track-way is probably a railway station. Blocks of flats from the sixties (recognisable by regular arrangement of their rectangular spacious outlines of foundations) have rather flat roofs, instead of tiled roofs typical of traditional one-family houses (tiny outlines of foundations surrounded by small enclosed areas). Additionally, roof shapes are specific for different regions of the country (e.g. roofs in the Tatra mountains). Longer distances between buildings are indicative of their greater height (building code). A shape and an area of foundations can also be helpful for estimating the height of a building (the wider and longer, the higher) and sometimes for prediction of its appearance (e.g. cross-like outline means most likely a church).

Other objects like roads, railways, rivers, water reservoirs (lakes), fences, power lines etc. are represented in GIS data in simplified form, too. Taking neighbourhood or geometry into account, we can predict lacking information describing object appearance. For example, we can assume most certainly that a surface of a wide city street is asphalt and contains white lines, whereas a narrow field road is rather made from broken stone. Similarly, sleepers of multitrack railway line are rather made from concrete instead of wood that is component of narrow-gauge cross-ties. Undulation and colour of a river or lake surface depends on water depth, which varies according to shape (width, meanders) of the river or lake. A cemetery railing or a factory wall is usually high and solid in contrast with a low country fence round the farm. Overhead transmission line supports are usually the same type for one line.

Unfortunately the heuristics that allows to describe appearance of objects cannot be hundred per-cent accurate. Therefore the special tool for manual correction (editor) is needed, particularly useful for distinctive objects like churches with towers among buildings.

3   Terrain Modeling

The most important task of the terrain modeling subsystem is a conversion of data from GIS formats to the terrain model for TMV visualisation, i.e. to a form adapted for rendering algorithms. The conversion deals with hypsometric data given as contour lines and generates triangle mesh described by their vertices. Since the locations of points between contour lines are unknown, conversion algorithm must approximate their heights. Instead of simple interpolation the converter should use clever methods taking typical configurations of terrain into account (Fig. 4).

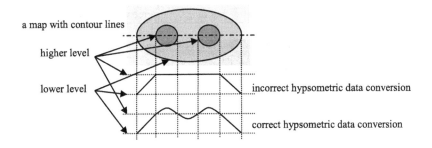

Fig. 4. Traps of conversion of hypsometric data

To obtain high efficiency of visualisation it is worth binding the triangles from terrain model into fans and strips. Such figures (Fig. 5) can be drawn faster than a set of isolated triangles. Hence the terrain modeling subsystem should also group the triangles into fans and strips optimised for rendering.

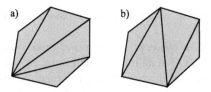

Fig. 5. A polygon that may be described as a set of triangles grouped into a fan (a) or into a strip (b)

Another task of the terrain model subsystem is completing lacking information necessary for high terrain fidelity. Due to dissimilarity of heuristics relating to trees, buildings and other objects, we have decided to isolate them into three modules: a module of conditioned by geographical-natural environment completing of information about trees and bushes, a module of conditioned by geographical-cultural environment completing of information about buildings, and a module of completing of information about objects the shapes of which agree with terrain topography (i.e. other objects than trees, bushes, and buildings). Because the results generated by these modules may not be in conformity with reality, there is a need for possibility of manual correction (editor) of data recorded in the terrain model for TMV visualisation.

Decomposition of terrain modeling subsystem is shown in Fig. 6.

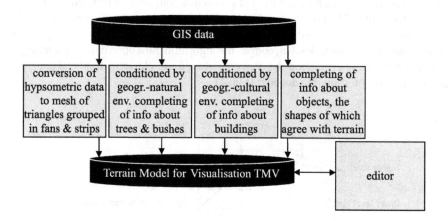

Fig. 6. Scheme of terrain modeling subsystem

4   Image Realism

To obtain the best level of created picture reception, it requires obtaining as good as possible reality with simultaneously smooth visualisation. Render application must deal with very high demands. Therefore it is important to constantly balance the scene complexity and the reality of render picture. This requires that levels of details of projected objects and area shape change dynamically. The levels of details selection must be based on distance from the observer, and ipso facto the size of drawn object maintaining high level of reality. Therefore it is necessary to create models with precisely analysed shape and specific presenting methods, often different for each of the levels of details and for several directions from which the object is seen. For example, forest area can be seen quite differently from above (treetops) and a side (tree wall). An angle of sun-beams falling on branches of trees has additional influence on appearance of the forest. Similar situation refers to buildings, where a form of windows is important only for observation from near and a side. Analogously other objects are differently seen from various distances and angles of inclination.

Area with placed objects creates very irregular data structure, which depends on many geographical and cultural factors as well as from area shape. One of the quick access methods is to divide the whole area into sectors. Such a division additionally facilitates to use different levels of details. The sectors that are closer to the observer should be rendered with greater precision than the far sectors. Knowing the complexity of each sector it is easier to estimate request of computing power. It is important not only for keeping of animation smoothness (limited time of frame generation) but also for parallel processing.

Realism of a scene is determined not only by appearance but also by behaviour of objects. Therefore terrain model should allow for entire interaction of physical model (e.g. a vehicle of the observer) with virtual environment. Terrain model should make it possible to detect collision between scene objects and to take into consideration type of base and its friction rate during ride on virtual terrain. Moreover, realism of presentation can be increased by stereoscopy or by other three-dimensional techniques (Fig. 7).

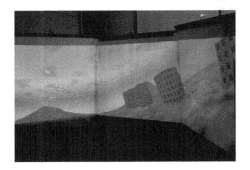 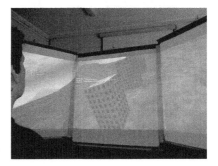

Fig. 7. An example of visualisation with three displays [4]

5 Image Generation

The basic task of the image generation subsystem is producing view of terrain enriched with objects on the basis of data stored in the terrain model for visualisation TMV.

Because the TMV ought to be versatile (i.e. not dedicated to given graphics system), before generating of image it needs to be transformed to a form optimised in respect of rendering methods. Such a transformation should consist of converting indexes to pointers, grouping vertex coordinates in arrays (redundancy possible), etc.

For graphics system with low calculating power it is proper to prepare various levels of details for each object and segment of terrain before image generating (off-line). For graphics system with high calculating power (e.g. cluster) the levels of details can be constructed just in real time when the image is generated (on-line). It means that contents of terrain model may be modified (e.g. by adding some moving objects) while performing animation controlled by interaction.

We have decided to effect simultaneously both approaches: off-line on the basis of PC-computer, and on-line using cluster. We are going to compare obtained results considering time and accuracy of visualisation. Construction of the image generation subsystem (Fig. 8) allows for employing both approaches.

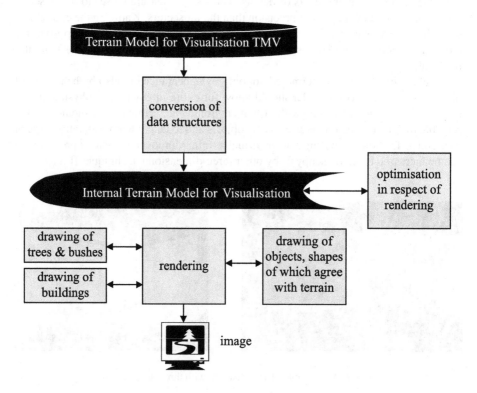

Fig. 8. Scheme of image generation subsystem

Additional acceleration of image generation can be obtained by using specialised procedures for drawing trees (also bushes), buildings, and objects the shapes of which agree with terrain topography (roads, railways, rivers, water reservoirs, fences, power lines, etc.).

6   Terrain Model for Visualisation

Efficient rendering of terrain needs to apply suitable data structures that allow for generating realistic terrain view for relatively low complexity. The best solution is using special structures for different levels of details. Such an approach is effected by the proposed terrain model for visualisation TMV, presented in Fig. 9.

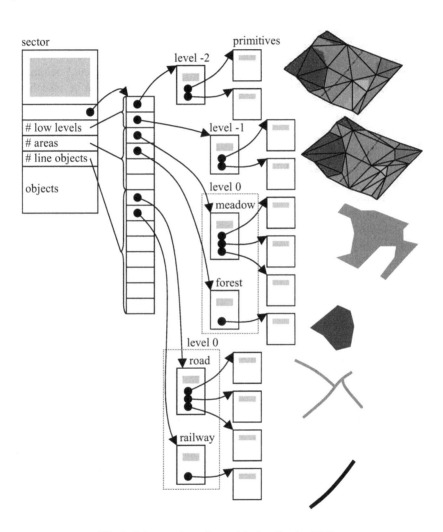

Fig. 9. Scheme of terrain model visualisation TMV

In the TMV all information about terrain is divided into square sectors. Small details of the sector can be seen only when they are close to the observer. The most detailed information about terrain, needed only for the close observer, is stored on the level 0 of the sector. The level 0 contains information about configuration of the terrain recorded in form of geometrical primitives like triangles, fans, and stripes. Each geometrical primitive can have only one texture, which may be common for a few primitives. The same texture groups primitives in one area like meadow, forest, lake, etc.

Line objects (like roads, railways, rivers, etc.) are described as independent stripes coating terrain primitives. Buildings, trees and other point objects are also represented independently of terrain description. Additionally, their description must take their individual character into account. Particularly, trees need different description model.

The above presented model of level 0 facilitates checking collision tests between moving object (e.g. plain) and terrain. It also allows for generating sector bitmaps useful for low levels of details. Such a sector bitmap contains all areas (forests, lakes, etc.), line objects (roads, rivers, etc.), and point objects (trees, buildings, etc.) belonging to the sector. When the observer is far from the sector, this sector can be visualised as a sector bitmap (texture) coating primitives (triangles, fans, strips) that approximate terrain configuration. Each sector can have a few sector bitmaps for different levels of details, i.e. for various distances from the observer. Moreover, each level of details can have quite different mesh of primitives. These meshes should be raised a little for bigger forests and buildings. Additionally, the sectors of low level of details are stuck together into supersectors according to quadtree principles. Within the described method far sectors can be rendered only as properly textured triangle mesh.

Since some objects like aerial masts are visible from far distance, they cannot be drawn by described method. Even the smaller objects like buildings and trees stick out from surface of terrain. Therefore, these objects should be drawn independently of rendering of sectors. Fortunately, their representation in terrain model for visualisation TMV permits independent rendering of them. All objects are assigned to different levels of details. The objects that have similar height like trees or buildings with the same number of floors are grouped into one level of details. Typical trees and one-family houses are rather visible only in area of a sector of terrain. Therefore, they belong to one level of details (level 0). The highest level of details contains the smallest registered objects like traffic signs that can be more or less seen only in area of a subsector that is one sixteenth of sector. The lowest level of details is composed of the highest objects like aerial masts visible from far distances. A given object is rendered only if its level of details is lower or equal to the level of details for the sector of terrain that contains the object. Small objects from level of details higher than zero (e.g. traffic signs) are rendered only if they belong to r subsectors the closest to the observer. Moreover, each object (excluding these from the highest level) can be rendered using different patterns depending on the level of details for terrain sector containing this object.

7   Conclusion

We have described an idea of real terrain visualisation based on GIS data. Main difficulties have been indicated and methods for their overcoming have been depicted. To reach acceptable quality we need to develop heuristic algorithms for fidelity of presentation and algorithms for realism (dynamic level of details).

Creating visualisation system is mainly designed for training units operating directly in the area. It can be with success used for group and individual training, for action in different weather conditions and in different daytime. Additional advantage is possibility to train in real locations due to use of GIS.

References

1. Varshney, A., Evans, F., Skiena, S.: *Optimising Triangle Strips for Fast Rendering*, IEEE Visualisation '96, 1996
2. Hoppe, H.: *View-dependent refinement of progressive meshes*, Proceedings of the 24th Annual Conference on Computer Graphics and Interactive Techniques SIGGRAPH'97, ACM Press, Addison-Wesley Publishing Co., 1997, pp. 189–198
3. Chrząszcz, J., Zabrodzki, J.: *Visualisation in flight simulators*, in J. Zabrodzki (ed.): Computer Graphics – Methods and Tools (in Polish). WNT, Warszawa 1994, pp. 291–309
4. Mieloszyk, K.: *Flight Simulator of Battle Helicopter – Flight Model*, MSc Thesis (in Polish), Gdańsk University of Technology, Gdańsk 2003
5. Kwoska, A.: *System of Visual Representation of Terrain for Dynamic Observer*. MSc Thesis (in Polish), Gdańsk University of Technology, Gdańsk 2003
6. Akenine-Moller, T., Haines E.: *Real-Time Rendering*, A.K. Peters Ltd., 2002
7. Environmental Tectonics Corporation: *Simulation*. http://www.etcsimulation.com
8. Olson, C. L.: *FlightGear – Open-Source, Multi-Platform Flight Simulator*. http://www.flightgear.org

Reliable Data Acquisition Systems
for Robotics and Multimedia Applications

Krzysztof Luks

Polish-Japanese Institute of Information Technology,
ul. Koszykowa 86, 02-008 Warsaw, Poland
kluks@ai.pjwstk.edu.pl

Abstract. This paper presents basic conceptions and classification of a data acquisition system for multimedia and robotic applications. A DAQ system designed for humanoid head robot built at PJIIT Robotics and Multiagent Systems Laboratory is described. The main goal of the system was to provide robust data acquisition architecture that would reliably provide data to processing modules. A real time operating system QNX Neutrino was used together with a dedicated hardware driver to provide a low overhead, high throughput data acquisition system. The driver architecture was determined by the environment it was operating in and software it interfaced with.

1 Introduction

In many applications in multimedia and robotics one needs to gather data from sensors probing the outside environment. Typically, sensors in robotic applications range from CCD cameras to sonars and gyroscopes to simple temperature sensors. In multimedia systems sensors used are mainly (but not limited to) cameras and microphones. In all cases the results of sensor measurement have to be converted into a digital form and transferred via some kind of interface to computer's memory. Only then can the processing software gain access to it.

2 Data Acquisition Systems Design

Sensing information flow model (Fig. 1) described in [1] is often used in robotic systems. It can be also applied to many multimedia applications. Data acquisition system can be divided into hardware and software layers.

The system may also need to provide feedback link to enable applications to send control commands to hardware components. Possible commands include controlling camera focus, picture resolution or data sampling frequency. Some of the sensors are more "intelligent" than others and require less sophisticated controlling software. E.g., cameras can implement picture adjustment algorithms such as white balancing or autofocus, in hardware significantly reducing processing power required to acquire satisfying quality images. Microphone headsets commonly used in multimedia setups often employ noise reduction algorithms implemented in hardware.

L. Bolc et al. (Eds.): IMTCI 2004, LNAI 3490, pp. 50–57, 2005.

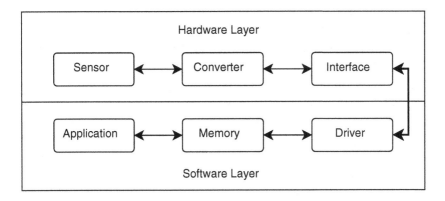

Fig. 1. Generic sensing information flow model used in robotic systems, based on [1]

2.1 Data Transfers

Difficulty in getting sensor data to the computer depends mainly on the nature of the data – amount and transfer speed. In its case of streaming high resolution video special care has to be taken to reduce transfer overhead to minimum.

A single camera with 512 by 512 pixel image with 256 intensity levels per pixel generating 30 images per second produces 24 megabytes of data every second [2]. Specialised dedicated processors such as the Imagine stream processor [6] can provide much greater performance than general purpose ones. The Imagine processor reduces the global register and memory bandwidth required by typical applications by factors of 13 and 21 respectively [6]. Systems not dealing with image processing typically require much less bandwidth.

Modern cameras can use high speed data transfer interfaces such as IEEE-1394, that are capable of transferring up to 400 megabits per second. With such interface it is possible to transfer 9 high resolution (1600 by 1220 pixels) true colour images per second.

2.2 System Environment

System environment in which data processing application will run has to be taken into an account. With many processes running on the same computer system proper care needs to be taken to ensure uninterrupted and timely execution of all programs.

In the most basic case data acquisition system will consist of a simple sensor integrated with analogue to digital converter connected via a serial port to, possibly embedded, dedicated computer system. A good example of such a setup is the temperature sensor from which only few bytes of data are being read every few seconds.

3   Application and System Classification

Multimedia applications can be divided into three groups, based on how they acquire the data [7]:

Continuous. Such as audio/video applications that require guaranteed bandwidth and processing resources. They typically require constant time to process a data unit. Their quality depends on how their periodic nature can be preserved. The quality is largely degraded when transfer or processing interruption occurs.

Interactive. They are highly delay sensitive and require low scheduling overhead and network delay. Applications of this type are event driven and initiate certain tasks depending on external conditions (user input, state of other programs). While executing those tasks they can become continuous applications. Interactive applications are often used to control or monitor parameters of sensing devices.

Bulk. They do not have strict bandwidth or latency requirements and their quality is not degraded by changes in available processing of transfer resources.

Such a classification can also be applied to many robotic systems. Each of the above mentioned types depends on different aspects of resources to provide high quality output. Specific requirements have to be taken into account when designing data acquisition system.

Based on types of hardware resources we can classify data acquisition systems into the following categories:

Embedded. Based on hardware especially designed for certain tasks, such as micro controllers or System-On-Chip computers. Such systems often employ special purpose embedded operating systems.

Dedicated. Built upon general purpose PCs, PC-140 computers or workstations. Each computer performs only one function. These can be thought of as embedded systems using general purpose hardware.

Cooperative. Systems use multi-tasking environment. Sophisticated time sharing algorithms have to be used to ensure proper execution of concurrent tasks. Best suited for this task are hard real-time operating systems.

4   Concepts of Real-Time Computing

Real-time system is the one in which the correctness of the computations not only depends upon the logical correctness of the computation but also upon the time at which the result is produced. If the timing constraints of the system have not been met, system failure is said to have occurred.

Traditionally, real-time operating systems have been used in "mission-critical" environments requiring real-time capability, where failure to perform computations in a certain time frame can result in harm to persons or property. Such systems are included for example in medical equipment or industrial process monitoring.

Recently, however, another field of application of real-time computing has become popular: systems where failure to meet time constraints results in financial penalty or considerable loss of quality of service. Such systems include consumer multimedia devices where dropped video frames exceeding certain amount make such device unacceptable to the customer.

4.1   Non Real-Time Operating Systems

The key characteristic that separates an RTOS from a conventional OS is the predictability needed in order to meet the above requirements. Conventional (monolithic) OS uses "fair" process and thread scheduling algorithms. This does not guarantee that real-time threads finish their processing on time. Also, priority information is, in most cases, lost during kernel calls being performed on behalf of a client thread. This results in unpredictable delays preventing an activity from being completed on time.

4.2   Real-Time Microkernel Architecture

The microkernel architecture used in QNX RTOS leaves only the most basic tasks to be performed by OS kernel. This tasks include managing threads and processes and passing messages between them. Scheduling for execution is done at per thread basis and high-priority threads can preempt lower-priority ones when they become ready for execution.

All other functionality, such as device drivers and OS services exists as separate processes and do not run within the kernel. In QNX such processes are called resource managers and use IPC interface provided by the microkernel as a message bus to exchange data (Fig. 2). This provides complete network transparency as the microkernel automatically recognises if data transfer can be accomplished by simple memory copy operation or by use of local area network.

Separating device drivers from the core kernel has additional benefits of protecting the system from accidental memory corruption caused by badly written code. Also,

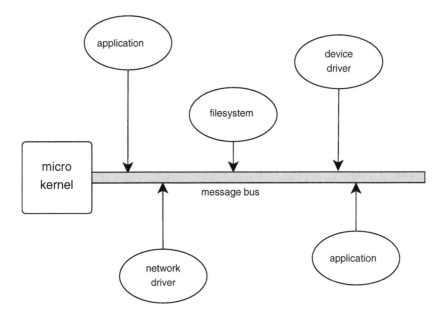

Fig. 2. Microkernel message bus

all processing is done at a priority determined by the thread on whose behalf they are operating [3].

4.3 QNX Resource Managers

Resource managers register a pseudo-file element in pathname space. Such pseudo-files can be accessed by standard POSIX I/O functions like `open()`, `read()`, `write()`. When this happens, the resource manager receives an open request, followed by read and write requests.

Resource managers not only deal with hardware devices, but can also provide functionality like filesystem interfaces. They are not restricted to handling just open(), read() and write() calls but can support any functions that are based on a file descriptor or file pointer, as well as other forms of IPC.

In QNX Neutrino, resource managers are responsible for presenting an interface to various types of devices. In other operating systems, the managing of actual hardware devices (e.g. serial ports, parallel ports, network cards, and disk drives) or virtual devices (e.g. /dev/null, a network filesystem, and pseudo-ttys), is associated with device drivers. But unlike device drivers, the Neutrino resource managers execute as processes separate from the kernel.

5   Data Acquisition System in the Paladyn Project

The data acquisition system developed for the humanoid head robot Paladyn was split into two parts: video acquisition module (Fig. 3) and sound and gyroscope data acquisition module (Fig. 4).

The whole system is of continuous nature and runs in cooperative environment. The video subsystem is the most bandwidth-dependant part. Images are grabbed from four cameras, each running in 360 by 243 pixels (half of standard PAL resolution). The frame grabber card is connected to the PCI bus and transfers images to operating memory using the Direct Memory Access mechanism.

The sound and gyroscope subsystem uses NuDaq 9112 Data Acquisition PCI board sample data from two microphones and 3 axis gyroscope and accelerometer board.

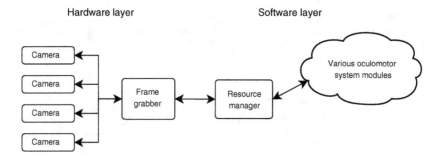

Fig. 3. Video acquisition module

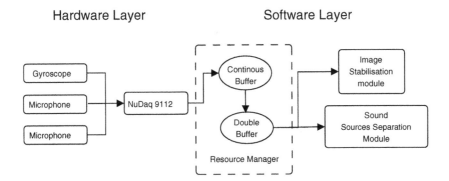

Fig. 4. Sound and 4gyroscope data acquisition module

Sound data was used by the auditory perception module [5] and data from gyroscopes by the image stabilisation module [4].

6   NuDaq 9112

The analogous to digital converter used for data acquisition purposes in project Paladyn was NuDaq 9112 32 bit PCI card. It has 16 single-ended or 8 differential analogue inputs and it's own FIFO buffer. The card supports sampling with frequency up to 110kHz.

Conversion can be initiated by one of three sources:

Software Trigger. A single value conversion is performed when a 1 is written into NuDaq's STR register. This mode is suitable for low frequency conversion because of big CPU overhead imposed by subsequent writes to STR registry.

Timer Pacer. NuDaq card is equipped with 3 programmable counters that can be used to trigger conversion at fixed frequency. When used together with DMA data transfer this mode is suitable for high speed conversion with very low CPU usage.

External Trigger. External frequency generator can be used to synchronise NuDaq's conversion speed with external devices.

6.1   Data Transfer Modes

When the conversion is complete and data is stored in card's internal buffer one of the following modes is used to transfer data to computer's memory:

Polling. Used in conjunction with software trigger. The software must check the state of a DRDY bit, which is set to 1 when data becomes available. Then it can read the converted value from data registry.

Interrupt Driven Transfer. NuDaq 9112 can use hardware interrupts to send data to the PC. In this mode the card generates an interrupt each time the conversion is completed. One can set up an interrupt handler that will copy the data from card's buffer to PC memory. This mode is asynchronous.

Direct Memory Access. The card "pushes" data to pre-allocated buffer in computer's memory and notifies it by signalling an interrupt when the transfer is complete. This method uses double buffering technique that combined with DMA transfer reduces CPU usage to almost 0%.

6.2   Driver Architecture

The core element of NuDaq driver is double buffer holding data transferred by the card and making it available to other processes via shared memory. One half of the double buffer holds samples that are being transferred from the A/D converter while the other half holds samples that can be read by other processes. When the first half becomes full their roles are exchanged.

During driver initialisation PCI bus is programmed with physical address of intermediate continuous buffer that is used as a temporary storage for data copied from NuDaq's FIFO buffer to main drive buffer (Fig. 5). Each time the FIFO buffer fills NuDaq card orders PCI controller to copy data to the continuous buffer.

DMA architecture requires that memory area, to which data is copied by PCI controller, is continuous and is located in first 16 megabytes of computer memory. Additionally, a buffer address passed to PCI controller must be a physical memory address. Therefore, an additional intermediate buffer was added to comply with the above requirements.

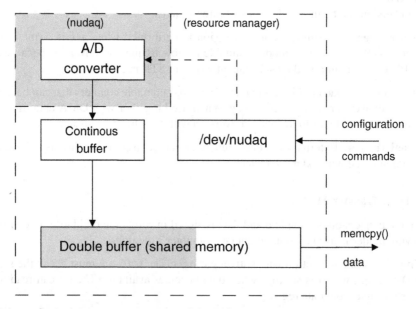

Only configuration requests are passed through /dev/nudaq. Data is read from shared memory segment pointing to filled half of driver's double buffer.

Fig. 5. Driver architecture using shared memory

6.3   Driver Operation

During startup the driver performs initialisation of PCI bus and NuDaq card. Next, all buffers are allocated and interrupt handler thread is spawned. This handler is responsible for copying data from intermediate buffer to double buffer. Then two files are registered in a local namespace, one of them is used by clients to send control commands and the other is an access point to shared memory area containing sampled data.

Driver then awaits incoming events. The main thread responds to opening of `/dev/PCI9112W0` file, while the interrupt handler thread sleeps and is awaken when NuDaq's FIFO fills up and PCI controller finishes transferring this data to the intermediate buffer. It then copies the data to appropriate half of the double buffer and checks if the active half needs to be changed. In such event the driver changes the beginning of shared memory area address to the address of the currently active half of double buffer. This way clients only deal with a single buffer available through a shared memory access point `/dev/shmem/nudaq`.

The client library offers function `AI_AsyncDblBufferHalfReady`, which checks if the current half of double buffer is ready to be read. It uses resource manager `/dev/PCI9112W0` interface to complete this task. If this function returns non zero values the client can copy data from a shared memory region to its local buffer.

7   Applications

NuDaq board controlled by the described driver was successfully used in project Paladyn for reading data from microphones and gyroscopes. The board was set up to sample data from two microphones at 44 kHz frequency and at 2 kHz frequency from piezoelectric gyroscope.

Sampled data was read by two concurrently running applications: image stabilisation module [4] and sound separation engine [5]. They both run wait for data become available for them and copy samples from a shared memory buffer to their local address space.

References

1. Xie, M.: (2003) Fundamentals of robotics. Linking perception to action. World Scientific, New Jersey London Singapore Hong Kong
2. Arkin, R.C.: (1998) Behaviour-based robotics. MIT Press, Cambridge, London
3. QNX Software Systems 2003 QNX system documentation
4. Luks, K.: (2003) System stabilizacji obrazu i akwizycji danych dla głowy robota humanoidalnego. MA Thesis, Polish-Japanese Institute of Information Technology, Warsaw
5. Blazejewski, L.: (2004) Separation and Localization of Binaural Sound Sources. Proceedings MSRAS (Monitoring, Security and Rescue in Multiagent Systems), Plock, June 2004, Warsaw Univ. Press. 2004
6. Rixner, S., Dally W.J., Kapasi U.J. Khailany B., López-Lagunas A., Mattson P.R., Owens J.D.: (1998) A Bandwidth-Efficient Architecture for Media Processing. Computer Systems Laboratory, Stanford University
7. Shi, S.Y., Parulkar G.M., Gopalakrishnan R.: (1998) TCP/IP Implementation with Endsystem QoS

Multi-level Annotation in SpeeCon Polish Speech Database

Krzysztof Marasek[1] and Ryszard Gubrynowicz[2]

[1] Polish-Japanese Institute of Information Technology,
ul. Koszykowa 86, 02-008 Warsaw, Poland
Krzysztof.Marasek@pjwstk.edu.pl
[2] Institute of Fundamental Technological Research PAS,
ul. Świętokrzyska 21, 00-049 Warsaw, Poland
Ryszard.Gubrynowicz@ippt.gov.pl

Abstract. SpeeCon Polish Speech Database was collected within the framework of the SpeeCon project partially sponsored by the EC (IST-1999-10003). The database contains two sets of data, which comprise 550 adults' recording sessions and 50 sessions from children, respectively. The adult speakers were recorded in various environments: offices, living rooms, cars and public places. Recordings contain free spontaneous speech passages, elicited spontaneous speech, phonetically compact words and sentences, general-purpose words and phrases, specific application words and utterances. One of the most important problems in the construction of the database is to define bases for multi-level transcription composed of several tiers. They could be grouped into three classes – linguistic, symbolic and physical representation. The orthographic transcription is applied to the sentence, phrase and word tiers, symbolic transcription related to grammar and articulation – to part of speech, phoneme and syllabic tiers and mnemonics – to the description of some characteristic of the measurable physical data. The paper presents the rules applied to text, speech and noise transcriptions and remarks on pronunciation varieties found in the database. The final part of the paper discusses the problem of the lexicon creation, which is an alphabetically ordered list of distinct lexical items occurring in the recorded corpus. The Polish lexicon has been built up by various methods, including hand-annotation and generation by rule with subsequent manual check.

1 Introduction

The recent development of large corpus-based studies has considerably improved the effectiveness of speech dialog system. This progress is observed for systems based on English language. However, until now there is no database for Polish suitable for training of the speaker independent large vocabulary continuous speech recognition systems (LVCSR) which is the crucial part of these systems. Nor are there sufficiently developed speech databases including prosodic descriptions. There are only two relatively small databases resulted from preliminary

L. Bolc et al. (Eds.): IMTCI 2004, LNAI 3490, pp. 58–67, 2005.
© Springer-Verlag Berlin Heidelberg 2005

studies on this subject [1, 2]. The lack of large speech databases for Polish is a serious obstacle to development not only of LVCSR systems, but of speech synthesis systems based on corpus approach, too, whereas intensive studies on designing large spoken databases to support training and testing of dialogue systems have been carried on for many years for other languages (for ex. [3,4]). These works result in evident progress of speech recognition and synthesis technology observed in recent years, especially for English, French and other European languages. Quite recent trend is toward designing of multi-language dialogue speech databases (e.g. [5]).

The presented Polish speech database has recently been created within the framework of SPEECON, a shared-cost project funded by the European Commission under Human Language Technologies, which was a part of the Information Society Technologies Programme (IST-1999-10003) [6]. The purpose of the project was to develop bases for voice-driven interfaces for consumer applications, but it could be applied to other studies, too.

The main target of the project was the collection of speech data for at least 20 languages (regional dialects, too) including most of the languages spoken in Europe. Recordings of Polish texts have been done at the PJIIT under the contract with Sony.

The database consists of 550 recordings of adults and 50 recordings of children. In this paper design and multi-level annotation of adults' database is described.

2   Speaker Population

The Warsaw version of Educated Polish (WEP) [7] does not differ significantly from the speech of educated Poles living in other regions of Poland. The WEP accent is most often regarded as the contemporary standard Polish speech style. Thus, the accent and articulatory variations are more related to the social status of the speaker than to his/her region provenance. For these reasons, the speakers' recruitment area was not limited to university/research centers. Although the Educated Warsaw Polish seems to be almost universal and the most frequent version used by population, an effort was made to diversify recruitment of speakers by their provenance and social stratum.

To obtain this goal several recording sessions were done outside Warsaw, mainly in the north-east and the south-west of Poland. In total, 307 speakers' origins (the places of birth and school education were in the same region) are outside Warsaw. We noted for this group 151 different cities and villages. The other 243 speakers originate in Warsaw but it does not mean that this group of speakers is homogeneous. A relatively large group of speakers are first generation Varsovians and it is hard to detect some common characteristics in their speech. An important factor, which has a significant impact on the quality of voice and speech, is a smoking habit (still very popular in Poland).

3   Recording Scenarios

Recordings were done in several real recording environments, defined as follows:

a) Office – a room where people are working at desks, usually or possibly with a computer. Noise level Leq = 30 – 60dBA

b) Entertainment environment – it refers to a living room with some furniture, places where people may sit down. A TV or other audio equipment may be turned on. Leq = 30 – 65dBA

c) Public Place – it can be a very large room (hall) or an open-air area. A hall should have at least 3 walls and a ceiling; more or less busy people; not too quiet. An open area has no walls and no closed ceiling. In all cases small shops, an open cafe area, traffic as well as a pedestrian way are possible. Leq = 45 – 90dBA

d) Car – a vehicle for 4 or 5 passengers, in motion or not, Leq = 28 – 80dBA
The recording time of one speaker was in the order of 1 hour, depending on his fluency and the number of repetitions due to errors. Ca. 320 prompts per speaker were recorded. For each recording condition additional measurements of noise level and room impulse response were done.

4   Recording Platform

The recording platform consists of a suitcase, which contains all necessary audio equipment (microphones, preamplifiers, etc.) as well as cables and adapters. The platform is mobile and contains a battery to make the platform independent of the main power supply. Four microphone channels are recorded simultaneously: close-talk, lavalier, desktop and far-field. The recording platform is based on a laptop, with two Type II PCMCIA slots as interface to the audio equipment. Two VXpocket V2 interface cards and special recording software are used. The software provides full control, prompting and monitoring facilities during the recording. The software allows the prompts to be presented to the speaker on a second LCD screen. Speech signals are stored with 16-bit, 16 kHz, header-less files.

5   Corpus Selection

The database is composed of read and spontaneous items.

The read part contains:

- Phonetically compact sentences, 30 per speaker
- Phonetically rich words, 5 per speaker
- General purpose words and phrases, 30 per speaker
- Application specific words and phrases, 220 per speaker

The spontaneous part is composed of:

- Free spontaneous items, ca. 15 per speaker,
- Elicited answers, 17 per speaker.

5.1   Phonetically Compact Sentences

The source text consisted of contemporary newspaper texts available in the Internet. A primary text was preprocessed to eliminate all incomplete sentences and remove formatting and orthographic errors. Then pre-selection was done – sentences of 5-20 words long, rather comfortable to read have been chosen resulting in the corpus of 3700 sentences with ca. 39000 words. The sentences were randomly selected, each prompt sheet allowing maximum 5 repetitions of a sentence in the whole database.

5.2   Phonetically Rich Words

Histograms of phone's occurrences in the sentences were used to identify Polish rare phones (N, dZ, dz, z'). To increase the amount of rare phones in the database special words (300) have been prepared (e.g. âÃIJmiaĹźdĹźycaâÃI - *atherosclerosis*).

5.3   General-Purpose Words and Phrases

The database contains also a set of 31 common words and phrases containing isolated digits and strings, natural numbers, telephone numbers (GSM and stationary), money amounts (in PLN and €), time and date expressions (including names of holidays and relative time & date expressions), spelt words (3 words 7 letters long), names of people, cities and streets, yes/no answers, e-mail and web addresses, and special keyboard characters.

5.4   Specific Application Words and Phrases

These were chosen to add some functionality: basic Interactive Voice Response (IVR) commands, directory navigation, editing, output control, messaging and Internet browsing, organiser functions, routing, automotive, and audio/video. From 533 commands and their synonyms (translated from common English lists) each speaker reads 220 randomly chosen items.

5.5   Unrestricted Items of Spontaneous Speech

Speakers were asked to respond to task specific situations related to mobile phone and PDA applications, automotive and information kiosks, audio/video and toys. For instance, in the mobile phone category speakers could be prompted: *Imagine that you are calling a [book store | music shop] to inquire about the availability, price (and edition) of a [book | CD]*.

5.6   Elicited Answers

A set of 17 questions is used to elicit spontaneous responses containing times, dates, city and proper names, spellings, yes/no answers, languages and telephone numbers. For example: *What time is it now?*

6   Annotation

At the first stage of the processing the recordings the orthographic transcription was used, applied to sentence, phrase and word level descriptions. For other levels of transcription the two SAMPA alphabets (a computer readable phonetic alphabet) were applied – SAMPA Polish version [8] for a phonetic (segmental) transcription and SAMPROSA [9] applied for a prosodic labelling. The tool applied to a multi-level speech annotation is based on Praat [13]. For this reason, the former orthographic transcriptions done under the SpeeCon project were converted into the Praat format and time-aligned. An example of a multi-level transcription for a Polish sentence "Wiewiórka siedzi na drzewie i gryzie orzech" is presented in Fig. 1.

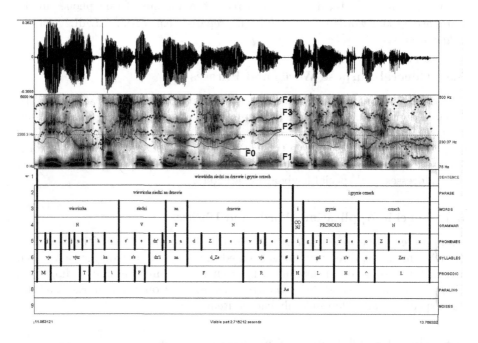

Fig. 1. An example of a multi-level transcription of a Polish sentence: *A squirrel is sitting on the tree and biting a nut.* The speech signal is on the top of the figure, below a dynamic spectrum representation with 4 formants and F0 time evolution. 8 levels of signal description are given: sentence, word, grammar, phonetic, syllabic, prosodic, paralinguistic and noise tier.

6.1   Orthographic Annotation Procedure

During the realisation of the SpeeCon project a special tool (based on the wavesurfer [10]) for a sound editing and an orthographic transcription and a non-speech event annotation has been used. Apart from orthographic transcribing speech signal the most important acoustic (non-speech) events present in the

Table 1. Annotation marks used to indicate words deformations and the presence of acoustic events

Symbol	Meaning
*xxx	Mispronounced word
**	Non-intelligible word(s)
˜xxx, xxx˜	Truncated word
[sta]	Stationary background noise
[int]	Intermittent noise
[spk]	Speaker noise (lip smack, breathing, etc.)
[fil]	Hesitations (hmm, uhm, etc.)

corresponding waveform files are additionally marked [11]. The symbol set of 7 markers is applied to indicate the presence and coarse categorisation of the main speech distortions and acoustic events. This enables to keep as much speech in the database as possible avoiding the need for taking out recordings from the corpus through some extra noises, disfluences or other events (see Table 1).

The orthographic transcription was formerly not time-aligned to the speech signal. No punctuation marks were used, and only small letters were applied with ISO8859-2 encoding. The waveforms visualisations were applied as well to locate certain noises or to determine their time sequence. Nevertheless, transcribers were clearly instructed to transcribe only what they really hear. However, the non-speech events level evaluation is not explicit and strongly depends on two factors – on a signal amplification level applied during an annotation session and on the level of the recorded speech. So the decision whether to mark or not the presence in the signal of non-speech events is in some cases uncertain. To reduce to some degree the transcribers' incertitude, the adopted level of reference below the non-speech events are not annotated is the level of weak speech sounds like unvoiced plosives or fricatives /f or x/. Transcriptions were done by experienced listeners and finally verified by a phonetician.

Letter sequences which occur in spelled words, ZIP-codes, e-mail and web addresses, acronyms and abbreviations were transcribed in capital letters separated by spaces (e.g. "PKO" spelled as "pekao" was transcribed as "P K O"). When the letter sequence was pronounced phonetically, then letters were written within //, e.g. "PKO" spelled as "py ky o" was transcribed as /P/ /K/ O.

Words of foreign origin and not commonly known in Poland, are prompted in a way to suggest the speaker their pronunciation (e.g. "DżiPiEs"). Words composed of a capital letters sequence and a "normal" word were transcribed as listed in Polish with spaces separating the letters: "odtwarzacz CD" → "odtwarzacz C D". Some speakers uttered letters sequences following spelling rules of English. In such cases, the letters sequences were transliterated, for example: "CD" is transcribed "si di".

Especially, Internet and e-mail addresses were transcribed as follows:
http://www.kbn.gov.pl   H T T P dwukropek slesz slesz W W W kropka K B N kropka gov kropka P L

Foreign words were transcribed in their original orthographic form.

For example, for the spontaneous prompt: *Pretend that you are sending a voice-mail message to a friend (phone number, reason of call, etc.)* one of the recorded answers was transcribed as follows: *[fil] [spk] witaj sławku ** mnie nie będzie w piątek [fil] o o piętnastej [spk] nie będzie mnie w domu bo wyjeżdżam za chwilę więc ja ci podam mój numer telefonu gdybyś chciał się ze mną skontaktować to proszę [spk] pięćset sześćdziesiąt siedem dwadzieścia sześć dwadzieścia osiem.*

6.2   Word Tagger

The first two orthographic levels of transcription, i.e. phrase and word are the basis for tagging of words items in one of following classes:

Table 2. Part of speech tags used in a multi-level annotation

Symbol	Meaning
V	Verb, e.g. *biegną*
ADJPAP	adjectival past participle e.g. *chowany*
ADJPRP	adjectival present participle e.g. *mierzący*
INF	Infinitive verb, e.g. *kochać*
ADVANP	Adverbial past participle, e.g. *ujżawszy*
ADVPRP	Adverbial present participle, e.g. *celując*
VNONP	Verb impersonal form, e.g. *mówiono*
N	Noun, e.g. *pies*
ADJ	Adjective, e.g. *biały*
ADV	Adverb, e.g. *daleko*
PRON	Pronoun, e.g. *ja*
INTER	Appeal, e.g. *och*
NUM	numerals
NUMCRD	Cardinal numeral, e.g. *jeden*
NUMORD	Ordinal numeral, e.g. *pierwsza*
P	Preposition, e.g. *przy*
PART	Particle, e.g. *że*
CONJ	Conjunction, e.g. *oraz*
$., $,	End of sentence, end of phrase

Tagging has been done automatically using a rule-based tagger (so called "Brill tagger" [15]). Simplifications of the tagging have been done. First, we decided to mark each word with only one POS (part-of-speech) tag taking only the one we expect to be the most frequent one (disambiguation). Second, each word has got a POS tag, so we did not consider the sequences of words. Those simplifications are perhaps too strong for the linguistic analysis of texts [16], however they are sufficient for our task targeting speech synthesis and intonation analysis.

The Brill tagger has been trained on ca. 3700 newspaper sentences (ca. 9000 words vocabulary) for which the POS tags have been manually set.

6.3 Phonetic Transcription

This process is done with a speech signal alignment. The phonetic transcription of the text is made automatically and aligned to the recorded speech signal automatically with hand-made corrections. The align program consists of three parts: a grapheme-to-phoneme converter, acoustic models and an align program.

In the automatic grapheme-to-phoneme converter the text is observed through a window of constant length where three graphemes to the left and three graphemes to the right serve as a context for a given character. A classification is performed by the decision tree. For each word only one pronunciation is generated. Foreign words have to be converted by hand [12]. Post-processing rules are used to refine generated transcriptions of pronunciations (e.g. devoicing final consonants if the next word starts with unvoiced consonant).

The aligner uses acoustic models prepared for the Polish speech recogniser [12]. A set of 1069 states (after state-tying) of triphones is modelled with 3 continuous density Gaussians per state. A feature vector comprises of 38 parameters (12 cepstral coefficients, 12 delta-cepstrals, 12 delta-deltas, delta of energy and delta-delta energy) and is extracted every 10 ms with observation window of 25 ms.

The aligner program is based on HVite from HTK tool [14]. Given the orthographic text and acoustic models the label file is generated and converted to the Praat label format. Phones and words are than time-aligned with the signal.

6.4 Syllabic Transcription

This level follows the phonetic transcription and is created semi-automatically taking into account that the nucleus of a Polish syllable is a vowel. The syllabic description aligned to the speech signal is the basis for a word and a phrase accent. Polish is traditionally described as having a systematic word accent on a penultimate syllable. However, there some exemptions from this rule and in case of a spontaneous speech the prominence of the penultimate syllable can be changed.

6.5 Prosodic Transcription

This transcription is mainly based on the analysis of F0 time evolution, although it seems that for Polish also a syllabic duration influences the accent perception. It is possible that another tier describing syllabic duration variations would be useful. At first approximation the SAMPROSA tone transcription system enables to code pitch patterns using a limited set of abstract tonal symbols like H (High pitch), L (Low pitch), T (Top pitch), B (Bottom pitch), M (Mid pitch), F(Falling pitch), R (Rising pitch) and others.

7 Observations

However, it should be observed that diversification of speakers over their provenance and social stratum has an evident influence on the quality of recorded speech. Some of the speakers have not a habit to read aloud a long list of iso-lated words; some of them do not know often the meaning of technical words they have to read. Many of these words are adopted from English. Especially difficult were e-mail and URL-addresses, usually build of foreign words or ab-breviations. There are no standard pronunciations, making reading this kind of prompts even more difficult.

Speakers were asked to speak clearly and precisely. For many of them it was a hard task. In some cases of isolated short phrases, like command words, we observed the accent shift. They accented the first syllable instead of the penultimate. In longer utterances the first part was spoken rather loudly, while the second was spoken often almost voiceless at the end of the phrase, even for final vowels.

Spontaneous items were particularly difficult. Most of the speakers cannot speak fluently, even if they have time to prepare the talk. Breaks, hesitations, verbal deletions, un-grammatical expressions, problems with a proper sentence formulation and first of all, careless articulations were often observed.

Conforming our expectations we did not observe dialectal differences: the pronunciation was very similar for almost all speakers. But individual habits, for example, smoking habits can hardly influence voice quality.

8   Lexicon

The lexicon has been built up by various methods, including hand-annotation and generation by rule [12] with a subsequent manual check. SAMPA phone sym-bols were used [11]. The pronunciation lexicon contains, alphabetically sorted, all transcribed words, their number of occurrences and the list of their phone-mic representations. In the lexicon only small letters are used. All truncated, mispronounced words and non-speech events are not included.

Multiple transcriptions are supported in case of foreign words and spelling. It is worth to mention that the URL and email addresses as well the com-pany/agency names in almost all cases do not correspond to Polish words. They are phonetically transcribed using Polish phone set, thus this transcription has an approximate character, only.

9   Final Remarks

Some of the design considerations of the SpeeCon Polish database annotation have been presented, including preprocessing and a multi-level speech signal description. A described transcription of recordings could be directly used in the training of speech recogniser [12], but could be also a starting point for a more detailed annotation which could be an effective tool in rather an indi-rect process extracting linguistic information from measurable speech data. Four channel recordings with annotations files are stored on 23 DVDs (213 CD-Rs). The eperience from the design and recording of the SpeeCon database for Polish presented in this paper shows efficient means of obtaining and its annotation of speech recorded in real conditions.

Acknowledgement

The authors are grateful to Dominika Oliver from Saarland University in Saarbrücken for helpful comments and proposals on levels of representation and analysis of speech.

References

1. Gubrynowicz, R.: The Polish Database of Spoken Language, Proc. First Int. Conference on Language Resources and Evaluation, Granada, 28–30 May 1998, 1031–1037
2. Grocholewski, S.: First Polish Database Proc. First Int. Conference on Language Resources and Evaluation, Granada, 28–30 May, 1998, 1059–1062
3. Lamel, L.F., Kassel, R.H., and Seneff, S.: Speech database development: Design and analysis of the acoustic-phonetic corpus, Proc. DARPA Speech Recognition Workshop, 1986, 100–109
4. Damhuis, M., Boogaart, T., in: Veld, C., Versteijlen, M., Schelvis, W., Bos, L., Boves, L.: Creation and analysis of the Dutch POLYPHONE corpus, Proc. Int. Congress on Speech and Language Processing, Yokohama, 1994, 1803–1806
5. Höge, H., Draxler, C., van den Heuvel, H., Johansen, F., Sanders, E., Tropf, H.: SpeechDat Multilingual Speech Databases for Teleservices: Across the Finish Line. Proceedings of Eurospeech'99, Budapest 1999. vol. 6, pp. 2699–2702
6. http://www.speecon.com/
7. Biedrzycki, L.: Phonology of English and Polish resonants (in Polish), PWN, Warszawa, 1978
8. http://www.phon.ucl.ac.uk/home/sampa/polish.htm
9. http://www.phon.ucl.ac.uk/home/sampa/samprosa.htm
10. http://www.speech.kth.se/wavesurfer/
11. http://www.speecon.com/public_docs/D21.zip
12. Marasek, K.: Large Vocabulary Continuous Speech Recognition System for Polish, Archives of Acoustics, vol. 28, 4, 293–303
13. http://www.praat.org
14. http://htk.ca.ed.uk
15. Brill E., A Corpus-Based Approach to Language Learning. PhD Dissertation, University of Pennsylvania, 1996
16. Przepiórkowski A., The IPI Corpus, http://dach.ipipan.waw.pl/~adamp/Papers/2004-corpus/book_en.pdf

Intelligent Content Extraction
from Polish Medical Reports

Małgorzata Marciniak[1], Agnieszka Mykowiecka[1], Anna Kupść[1],
and Jakub Piskorski[2]

[1] Institute of Computer Science, Polish Academy of Sciences,
ul. Ordona 21, 01-237 Warsaw, Poland
[2] DFKI GmbH, Stuhlsatzenhauseweg 3, D-66123 Saarbücken, Germany

Abstract. The paper presents a method for intelligent automatic processing of medical reports. First, we extract single pieces of information using SProUT (a general-purpose Information Extraction platform), and then, externally merge the results in order to obtain a detailed formalised description of the reports.

1 Introduction

The paper presents a method for intelligent automatic processing and understanding of Polish medical texts. In particular, we aim at standardising and formally representing data from mammogram reports so that they can be stored in a database which can support physicians in decision making and diagnosing.[1] Our processing method consists of two phases: template extraction and merging these templates into more complex structures.

We obtain single pieces of information using SProUT (Shallow Text Processing with Unification and Typed Feature Structures, version 2.11.2[2]) [3] which has been adapted to processing of Polish [2],[7]. The extracted information is represented as attribute-value pairs, according to the domain model specified in [6]. The model comprises a simplified ontology which represents main mammographic concepts. The extracted data is normalised and linked to the ontology elements, which will enable concept-driven querying of the final database.

In the second phase, the templates are merged in order to obtain more complex structures defined in the model. This phase consists of cleaning up the results, performing pseudo-unification and grouping the attributes so that they describe appropriate objects. The latter operation is crucial, as a single report often contains several mammographic findings or other objects of the same type. In order to separate their descriptions, we have implemented several heuristics for automated tags insertion to the reports.

The organisation of the paper is as follows. First, we present the general system architecture (sec. 2), with a more detailed description of its components in the subsequent sections (sec. 3–5). An evaluation of the algorithm inserting tags is presented in sec. 6, whereas final conclusions and future work are given in sec. 7.

---

[1] A similar task for English mammogram reports was undertaken in [5] and [4].

[2] This version of SProUT does not require strong typing introduced in later versions [1] of the system.

L. Bolc et al. (Eds.): IMTCI 2004, LNAI 3490, pp. 68–78, 2005.

2   System Architecture

Breaking a problem into simpler subtasks highly facilitates the general task. In the system, we adopted this strategy and dedicated submodules are delegated to solving particular subtasks. The extraction process has been divided into four stages: pre-processing, basic Information Extraction (IE), cleaning-up the extracted data, and final merging of the data into more complex structures, see Fig. 1.

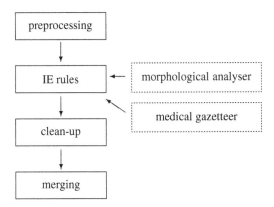

Fig. 1. System architecture

The pre-processing stage was motivated by low quality of the texts produced by physicians. There are many spelling errors (mostly lack of Polish diacritics but also other misspellings) and punctuation errors (lack of commas or periods and their non-standard usage). There are also many domain-specific abbreviations. Using uncorrected data would result in a severe data loss and, therefore, the first step is data correction.

The corrected text is then processed by the SProUT IE system. Polish is a language with rich inflection, so extraction from Polish medical texts requires not only medical term recognition, but also identifying various inflectional forms of the same term. To the best of our knowledge, there is no electronic medical lexicon for Polish available publicly. Fortunately, many medical terms are also present in everyday speech and are covered by general-purpose dictionaries. To this end, we use a morphological analyser integrated with SProUT [7]. This allows us to recognise more complex syntactic forms as well, not just isolated words. We employ the SProUT grammar formalism (see sec. 3) to build phrases based on morphological features of their components. Since only part of the medical terminology can be recognised (and inflected) by the general-purpose morphological analyser, we also employ a specialised lexicon integrated with SProUT, the so-called gazetteer, where we store domain-specific inflected forms of words or phrases unrecognised by the morphological module.

IE from unstructured texts requires a tradeoff between simplicity and extraction completeness. The more sophisticated rules we produce, the more precise information we can get; but at the same time the rules become less general. This problem begins to be extremely important when dealing with data corresponding to related features appearing freely in the text. In our application domain, this happens if we want to collect all information about a particular finding (its shape, size, contour, density, change in

ATTRIBUTE NAME	MEANING
attributes with general information	
EXAM_ID	examination identification number
PATIENT_ID	patient's identification number
EXAM_DATE	examination date
BREAST_TISSUE	an AVM with attributes describing breast tissue
FINDINGS	a list of AVMs describing mammographic findings (see below)
SUMMARY_INFO	an AVM with attributes used in the report summary
attributes used in the report summary	
DIAGNOSIS_RTG	radiological diagnosis
DIAGNOSIS_RTG_LOC	diagnosis combined with localisation
RECOMMENDATION	recommendation, e.g., biopsy, USG
TIME	time of the recommended examination
RECOMEND_REASON	the reason of the recommendation
attributes used for findings' description	
ANAT_CHANGE	what the finding looks like on the film, e.g., darkness, tumour
LOCALISATION	an AVM describing localisation (see below)
DENSITY	finding's density, e.g., high, low
SHAPE	shape
CONTOUR	contour
SATURATION	saturation
MULT	for phrases such as *liczne torbielki* 'numerous small cysts'; one structure describing a cyst is created with the value of the attribute MULT: *numerous*
SIZE	an AVM describing finding's size (up to three dimensions and a measurement unit)
WITH_CALCIF	information about accompanying calcifications (micro or macro)
C_MULT	similar to MULT but used only for calcifications
WITH_APPEND	information about the presence of appendices
APP_MULT	number of appendices
APP_CHAR	shape of appendices
PALPABILITY	a boolean value 'yes' or 'no'
SUGGESTION	maculation
PROJECTED	information if the finding has been dispersed in a different projection
PROJECTION	in which projection the finding is visible
INTERPRETATION	medical interpretation of the finding: cyst, cancer, etc.
DIAGNOSIS_RTG	whether the finding seems to be benign, suspicious or malignant
RECOMMENDATION	further examinations of the finding required
PREVIOUS_EXAM	date of the previous exam, combined with the next three attributes
SIZE_CHANGE	comparison of finding size
QUANT_CHANGE	comparison of finding quantity
SATURATION_CHANGE	comparison of finding saturation
attributes used for the localisation (LOC) description	
BODY_PART	body part, e.g., breast, armpit
L_R	lateralization: left or right
LOC_A	anatomic part, e.g., nipple, lymph node
LOC_CONV	conventional localisation e.g., quadrants of a breast
LOC_CONV1	conventional localisation indicating depth in the breast

Fig. 2. Attributes used in the representation and their meaning

time, localisation and so on). In addition to various permutations, pieces of relevant information can be scattered in the document and it will be impossible to merge them locally. Therefore, we decided to process the data sequentially. First, we use SProUT for extracting simple phrases: using the gazetteer and the morphological analyser we can identify all relevant data. Then, the results stored in a separate file are externally processed and combined into more complex structures consisting of attribute-value pairs (Attribute Value Matrices, AVM).

The list of attributes, specified by our domain model in [6], and their meaning are presented in Fig. 2, whereas the resulting AVM structure is sketched in (1).

$$(1) \quad \begin{bmatrix} \text{EXAM\_ID } \textit{exam\_id} \\ \text{EXAM\_DATE } \textit{exam\_date} \\ \text{PATIENT\_ID } \textit{pat\_id} \\ \text{BREAST\_TISSUE } \textit{breast\_desc} \\ \text{FINDINGS } \langle \begin{bmatrix} \text{ANAT\_CHANGE } \textit{change} \\ \text{LOC } \textit{loc} \\ \dots \end{bmatrix}, \dots \rangle \\ \text{SUMMARY\_INFO } \textit{summary\_info\_desc} \end{bmatrix}$$

3   IE Using SProUT

SProUT is a multilingual NLP platform equipped with a set of reusable Unicode-capable processing components for various linguistic operations, including tokenisation, morphological analysis, gazetteer lookup, basic coreference resolution, etc. Since AVMs are used as a uniform I/O data structure by each of these processing resources, they can be flexibly combined into a pipeline that produces several streams of linguistically annotated structures, which serve as an input for the shallow grammar interpreter, applied at the next stage. The grammar formalism in SProUT is a blend of efficient finite-state techniques and unification-based formalisms which are known to guarantee transparency and expressiveness. To be more precise, a grammar in SProUT consists of pattern/action rules, where the LHS of a rule is a regular expression over AVMs with functional operators and coreferences, representing the recognition pattern, and the RHS of a rule is an AVM specification of the output structure. Coreferences express structural identity, create dynamic value assignments, and serve as means of information transport. Generally, variables can be assigned arbitrarily complex AVMs as their values. All necessary types are arranged in the system's type hierarchy, which can be modified by the user. Furthermore, grammar rules can be recursively embedded, which provides grammar writers with a context-free formalism. Functional operators are primarily utilised twofold: first, for forming the output of the rules and second, for introducing complex constraints in the rules.

The SProUT grammar used in this paper consists of 221 extraction rules. Each rule detects words or phrases which describe information presented in Table 2. For example, the rule in (2) recognises different preposition phrases identifying calcifications.

```
(2)   with_calc:>
         ((morph & [POS prep, STEM 'z', INFL [CASE_PREP ins]] |
           morph & [POS prep, STEM 'ze', INFL [CASE_PREP ins]])
```

```
      (morph & [POS noun, STEM 'obecność']) ?
      (@seek(multiplicity) & [MULT #mu]) ?
      (gazetteer & [GTYPE gaz_med_zmiana,
                         CONCEPT mikrozwapnienie & #zm,
                         G_NUMBER #li] |
        gazetteer & [GTYPE gaz_med_zmiana,
                         CONCEPT makrozwapnienie & #zm,
                         G_NUMBER #li] |
        morph & [STEM 'zwapnienie' & #zm,
                     INFL[ NUMBER_NOUN #li]]))
   -> [WITH_CALCIF #zm, C_MULT #mul],
      where #mul = ConcWithBlanks(#mu,#li).
```

The first AVM matches a preposition *z(e)* 'with'. It is followed by at most one noun (a form of the noun *obecność* 'presence'). The variables #mu, #li, #zm establish coreferences between values of the component AVMs (on LHS) and the resulting structure (on RHS). Concepts corresponding to (micro- and macro-) calcifications are taken from the gazetteer, whereas their quantity is recognised by the multiplicity rule called (via the @seek operator) by the with_calc rule. The quantity of calcifications is either expressed directly, e.g., *bardzo liczne* 'numerous', *nieliczne* 'a few', etc., or by the grammatical number (singular/plural) of a word corresponding to the calcification. The accompanying calcifications are transported to the slot WITH_CALCIF on RHS via the variable #zm. The quantity of the detected calcifications and their grammatical number are concatenated by the functional operator ConcWithBlanks and kept in the C_MULT slot of the resulting output structure.

4 Post-processing

Every phrase recognised by SProUT is stored with all alternative analyses if more than one grammar rule has been applied to the phrase. In postprocessing, the disjunctive results for each recognised phrase are separated and cleaned up.

First, all variable coreferences are resolved. In many cases, an attribute's value is given indirectly, by a reference to a different value. Therefore, we substitute all references with the corresponding values. Then, duplicate analyses are removed. Grammar rules often output morphological information (case, number and gender) in order to ensure agreement between elements in the identified phrases. Maintaining this information in the output structures usually produces alternative analyses. As morphology is irrelevant for our final results, it is deleted from the output structures and duplicate analyses are removed. Finally, in order to simplify annotation heuristics, we perform a pseudo-unification of some attribute-value pairs. Although we attempt at collecting all information about localisation in a single structure, it is not always possible. Usually different pieces of information about localisation are recognised one after another but, due to numerous paraphrases, they are separated by miscellaneous text and extraction rules cannot group them in a single structure. If the two adjacent pieces of information are complementary, e.g., the first recognised localisation concerns a body part and lateralization, whereas the second lacks this information but specifies conventional localisation, the two pieces are merged into a single structure.

The postprocessed report is a text document containing a sequence of attribute-value pairs. If the output structure consists of several attribute-value pairs, as in (3b), they are treated as one result in the document. Each result is stored in one line, with attributes separated by '$||$', i.e., (3a)–(3b) correspond to (4).

(3)   a. $\begin{bmatrix} \text{EXAM\_ID} & 237 \end{bmatrix}$ b. $\begin{bmatrix} \text{RECOMMENDATION} & USG \\ \text{TIME} & za\_rok \end{bmatrix}$

(4)   EXAM_ID:237
RECOMMENDATION:USG||TIME:za_rok

5   Merging and Automatic Annotation

The most complex structures in the adopted mammography model are descriptions of breasts' composition and findings. In order to delimit their descriptions in processed

```
while not end-of-file
    // initialisation
    find the beginning of the report and mark it as bp;
    copy one report to table TAB and set table TAB_TAG's rows to:
        ut if BTISSUE is found,
        a_ch if ANAT_CHANGE,
        i_ch if INTERPRETATION,
        dloc if DIAGNOSIS_RTG_LOC or attributes concerning breast composition,
    skip the last RECOMMENDATION lines and put mark rp to the first of them;
    skip identification information;
    checkpoint=beginning_of_report;
    // basic annotation
    while not end-of-report and not rp
        find next ut, a_ch or i_ch;
        go back to the nearest block boundary (zk, uk, dloc, bp);
        check whether unique attributes are not repeated and correct the boundary;
        mark the boundary as up or zp;
        while tag not-equal to ut, a_ch, dloc, rp or (i_ch if started from i_ch)
            go forward
            check if unique attributes are not repeated and correct the boundary;
        mark the boundary as uk or zk;
    checkpoint=the_last_boundary+1;
    // correcting localisation
    if there is a localisation (LOC) outside blocks boundaries
        if the previous line is not marked i_ch and
        inside the block there is another i_ch or a_ch tag
            move the zk tag above the i_ch tag;
    if there are blocks without a localisation (LOC)
        if the up/uk block ends with a localisation (LOC)
            move the uk tag above the LOC line and redo the annotation from that line;
    print out the results;
```

Fig. 3. Algorithm for identifying findings' boundaries

reports, we introduce several tags and use a few heuristics to insert them at the beginning and at the end of each block. The two main blocks are indicated by up/ uk, start/end of the breast's composition description, and zp/zk tags, start/end of a finding description.

The annotation of each report is built around the attributes representative for each block, i.e., ANAT_CHANGE, INTERPRETATION for findings, and BTISSUE for breast's composition. Lines containing these attributes are tagged, respectively, a_ch, i_ch and ut. All lines with attributes which do not belong to any block (e.g., DIAGNOSIS_RTG_LOC or attributes belonging to the breast's composition block) are marked as dloc. The last part of the report, containing general recommendations, is marked with the rp tag. The process of identifying blocks is repeated starting from the first line marked with a_ch, i_ch or ut tags. From that line we go back to the previous block's opening or closing tag, and then go forward, trying to cover the maximal part of the report unless the dloc tag or the second occurrence of attributes unique for a finding (e.g., localisation, shape, size) are found. In this case, the corresponding closing tag (uk or zk) is inserted. A pseudo-code of the algorithm is given in Fig. 3.

Sample processing results for reports in Fig. 4 and 6 are presented, respectively, in Fig. 5 and 7. In Fig. 5, identifying a new localisation (the attribute unique for a finding)

---

775 W sutku prawym przybrodawkowo widoczny guzek o śr. 10mm z makrozwapnieniami w jego obrębie odpowiadający f-a degenerativa (zmiana łagodna). W sutku lewym w KGZ wewnątrz-sutkowy węzeł chłonny.
[In the right breast in subareolal, there is a tumour of 10mm diameter with calcifications corresponding to f-a degenerativa (bengin finding). In the left breast, there is an intramammary lymph node in the upper outer quadrant.]

Fig. 4. Sample mammogram report

```
bp
    EXAM_ID:775
zp
    LOC|BODY_PART:sutek||LOC|LOC_CONV:
    ok._brodawki_sutkowej||LOC|L_R:prawy
    ANAT_CHANGE:guzek||MULT:singular
    DIM:mm||NUM1:10||NUM2:10
    C_MULT:plural||WITH_CALCIF:makrozwapnienie
    INTERPRETATION:f-a_degenerativa
    DIAGNOSIS_RTG:zmiana_lagodna
zk
zp
    LOC|BODY_PART:sutek||LOC|LOC_CONV:loc_KGZ||LOC|L_R:lewy
    INTERPRETATION:wewnątrzsutkowy_węzeł_chłonny
zk
bk
```

Fig. 5. Processing results for report 775 (Fig. 4)

123 Sutek prawy – w kwadrancie górnym zagęszczenie dobrze wysycone o średnicy około 20 mm i zatartych granicach. Wymaga ona dalszej diagnostyki – konieczne wykonanie badania USG i PCI. Wewnątrzsutkowy węzeł chłonny w kwadrancie górno-zewnętrznym sutka lewego.
[The right breast – in the upper outer quadrant there is a high density finding of about 20 mm diameter and obscured margins. Requires further examination – USG and biopsy compulsory. An intramammary lymph node in the upper outer quadrant.]

Fig. 6. Sample mammogram report

```
bp
    EXAM_ID:123
zp
    LOC|BODY_PART:sutek||LOC|LOC_CONV:loc_KG||LOC|L_R:prawy
    ANAT_CHANGE:zagęszczenie||MULT:singular
    SATURATION:dobrze_wysycony
    DIM:mm||NUM1:20||NUM2:20
    CONTOUR:zatrzeć_zarysy
    RECOMMENDATION:USG_PCI||TIME:unknown
    INTERPRETATION:wewnątrzsutkowy_węzeł_chłonny
zk
    LOC|BODY_PART:sutek||LOC|LOC_CONV:loc_KGZ||LOC|L_R:lewy
bk
```

Fig. 7. Initial processing results for report 123 (Fig. 6)

is a good criterion for separating findings' descriptions. However, in some reports this strategy leads to wrong segmentations. In Fig. 6, for the second finding only its interpretation is given. As its localisation occurs after the finding and there is no interpretation for the first finding, 'intramammary lymph node' is classified as an interpretation of 'density'. To correct some of such improper segmentations, two procedures have been implemented. After processing, the report is checked whether there are no localisation

```
bp
    EXAM_ID:123
zp
    LOC|BODY_PART:sutek||LOC|LOC_CONV:loc_KG||LOC|L_R:prawy
    ANAT_CHANGE:zagęszczenie||MULT:singular
    SATURATION:dobrze_wysycony
    DIM:mm||NUM1:20||NUM2:20
    CONTOUR:zatrzeć_zarysy
    RECOMMENDATION:USG i PCI
zk
zp
    INTERPRETATION:wewnątrzsutkowy_węzeł_chłonny
    LOC|BODY_PART:sutek||LOC|LOC_CONV:loc_KGZ||LOC|L_R:lewy
bk
```

Fig. 8. Final processing results for report 123 (Fig. 6)

attributes outside tagged blocks. If there is such a localisation, it is checked whether the previous line contains an interpretation. In such a case, if the previous block contains more interpretation lines or a line with ANAT_CHANGE attribute, the block's boundary is moved above the interpretation line and the new (finding's) opening tag is inserted (see Fig. 8). The second correction is made if there is a block without any localisation attribute. In such a case, if the first part of the report (the breast composition block) ends with a localisation line, this line is moved to the previous finding segment and the tags in the rest of the report are corrected accordingly.

6   Evaluation

6.1   Methodology

The evaluation consisted in checking how many findings were identified by our algorithm and how many of their attributes were adequately recognised. We used for evaluation 448 reports from two different health care providers, which constituted (a random) one third of all reports available for the system development. For evaluation, we selected only reports describing some irregularities, i.e., 361 reports. We processed them automatically and then manually examined the obtained results. All incorrectly inserted tags or attributes were marked as '−', whereas all missing tags and attributes were preceded by '+'. Then, we compared the original results with their manual corrections, counting the number of incorrectly recognised attributes and findings' boundaries. The obtained results are presented in Fig. 9.

6.2   Identified Problems

The evaluation presented in Fig. 9 concerned mostly identifying findings, recognising their beginnings and component attributes. The numbers are quite encouraging but several problems still remain. Although it is probably not surprising that accuracy of identifying complex structures (findings) is not optimal, a similar performance for single attributes is more puzzling. While analysing the results, the following main issues have been detected.

First, not all forms of negation have been captured by shallow extraction rules, which causes opposite interpretations. In (5), the grammar does not put the recognised finding (*zagęszczenie* 'density') in the scope of negation and the reversed meaning results.[3]

(5)   Opisywane [w badaniu poprzednim z dnia 18.10.99r] [zagęszczenie] [w sutku prawym] obecnie nie jest widoczne.
Density in the right breast, described previously in the report from 18.10.99, is not currently visible.

Second, some elements of conjoined phrases are not repeated and in most cases this results in obtaining only partial information. In (6), the information about the number

---

[3] Automatically identified phrases are delimited by square brackets '[', ']'.

	nb	%
patient records	361 (448)	
FINDINGS	496	100.00
correctly recognised beginning	416	83.87
unrecognised findings	13	2.62
incorrectly recognised findings	17	3.42
incorrectly recognised beginning	67	13.50
sample attributes:		
SATURATION	185	100.00
correctly recognised	182	98.38
WITH_CALCIF	40	100.00
correctly recognised	35	87.50

Fig. 9. Evaluation of automatically identifying findings' boundaries/attributes

of calcifications (*pojedyncze* 'single') refers to both terms but, due to lack of a proper treatment of coordination, they are recognised separately and the identified number is associated only with the first one.

(6)   [pojedyncze makro] i [mikrozwapnienia]
        single macro- and microcalcifications

Third, information carried by comparisons is often misinterpreted. For example, the phrase *najlepiej wysycone* 'with highest density' in (7) specifies which findings have **relatively** the highest density but there is no indication what their absolute density might be. There is no 'standard' or 'default' density level in mammography and, in fact, its value should be unspecified. Instead, IE rules assign to the corresponding attribute the value provided by the adjective's stem, i.e., high.

(7)   [W obu sutkach] widoczne [plamiste zagęszczenia] o [charakterze łagodnym].
        Największe i [najlepiej wysycone] zlokalizowane [w sutku prawym w KDW].
        In both breasts, there are visible benign maculated densities. The biggest and of highest density in the right breast in the lower-inner quadrant.

Finally, paraphrases present a notorious problem. Various ways of expressing the same concept make automatic extraction very difficult. Variants are abundant in natural language texts and only a few terms are coined. For example, *zaburzenie architektury* 'architecture distortion' seemed to us a fixed phrase at first, till we came across its 3 variants: *obszar zaburzonego utkania* 'an area of distorted tissue', *obszar zaburzonej architektury* 'an area of distorted architecture' and *obszar zaburzenia struktury* 'an area of distorted structure'. Without tools for capturing derivations or synonyms, identifying such variants automatically is quite challenging.

7   Conclusions

We presented a method for automatic processing of Polish medical texts. The extraction process has been split into several simpler submodules responsible for specific subtasks.

Although the approach described in the paper turned out to be quite effective, there is still room for improvement. Our future work will focus on: a) writing more complex grammar rules to cover problematic cases (e.g., different types of relations in comparisons or coordination); b) developing more fine-grained grouping heuristics; c) applying machine learning techniques to obtain paraphrases and extraction patterns (the manually corrected test results will be used to evaluate learning techniques); d) supporting processing with an inference mechanism. The latter enhancement would allow for filling in data missing from the reports but which can be inferred based on the general medical knowledge. After the amendments, data will be entered to a database where they can be further analysed.

References

1. Busemann, S., Krieger, H.-U.: Resources and Techniques for Multilingual Information Extraction. *Proceedings of LREC 2004, Lisbon, Portugal*, 2004, pp. 1923–1926
2. Drożdżyński, W., Homola, P., Piskorski, J., Zinkevičius, V.: (2003). Adopting SProUT to processing Baltic and Slavonic languages. In *Proceedings of the IESL Workshop in conjunction with the RANLP2003 Conference, Bulgaria*
3. Drożdżyński, W., Krieger, H.-U., Piskorski, J., Schäfer, U., Xu, F.: Shallow Processing with Unification and Typed Feature Structures — Foundations and Applications. *German AI Journal KI-Zeitschrift*, 01/04. Gesellschaft für Informatik e.V, 2004
4. Hahn, U., Romacker, M., Schultz, S.: MEDSYNDIKATE — a natural language system for the extraction of medical information from findings reports. In: *International Journal of Medical Informatics*, 2002, pp. 63-74
5. Jain, N.L., Friedman, C.: Identification of Findings Suspicious for Breast Cancer Based on Natural Language Processing of Mammogram Reports. In: *Proceedings of the American Medical Informatics Association Annual Fall Symposium*, 1997, pp. 829-833
6. Kupść, A., Marciniak, M. Mykowiecka, A., Piskorski, J., Podsiadły-Marczykowska T.: Information Extraction from Mammographic Reports. In: *KONVENS 2004*, Vienna, Austria, 2004, pp. 113–116
7. Piskorski, J, Homola, P., Marciniak, M., Mykowiecka, A., Przepiórkowski, A., Woliński, M.: Information Extraction for Polish using the SProUT Platform. *Proceedings of ISMIS 2004, Zakopane*, 2004, pp. 225–236
8. Ruch, P., Baud, R., Geissbruhler, A.: Evaluating and reducing the effect of data corruption when applying bag of words approaches to medical records, in *International Journal of Medical Informatics*, 2002

The Explanatory Experiment for Evaluation of SPOC System from Contents Creators' Perspective

Ken'ichi Matsumura[1], Yukiko I. Nakano[1], and Toyoaki Nishida[2]

[1] Research Institute of Science and Technology for Society (RISTEX),
Atago Green Hills MORI Tower 18F, 2-5-1, Atago Minato-ku, Tokyo 105-6218, Japan
{matumura, yukiko}@ristex.jst.go.jp
http://kaiwa.ristex.jst.go.jp
[2] Department of Intelligence Science and Technology,
Graduate School of Informatics Kyoto University,
Yoshida-honmachi, Sakyo-ku, Kyoto city, Kyoto 606-8501, Japan
nishida@i.kyoto-u.ac.jp

Abstract. In this paper, we will present an evaluation experiment of Stream Public Opinion Channel (SPOC) from contents creators perspective. This system allows a contents creator to publish programs using not only multimedia but also conversational information in sync with interface agent and multimedia. Contents creator of SPOC needs to make a story with consideration of agentçÛt' actions and their effect on audience. Therefore, it is important to evaluate the effect of interface agents on contents creators. Results of the experiment showed that contents creators positively accepted the SPOC in subjective evaluation, but they could not successfully embody what they want to express as a story. Additionally, we found correlations between the impressions of interface agent and factors which would form users behavioural intention. We need to measure not only subjective evaluation but also objective indicator in evaluation.

1 Introduction

The number of the Internet users is increasing, and the way to use it becomes diverse. Some of them use the Internet in order to collect and acquire information which they need, and others do for the purpose of sending messages to general public.

SPOC system aims to support communication through conversational contents in the network community and supports conversation and knowledge sharing among members of the network community [1]. This system allows a contents creator to publish programs using not only multimedia but also conversational information in sync with interface agent and multimedia [2]. SPOC provides a media technology which automatically embodies a story using speech, graphics, movie, and animated agent, and supports story-based communication in a network community. A story consists of a sequence of Knowledge Cards (Card), each of which consists of a visual material (movie or graphics) and a short explanation text about it. The story is presented by caster agent with speech and multimedia.

In SPOC system, the receiver of information watches conversational contents from caster agent with voice and multimedia. Therefore, contents creators making a story means that they make conversational contents presented by interface agent.

L. Bolc et al. (Eds.): IMTCI 2004, LNAI 3490, pp. 79–90, 2005.

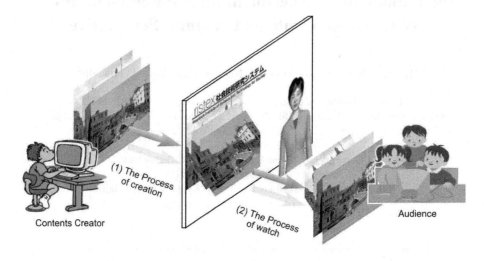

Fig. 1. Information flow in SPOC system

In SPOC, contents creators who want to send information can create a new story and edit existing stories. When they create a story, they make or edit cards, and put into a story by collecting some cards. In editing cards, users need to do only the following two things; (1) Editing a visual material by selecting a material from a menu, and specifying zoom scale and position of the focused area, (2) typing in a text which should be uttered by an animated agent. SPOC supports the user to create a story in this way. But SPOC does not directly give any advice to contents creators. Therefore, contents creators need to make a story with consideration of agent's action and its effect on audience.

How can we evaluate the communication tools with interface agents like SPOC? There are mainly two perspectives in evaluating such tools. One is perspective from audience and the other is from contents creators. Figure 1 shows two processes in SPOC. One is the process of creation, and the other is the process of watching. We need to evaluate both the process of creation and that of watching in order to evaluate communication tools like SPOC. But there are few researches from perspective of contents creators.

Andre [3] examined effectiveness of interface agents. The subjects evaluate presentations on technical and non-technical domains under two conditions: supported and not-supported by an interface agent. Craig & Gholson (2002) investigated effectiveness of animated agent on multimedia learning [4]. These studies discussed the effect of interface agent from perspective of audience. The other focus is the effect of interface agent on contents creators.

The usability test is from this perspective. Of course, usability test is an important aspect in evaluating communication tools. To evaluate communication tools with interface agent, we need to consider the effect of interface agent on contents creatorçÙ£ subjective evaluation. In this paper, we report the results of our evaluation experiment for SPOC system from contents creators, and we discuss the effect of interface agent on them. In addition, we report users actions seen in contents creation process on SPOC and time spent to conduct a story.

2   Approach to Evaluation

2.1   Evaluation Design

Fishbein & Ajzen (1975) presented the Theory of Reasoned Action (TRA) [5]. In this theory, the behavioural intention is influenced by attitude to behaviour and subjective social norm. Behavioural intention is the representation about the action exacted in the future [6]. TRA assumes that people act on the basis of behavioural intention. Therefore, it seems that behavioural intention is useful for predicting users future behaviours, and measuring behavioural intention is useful to reveal problems of a tool to be improved.

Davis et al (1989) claimed that TRA can be applied to acceptant of technology in an organisation [7]. Davis model predicts acceptance and usage of information systems in the organisation. In this model, behavioural intention is influenced by perceived usefulness, perceived ease of use, and subjective social norms. A subjective social norm is defined as perceived expectation from other members. Although a subjective social norm affects the intention in an organisation, it has little effect on a network community. This is because there is little information useful for judging a social norm in a network community. Therefore, in this study, in order to estimate users perceived usefulness and perceived ease of use in SPOC, we will use both (1) subjective measure using a questionnaire and (2) task performance time as an objective measure. Then, by calculating the correlation between subjective measures and a performance time for composing a story, we examine whether these two measures are consistent and useful to predict perceived usefulness and perceived ease of use.

2.2   Contents Creation Process

First, as an objective measure for predicting perceived ease of use in SPOC, we measure user's task performance time for creating SPOC contents. Task performance time is a useful measure for examining whether users can operate SPOC smoothly. If they spend much time to operate a tool, they would not feel ease of use for that.

2.3   The Image of a Story and the Impression of Interface Agent

As a behavioural measure for predicting perceived usefulness in SPOC, we measured user's impression of the contents created by herself/himself as well as the user's impression of the SPOC interface agent, which plays as a caster in SPOC contents. As SPOC system provides information to community members with the agent, users impression of the interface agent would affect the impression of a story itself. Based on this assumption, to measure the users impression, we compare the user's impression after a creating process (i.e., before watching the contents) with that after watching the contents that they created. If there is a discrepancy in user's impression between before and after watching contents, the users would not feel that they successfully embodied their image of a story which they wanted to express by using SPOC, and they underrate perceived usefulness and perceived ease of use for SPOC.

3   Method

3.1   Purpose

The purpose of this study is to find factors that correlate with behavioural intention, perceived usefulness, and perceived ease of use. In this study, we measured mainly behavioural intention, perceived usefulness, perceived ease of use, the image of a story and the impression of agent, and we examine the correlation between subjective evaluations of SPOC system by contents creators and the time required to construct a story with it.

3.2   Participants and Task

Two women and seven men participated in this experiment. The task in main session was creating a story about Tokyo city because all participants live in Tokyo. They could use 23 pictures and seven movies in creation of a story. All pictures and movies were taken of Tokyo scenery. They made Cards and a story with these materials.

3.3   Procedure

At the beginning of a session, an experimenter instructed how to use the Story Editor of SPOC. After instruction session, each participant tried to create a short story consisting of four cards with all functions by herself/himself. Main session started after an experimenter made sure that participants had no questions about operation of SPOC.

The task in the main session was creating a story about Tokyo city. They made Cards and a story with pictures and movies. A number of cards in a story and time for creation were not limited while creating story. After finishing creating a story, they were asked to answer the questionnaire.

We had taped the work process for story creation. We could not record one subject, because there were troubles with camera. Therefore, we analysed eight participants subjective evaluation and creation process in this study.

3.4   Questionnaire

The image of a story and the impression of caster agent were measured by semantic differential method (SD method). SD method has been developed by Osgood, Suci, & Turnnenbaum (1957) in order to measure peopl's psychological meaning about a target or words [8].

The questionnaire consisted of SD scales for the image of a story they had wanted to express (19 pairs of adjectives: see Figure 2), the impression of caster agent (12 pairs of adjectives: see Figure 3), and questions about behavioural intention, perceived usefulness, and perceived ease of use for SPOC.

3.4.1 Subjective Evaluation

Behavioural intention was measured by one item. Questions about perceived usefulness consist of the satisfaction to a story (one item), the easiness of expression (one item), usefulness (one item). As perceived ease of use, operationality (six items), the development of skills for using SPOC (two items), the impression of work with SPOC (three items). These items were measured on four-point scales.

3.4.2 The Image of a Story and the Impression of Caster Agent

In order to measure the image of a story created by himself with SPOC system and the impression of caster agent, participants were asked to answer 19 pairs of adjectives about the image of a story, and 12 pairs of adjectives about the impression of caster agent on five-point SD scales.

4 Results

4.1 Subjective Evaluation, the Image of a Story, and the Impression of Interface Agent

Subjective evaluation is measured on four-point scales, and higher score means that a user evaluates it more positively. We calculated mean value of factors composed by two or more items. This mean value was assumed the score of each factor.

Most of factors were evaluated positively, but satisfaction to the story created by her/himself was slightly negative. These results indicate that participants thought of SPOC system as a useful tool which was easy to embody what they wanted to express. And they thought that they could use SPOC easily. But they could not be satisfied with a story by them. Table 1 shows mean scores of each factor.

4.2 The Image of a Story and the Impression of Caster Agent

In order to examine the discrepancy of image of a story between at pre-trial and post-trial, we measured the image of the story at pre-trial and post-trial. The pre-trial image is the image that the creators wanted to express as a story. The post-trial image is the impression after watching the story created by a participant. We calculated difference between the image score at pre-trial and post-trial. And as the impression of caster agent, we calculated total impression score, which is the total of impression score for each pair. These scores were used in later analysis. Discrepancy and impression of caster agent are shown in Table 1.

Figure 2 shows the image profile at pre-trial and post-trial. T-test on each pair of adjectives indicated that there are significant differences between pre-trial image and

Table 1. The mean and SD of each score, discrepancy, and the impression of caster agent

	means	SD
Behavioural intention		
Behavioural intention in the future (one item)	2.78	0.83
Perceived usefulness		
The satisfaction to a story (one item)	2.44	1.13
The easiness of expression (one item)	3.00	1.00
The usefulness (one item)	3.00	0.87
Perceived ease of use		
Operationality (six items)	2.93	0.38
The development of skill for use SPOC (two items)	3.39	0.49
The impression of work with SPOC (three items)	3.33	0.50
Evaluation of SPOC		
The expectation to effect of SPOC (two items)	2.78	0.44
The image of a story and agent		
Discrepancy	13.33	4.85
The impression of agent	42.11	4.04

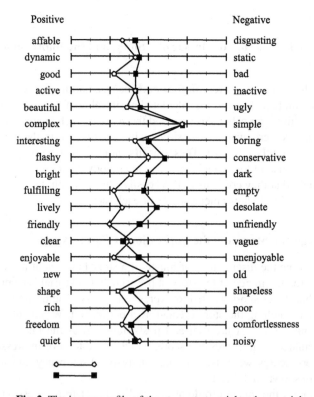

Fig. 2. The image profile of the story at pre-trial and post-trial

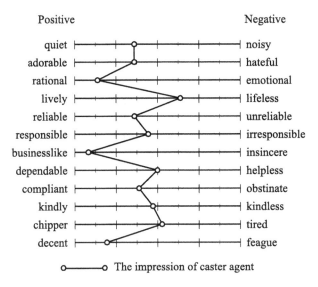

Fig. 3. The image profile of caster agent

post-trial image on "fulfilling-empty", "lively-desolate", "friendly-unfriendly", "enjoyable-unenjoyable". We calculate the image scores by totalising all the scores at pre-trial and post-trial. There is a significant difference between pre-trial image score and post-trial image score with T-test. These results indicate that users cannot successfully embody what they want to express. The image profile of the caster agent is shown in Figure 3. These results indicate that participants felt that the caster agent was businesslike, rational, and decent strongly but lifeless.

4.3   Analysis for Contents Creation Process on SPOC

A coder coded actions with watching the creation process taped. He coded actions in a story creation process and recorded starting time and finishing time of each action using a video camera counter. We could see the following eight actions in the process of story creation; (1) Selecting pictures or movies, (2) Lining up the position of materials and adjusted size, (3) Making narrations, (4) Saving card, (5) Creating new cards, (6) Changing order of cards, and (7) Watching a story created by themselves.

Figure 4 shows a screenshot of the card editor and corresponding users' action. In this screenshot, users (1) selected pictures or movies, (2) lined up the position of materials and adjusted size, (3) typed in narrations, and (4) saved the card. Figure 5 shows a screenshot of the story editor and corresponding users' actions. In this screen, they (5) created new cards, (6) changed order of cards, and (7) watch a story created by themselves. Modification means these actions to already existing cards. And other actions included blank time between actions.

Table 2 shows the average times for each action, total time to create a story, and percentage of each action in story creation process. Average total time is about

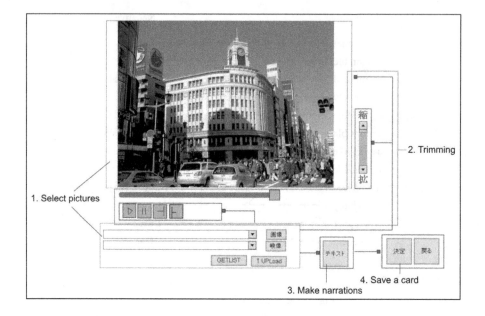

Fig. 4. The screenshot of card editor and corresponding users' action

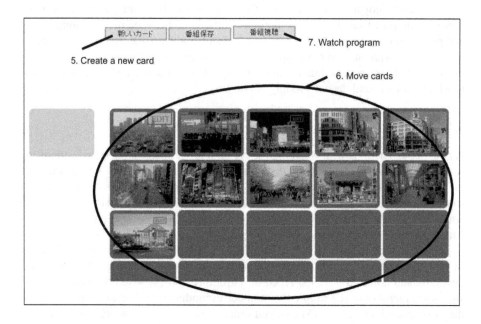

Fig. 5. The screenshot of story editor and corresponding users' action

Table 2. The average time of each action on the creation process of SPOC

	Average Time	SD	Percentage (%)
1. Select picture	6'39"22	2'38"24	26.51
2. Trimming	4'21"15	3'58"19	17.34
3. Make narrations	9'31"38	3'43"55	37.93
4. Save a card	2'24"45	1'19"51	9.61
5. Create a new card	0'07"00	0'04"56	0.47
6. Move cards	0'18"52	0'13"03	1.24
7. Watch a story	2'36"36	1'38"40	10.39
8. Modification	0'05"00	0'09"38	0.33
9. Other activities	0'01"07	0'03"11	0.07
Total time	25'06"53	8'37"32	

25 minutes. The process of story creation was mainly consisted of 5 actions. 5 actions were: selecting pictures, trimming, making narrations, waiting for saving cards, and watching the story which they created by themselves.

These results suggest that creators of SPOC stories spend much time in selecting pictures and making a narration. Most of participants selected visual materials at first and then made narrations about the visual materials selected. In other words, visual materials are in the centre of a story, and creators choose visual materials very carefully. Additionally, we can say that it took much time to make narrations, because creators should represent their image or thought in their mind in these activities.

4.4 Correlation Analysis

In order to examine the relation among factors, time for construction, the image of a story and the impression of caster agent, we calculated the correlation coefficient between each score of factors, the time, the image and the impression. Factors were behavioural intention to use SPOC in the future, perceived usefulness, perceived ease of use, the impression of the caster agent, and the discrepancy between images of the story measured at pre-trial and post-trial (discrepancy). Table 3 shows correlation coefficient among factors.

4.4.1 The Relation Among Subjective Evaluations

There were significant correlations between behavioural intention and perceived ease of use. Behavioural intention was associated with the impression of work process with SPOC, which is a factor of perceived ease of use. In other words, contents creator feeling that s/he can use SPOC easily heightens the behavioural intention. Additionally, the intention correlates with the satisfaction to a story and usefulness.

When we focus on the means of scores of factors which have significant correlation with behavioural intention, we can see that the impression of work process and usefulness were evaluated positively, but the satisfaction is not positively.

Table 3. The correlation coefficient of each score of factors

	Behavioural intention	Satis-faction	Easiness	Usefulness	Opera-tionality	Development of skill	Impression of work
Satisfaction to a story	0.52						
Easiness of expression	0.00	0.77**					
Usefulness	0.87**	0.51	0.14				
Operationality	0.27	0.09	−0.38	0.06			
Development of skill for use	0.09	0.67*	0.77**	0.15	−0.44		
The impression of work process	0.60*	0.29	0.00	0.77**	−0.07	0.26	
Expectation to effect of SPOC	0.19	0.35	0.43	0.33	−0.54	0.75*	0.38
Discrepancy	0.70*	0.43	−0.13	0.57	0.27	0.30	0.55
The impression of agent	0.68*	0.84**	0.59*	0.75*	−0.10	0.61*	0.45

* $p < .05$ ** $p < .01$

There are some receivers of information which somebody sends in communication. But we do not consider the presence of other persons in this study. Therefore they could not understand how other persons assess a story that they created. This might cause to reduce their satisfaction to the story.

4.4.2 The Correlation Between Subjective Evaluation and the Time for Creation of a Story

In order to examine the effect on time for making narration and selecting pictures, we calculated coefficient of correlation between time for action and subjective evaluation. Results showed that making narration had a correlation on operationality which was measured as subjective evaluation ($r = -0.71, p < .05$). And Selecting pictures has a correlation on the impression of working SPOC ($r = -0.74, p < .05$).

4.4.3 The Relation Between the Impression of Caster Agent and Subjective Evaluations

We calculated total score of the impression of the caster agent. The impression of the caster agent correlated with many factors. This means that the impression of the caster agent correlated with factors which would form behavioural intention. Therefore, we can say there is possibility that the caster agent does not affect only audience but also contents creators.

In the case of SPOC, contents creators need to make a story with consideration for actions of the caster agent in order to communicate accurately and comprehensibly what s/he wants to express. Therefore, the impression of the caster agent correlated with subjective evaluation.

5   Discussion and Conclusion

In this study, we discussed the effect of interface agent on contents creators. In general, we did not find any result showing that users had any trouble with operating SPOC. This suggests that the users easily create stories using SPOC. SPOC system was evaluated positively on subjective evaluation by contents creator. But their satisfaction to the story created by her/himself was slightly negative. Though there are commonly some receivers of information which somebody sends in communication, there were no receivers in this experiment. Therefore they could not evaluate the story which they created in comparison with others, so that there were no other stories which they could watch. This made them reduce satisfaction. We need to evaluate SPOC system in a community in the future in order to solve this problem.

The results of analysis of contents creation process indicated that creators of SPOC story spend much time in selecting pictures and making a narration. Most of the participants selected visual materials first and then made narrations about the selected visual materials. In other words, visual materials are in the centre of a story. Therefore we can think that creators choose visual materials carefully. Additionally, we can say that it took much time to make narrations, because creators should represent their image or thought in their mind in these activities.

The behavioural intention correlated with usefulness, and the impression of work process. Usefulness is a factor about perceived usefulness and the impression of work process is a factor about perceived ease of use. Results of correlation analysis indicate that there are relations between the impression of interface agents and subjective evaluation by contents creator. As perceived usefulness and ease of use will partly form the behavioural intention, we can say that these results indicate that we have to consider the effect of interface agent on contents creator in the evaluation of communication tools supported by interface agent not only from perspective of audiences but also from perspective of contents creators.

The intention has a relation with the impression of working with SPOC. And the impression correlated with the time for selecting pictures. Contents creators spend much time for selecting pictures and making narrations. Therefore the time for selecting materials and making narration had an impact on operationality and the impression of working with SPOC.

These results indicate that subjective evaluation was influenced by time for actions. Therefore we need to measure not only the subjective evaluation but also objective indicator. In the future, we will need to establish an evaluation method, and evaluate SPOC system from receivers of information in order to examine whether a story is communicated through the receivers easily.

Acknowledgement

This study is supported by Mission-oriented Program I in RISTEX, which was established under the joint auspices of the Japan Science and Technology Corporation (JST).

References

1. Nakano, I. Y., Murayama T., Nishida T.: *Multimodal Story-based Communication: Integrating a Movie and Conversational Agent,* IEICE Transactions, 2002
2. Murayama T., Nakano, I. Y., Nishida T.: *Participatory Broadcasting System Using Interface Agent and Multimedia*, in: Social Intelligence Design international workshop, 2004
3. van Mulken, S., Andre, E., Mfiller, J.: *The Persona Effect: How Substantial Is It?* in People and Computers XIII: Proceedings of HCI'98. 1998
4. Craig & Gholson Does an agent matter?: *The Effects of Animated Pedagogical Agents on Multimedia Environments.* in ED-MEDIA 2002: World Conference on Educational Multimedia, Hypermedia and Telecommunications, 2002
5. Fishbein, M., Ajzen, I.: *Belief, attitude, intention and behaviour: An introduction to theoryand research*, Addison Wesley, 1975
6. Bandura, A.: *Social Cognitive Theory: An Agentic Perspective*, Annual Review of Psychology, Vol. 52, 1–26, 2001
7. Davis, F. D., Baggozzi, R. P., Warshaw, P. R.: *User Acceptance of Computer Technology: A Comparison of Two Theoretical Models*, Management Science, Vol. 35, 8, 982–1003, 1989
8. Osgood, C. E., Suci, G. J., Turnnenbaum, P. H.: *The measurement of meaning*, Urbana: University of Illinois Press, 1957

Enriching Agent Animations with Gestures and Highlighting Effects

Yukiko I. Nakano[1], Masashi Okamoto[2], and Toyoaki Nishida[3]

[1] Japan Science and Technology Agency (JST), 2-5-1 Atago Minato-ku,
Tokyo 105-6218, Japan
yukiko@ristex.jst.go.jp
[2] Graduate School of Information Science and Technology, The University of Tokyo,
7-3-1 Hongo, Bunkyo-ku, Tokyo 113-8656, Japan
okamoto@kc.t.u-tokyo.ac.jp
[3] Graduate School of Informatics, Kyoto University, Yoshida-Honmachi,
Sakyo-ku, Kyoto 606-8501, Japan
nishida@i.kyoto-u.ac.jp

Abstract. Character agents have become more popular in the Internet due to its attractiveness. This paper proposes an agent animation generation system which automatically selects agent behaviours as well as highlighting animations to emphasise the agent actions. In order to produce appropriate animations according to the content of agent's spoken message, our system, first analyses the message text using natural language processing engine, and then selects animations based on the linguistic information calculated by the engine.

1   Introduction

Character animations have become popular on the Web pages, and the characters serve as news casters, clerks who advertise products, and teachers who explain scientific issues, etc.

The existence of characters on the Web pages has positive effect of attracting users attention and interest. Moreover, psychological studies reported that comprehension of spoken utterances accompanied by gestures is much better than those presented without gestures [1] These suggest that it is important to generate appropriate gestures according to the content of a message.

However, little has been studied about automatic gesture generation for animated agents. Most of the current web-based agent animations are produced by expert animation designers, or generated from a script which specifies a sequence of agent actions [2]. A problem of a script-based approach is that describing a script needs enormous time and effort. With the goal of improving expressiveness of agent animations, this paper proposes an agent animation system that automatically decides agent behaviours based on the linguistic information in a text, and produces an agent action script. Moreover, to emphasise important concepts clearly, we also propose a mechanism that generates highlighting animations, such as superimposition and illustrative animations, which synchronise with agent behaviours.

L. Bolc et al. (Eds.): IMTCI 2004, LNAI 3490, pp. 91–98, 2005.

This paper is organised as follows. The next section reviews theoretical issues about the relationships between gestures and syntactic information. The empirical study we conducted based on these issues is described in Section 3. In Section 4, based on the empirical results, we implement the CAST system that converts a text into a conversational agent gesticulating and speaking synchronously. In Section 5, a highlighting generation mechanism is proposed as an optional function of CAST. Finally, in Section 6, we discuss future directions of this research.

2   Linguistic Theories and Gesture Studies

In this section, we review linguistic theories and discuss the relationship between gesture occurrence and syntactic information.

Linguistic quantity for reference: [3] used communicative dynamism (CD), which represents the extent to which the message at a given point is "pushing the communication forward" [4], as a variable that correlates with gesture occurrence. The greater the CD, the more probable the occurrence of a gesture. As a measure of CD, McNeill chose the amount of linguistic material used to make the reference [5]. Pronouns have less CD than full nominal phrases (NPs), which have less CD than modified full NPs. This implies that the CD can be estimated by looking at the syntactic structure of a sentence.

Theme/Rheme: McNeill also asserted that the theme [6] of a sentence usually has the least CD and is not normally accompanied by a gesture. Gestures usually accompany the rhemes, which are the elements of a sentence that plausibly contribute information about the theme, and thus have greater CD. In Japanese grammar there is a device for marking the theme explicitly. Topic marking postpositions (or "topic markers"), typically "wa", mark a nominal phrase as the theme. This facilitates the use of syntactic analysis to identify the theme of a sentence. Another interesting aspect of information structure is that in the English grammar, a wh-interrogative (what, how, etc.) at the beginning of a sentence marks the theme and indicates that the content of the theme is the focus [6]. However, we do not know whether such a special type of theme is more likely to co-occur with a gesture or not.

Given/New: Given and new information demonstrate an aspect of theme and rheme. Given information usually has a low degree of rhematicity, while new information has a high degree. This implies that rhematicity can be estimated by determining whether the NP is the first mention (i.e., new information) or has already been mentioned (i.e., old or given information).

Contrastive relationship: [7] reported that intonational accent is often used to mark an explicit contrast among the salient discourse entities. On the basis of this finding and Kendon's theory about the relationship between intonation phrases and gesture placements [8], [9] developed a method for generating contrastive gestures from a semantic representation. In syntactic analysis, a contrastive relation is usually expressed as a co-ordination, which is a syntactic structure including at least two conjuncts linked by a conjunction.

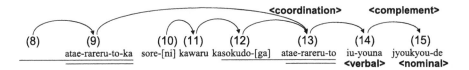

Fig. 1. Sample analysis of syntactic dependency and gesture occurence

Underlined phrases are accompanied by gestures, and gesture strokes occur at
double-underlined parts. Case markers are enclosed by square brackets [ ].

Fig. 1 shows an example of the correlation between gesture occurrence and the
dependency structure of a Japanese sentence. Bunsetsu units[1] (8)–(9) and (10)–(13) in
the figure are conjuncts. Each conjunct is accompanied by a gesture. Bunsetsu (14) is
a complement containing a verbal phrase; it depends on bunsetsu (15), which is an NP.
Thus, bunsetsu (15) is a modified full NP and thus has large linguistic quantity.

3   Empirical Study

To identify linguistic features that might be useful for judging gesture occurrence, we
videotaped seven presentation talks and transcribed three minutes of each of them. The
collected data included 2124 bunsetsu units and 343 gestures.

3.1   Gesture Annotation

Three coders discussed how to code the half of the data and reached a consensus on
gesture occurrence. After this consensus on the coding a scheme was established, one
of the coders annotated the rest of the data. A gesture consists of preparation, stroke,
and retraction [3], and a stroke co-occurs with the most prominent syllable [8]. Thus,
we annotated the stroke time as well as the start and end time of each gesture.

3.2   Linguistic Analysis

Each bunsetsu unit was automatically annotated with linguistic information using a
Japanese syntactic analyser [10]. The information was determined by asking the following questions for each bunsetsu unit.

(a) If it is an NP, is it modified by a clause or a complement?
(b) If it is an NP, what type of postpositional particle marks its end (e.g., "wa", "ga",
"wo")?
(c) Is it a wh-interrogative?
(d) Are all the content words in the bunsetsu unit have mentioned in a preceding sentence?
(e) Is it a constituent of a coordination?

---

[1] A "bunsetsu unit" in Japanese corresponds to a phrase in English, such as a noun phrase or a
prepositional phrase.

Moreover, as we noticed that some lexical entities frequently co-occurred with a gesture in our data, we used the syntactic analyser to annotate additional lexical information based on the following questions.

(f) Is the bunsetsu unit an emphatic adverbial phrase (e.g., very, extremely), or is it modified by a preceding emphatic adverb (e.g., <u>very</u> important issue)?

(g) Does it include a cue word (e.g., now, therefore)?

(h) Does it include a numeral (e.g., <u>thousands</u> of people, <u>99</u> times)?

We then investigated the correlation between these lexical and syntactic features and the occurrence of gesture strokes.

3.3   Result

The results are summarised in Table 1. The baseline gesture occurrence frequency was 10.1% per bunsetsu unit (a gesture occurred once about every ten bunsetsu units). A gesture stroke most frequently co-occurred with a bunsetsu unit forming a coordination (47.7%). When an NP was modified by a full clause, it was accompanied by a gesture 38.2% of the time.

For the other types of noun phrases, including pronouns, when an accusative case marked with case marker "wo" was new information (i.e., it was not mentioned in a previous sentence), a gesture co-occurred with the phrase 28.1% of the time.

Moreover, gesture strokes frequently co-occurred with wh-interrogatives (41.4%), cue words (41.5%), and numeral words (39.3%). Gesture strokes frequently occurred right after emphatic adverbs (35%) rather than with the adverb (24.4%).

Table 1. Summary of results

Case Id	Case			Frequenct per bunsetsu unit
[C1]	Quantity of modification	(a) NP modified by a class		0.382
[C2]		Pronouns, other type of NPs	(b) Case marker = "wo" & (d) New information	0.281
[C3]	(c) WH-interrogative			0.414
[C4]	(e) Coordination			0.477
[C5]	Emphatic adverb	(f) Emphatic adverb itself		0.244
[C6]		(f′) Following an emphatic adverb		0.350
[C7]	(g) Cue word			0.415
[C8]	(h) Numeral			0.393
[C9]	Other (baseline)			0.101

These cases listed in Table 1 had a 3 to 5 times higher probability of gesture occurrence than the baseline and accounted for 75% of all the gestures observed in the data. Our results suggest that these types of lexical and syntactic information can be used to distinguish between where a gesture should be assigned and where one should not be assigned. They also indicate that the syntactic structure of a sentence more strongly affects gesture occurrence than theme or rheme and than given or new information specified by local grammatical cues, such as topic markers and case markers.

4   Generating Agent Animations

This section describes an animated agent system, CAST (The Conversational Agent System for neTwork applications). CAST calculates the agent animation schedule as well as produces synthesised voice for the agent. CAST system architecture is shown in Fig. 2. The system consists of four main modules: (1) the Agent Behaviour Selection Module (ABS), (2) the Language Tagging Module (LTM), (3) a Text-to-Speech engine (TTS), and (4) Flash-based character animation system, RISA (The RIStex animated Agent system). When CAST receives a text input, it sends the text to the ABS. The ABS selects appropriate gestures and facial expressions according to the linguistic information calculated by the LTM. Then, the ABS obtains timing information by accessing the TTS, and calculates a time schedule for a set of agent actions. At the same time, the synthesised voice for the text is also generated and saved as an MP3 audio file.

The time schedule and the MP3 file generated by CAST are sent to a web-based presentation generation system, called SPOC [11], and the animations executed by RISA and the synthesised voice are played through SPOC in a synchronised manner.

4.1   Agent Behaviour Selection Module (ABS)

Input of the ABS is a plain text, and the output is an instruction set for RISA Animation System. Process in the ABS consists of two steps; (1) Annotating Japanese linguistic information useful for determining nonverbal behaviours, (2) Assigning nonverbal behaviours by applying behaviour selection rules to the annotated Japanese text. We will describe these steps in the following sections.

4.1.1   Tagging Linguistic Information

First, the LTM parses the input text and calculates the linguistic information described in Section 3.2. For example, bunsetsu (9) in Fig. 1 has the following feature set.

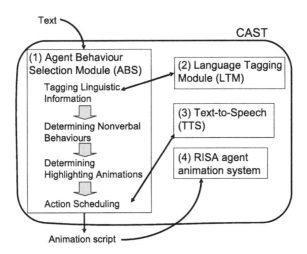

Fig. 2. CAST architecture

{*Text-ID: 1, Sentence-ID: 1, Bunsetsu-ID: 9, Govern: 8, De-pend-on: 13, Phrase-type: VP, Linguistic-quantity: NA, Case-marker: NA, WH-interrogative: false, Given/New: new, Coor-dinate-with: 13, Emphatic-Adv: false, Cue-Word: false, Nu-meral: false*}

The text ID of this bunsetsu unit is 1, the sentence ID is 1, the bunsetsu ID is 9. This bunsetsu governs bun-setsu 8 and depends on bunsetsu 13. It conveys new information and, together with bunsetsu 13, forms a parallel phrase.

4.1.2   Assigning Nonverbal Behaviours

Then, for each bunsetsu unit, the ABS decides whether to assign a gesture or not based on the empirical results shown in Table 1. For example, bunsetsu unit (9) shown above matches case [C4] in Table 1, where a bunsetsu unit is a constituent of coordination. In this case, the system assigns a gesture to the bunsetsu with 47.7% probability. In the current implementation, if a specific gesture for an emphasised concept is defined in the gesture animation library (e.g., a gesture animation expressing "big"), it is preferred to a "beat gesture" (a simple flick of the hand or fingers up and down [3]). If a specific gesture is not defined, a beat gesture is used as the default.

5   Adding Highlights to Gestures

As an optional function in CAST, we have also built a component called the Enhancement Generator that automatically adds highlighting animations to agent gesture animations after the gestures are determined by the ABS. We propose two types of highlighting methods to emphasise synchronization between verbal (speech) and nonverbal (gesture) behaviours [12].

(1) Superimposition with Beat Gesture: Beat gestures simply emphasise one part of an utterance without representing the meaning of a word. To visualise synchronization between the emphasised words and a beat gesture, the Enhancement Generator adds a superimposition of the emphasised words to the agent's beat gesture animation. Fig. 3(a) shows an example of superimposition with a beat gesture.

(2) Illustrative Animation with Metaphoric Gesture: When a specific shape of gesture is assigned to a metaphoric gesture, it is emphasised by illustrative animations, such

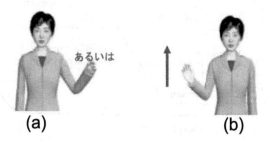

Fig. 3. Examples of (a) superimposition and (b) illustrative animation indicating "increase"

as an arrow and a line. If the emphasised concept implies motion or movement, such as "increase" or "decrease", the direction of the movement is illustrated by an arrow animation. An example of highlighting the concept of "increase" is shown in Fig. 3(b). If the emphasised concept expresses a static state, a motionless picture is used to emphasise the gesture. For example, when the agent is performing a "long" gesture, a rectangle shape is shown near the agent's hands to emphasise the length.

```
(1) shindo-ga
            <Gesture_right type="contrast" handshape_right="stroke1@2">
(2)         atae-rareru-to-ka
            </Gesture_right>
(3) sore-ni
(4) kawaru
(5) kasokudo-ga

            <Gesture_right type="contrast" handshape_right="stroke2@2">
(6)         atae-rareru-to
            </Gesture_right>
(7) iu-youna
            <Enhance type="superimposition" text="jyoukyou-de" layout="right">
            <Gesture_right type="beat" handshape_right="stroke1">
(8)         jyoukyou-de
            </Gesture_right>
            </Enhance>
      ...
```

Fig. 4. Example of CAST output

The output of the ABS is stored in XML format. The type of action and the start and end of the action are specified by XML tags. In the example shown in Fig. 4, the agent performs contrast gestures at the second and sixth bunsetsu units and a beat gesture at the eighth bunsetsu unit. The latter gesture is accompanied by a highlighting animation, which is specified by an Enhance tag. In this example, a superimposition of the emphasised word, "jyoukyou-de", is added to the beat gesture animation. The ABS also assigns facial expressions. Eyebrow raise co-occurs with a gesture. Head nod and blink occasionally occur at the end of an utterance.

6   Conclusion and Future Work

This paper described an agent behaviour generation system, CAST, aiming at enhancing expressiveness of agent animations by generating gestures and facial expressions automatically, and adding highlighting animations to the gesture animations. CAST selects agent behaviours and highlighting animations based on linguistic information calculated by a natural language processing engine.

Although in the current implementation the system uses only lexical and syntactic information, as a future direction, we plan to improve the system by incorporating more general discourse level information in the message text.

In addition, it is also necessary to evaluate the effectiveness of nonverbal agent behaviours in actual human-agent interaction. We expect that if CAST can generate nonverbal behaviours with appropriate timing for emphasising important words and phrases, users will perceive agent presentations as lively and comprehensible. An important future direction for our research will be conducting a user study to examine this hypothesis.

References

1. Rogers, W.: *The Contribution of Kinesic Illustrators towards the Comprehension of Verbal Behavior within Utterances.* Human Communication Research, 1978. **5**: pp. 54–62
2. Ishizuka, M., Tsutsui, T., Saeyor, S., Dohi, H., Zong, Y., and Prendinger, H.: *MPML: A Multimodal Presentation Markup Language with Character Agent Control Functions.* In *Proceedings of Agents2000 Workshop 7 on Achieving Human-like Behavior in Interactive Animated Agents*, 2000, (Barcelona, Spain), pp. 51–54
3. McNeill, D.: *Hand and Mind: What Gestures Reveal about Thought.* 1992, Chicago, IL/London, UK: The University of Chicago Press
4. Firbas, J.: *On the Concept of Communicative Dynamism in the Theory of Functional Sentence Perspective.* Philologica Pragensia, 1971. **8**: pp. 135–144
5. Givon, T.: *Iconicity, Isomorphism and Non-arbitrary Coding in Syntax*, in *Iconicity in Syntax*, J. Haiman, Editor. 1985, John Benjamins. pp. 187–219
6. Halliday, M.A.K.: *Intonation and Grammar in British English.* 1967, The Hague: Mouton
7. Prevost, S.A.: *An Informational Structural Approach to Spoken Language Generation.* In *Proceedings of 34th Annual Meeting of the Association for Computational Linguistics*, 1996, (Santa Cruz, CA)
8. Kendon, A.: *Some Relationships between Body Motion and Speech*, in *Studies in Dyadic Communication*, A.W. Siegman and B. Pope, Editors. 1972, Pergamon Press: Elmsford, NY. pp. 177–210
9. Cassell, J. and Prevost, S.: *Distribution of Semantic Features Across Speech and Gesture by Humans and Computers.* In *Proceedings of Workshop on the Integration of Gesture in Language and Speech*, 1996, (Newark, DE), WIGLS, pp. 253–270
10. Kurohashi, S. and Nagao, M.: *A Syntactic Analysis Method of Long Japanese Sentences Based on the Detection of Conjunctive Structures.* Computational Linguistics, 1994. **20**(4): pp. 507–534
11. Nakano, Y.I., Murayama, T., and Nishida, T.: *Multimodal Story-based Communication: Integrating a Movie and a Conversational Agent.* IEICE Transactions on Information and Systems, 2004. **E87-D, No.6**: pp. 1338–1346
12. Li, Q., Nakano, Y., Okamoto, M., and Nishida, T.: *Highlighting Multimodal Synchronization for Embodied Conversational Agent.* In *Proceedings of the 2nd International Conference on Information Technology for Application (ICITA 2004)*, 2004

Towards Intelligent Media Technology for Communicative Intelligence

Toyoaki Nishida

Dept. of Intelligence Science and Technology, Graduate School of Informatics,
Kyoto University, Yoshida-Honmachi, Sakyo-ku, Kyoto 606-8501, Japan
`nishida@i.kyoto-u.ac.jp`
`http://www.ii.ist.i.kyoto-u.ac.jp/~nishida/`

Abstract. One of the major problems that might hinder the construction of the knowledge society on the information network is what I call the understanding and communication bottlenecks, which might be caused by the limitation of human cognitive capability. In this paper, I present Communicative Intelligence as a step towards solving the understanding and communication bottleneck by inventing communicative artifacts that enable people and artifacts to interact with each other in a natural fashion. I focus on conversational communications in particular, for conversation is the most natural means for communication. I believe that making conversation-rich community contributes a lot to resolve the understanding and communication bottlenecks. Intelligent media technology aims at inventing communicative artifacts which allow people and artifacts to interact with each other in a natural fashion and thereby enable conversation-rich knowledge society. It consists of five subfields: conversation measurement and analysis, conversational artifacts, conversational environment design, conversational contents, and applied conversational systems. I will overview major results obtained in each subfield.

1 Communicative Intelligence as a Next Step of ICT

The recent advancement of information network and intelligent robotics technologies has produced a firm ground that permits us to think realistically about the next stage. The Internet and ubiquitous network technologies have brought about a huge amount of knowledge sources that can serve as a seed for a super intelligence by accumulating pieces of knowledge sources into an ultra-large-scale knowledge base. The intelligent robotics technologies have established a basis of building embodied artificial intelligence systems that might be able to continuously learn from experiences in the real-world physical environment. They are considered to contribute to the resolution of two major bottlenecks of Artificial Intelligence: the lack of commonsense knowledge and embodiment.

In the meanwhile, we are still suffering from what I call the understanding and communication bottlenecks, which might be caused by the limitation of human cognitive capability. Even though a huge amount of knowledge is accessible, we can only understand and communicate only a little portion of knowledge at a time. The understanding and communication bottlenecks may become a major cause that hinders the entire knowledge process.

L. Bolc et al. (Eds.): IMTCI 2004, LNAI 3490, pp. 99–110, 2005.

In order to look at the problem of understanding and communication bottlenecks in more detail, let us take risk communication as an example. In risk communication, various kind of risks in the society needs to be identified, understood, and shared so that the society as a whole recognises them and acts to minimise them. In earthquake disaster prevention, for example, the society needs to develop the shared knowledge and consensus about the earthquake disaster and its prevention so that the government and individuals can act to prepare for earthquake. The knowledge cannot be in effect unless it is understood and action is taken based on it. The existence of knowledge does not mean that individual people may be aware of knowledge and actively take action for it, even though the information infrastructure is built. People might be indifferent to earthquake disaster prevention, they might not be aware of the existence of knowledge about earthquake disaster prevention, or they may not understand what is implied by the knowledge even though they access it. Even active or knowledgeable people may not be able to find a proper means for accomplishing their goal.

Communicative Intelligence is a step towards solving the understanding and communication bottleneck by inventing communicative artifacts that enable people and artifacts to interact with each other in a natural fashion and build their personal or collective persistent memory. To put it in another way, the goal of Communicative Intelligence is to establish a method of understanding and augmenting social interactions that permits social actors, either natural or artificial, to coordinate their activities in the environment augmented by information and communication technology.

We focus on conversational communications, for conversation is the most natural means for communication. In some occasions, new ideas may evolve in conversation and spread in the community. In other occasions, tacit dimensions of knowledge may be disclosed. In many cases, conversation helps participants gain sympathetic understand-

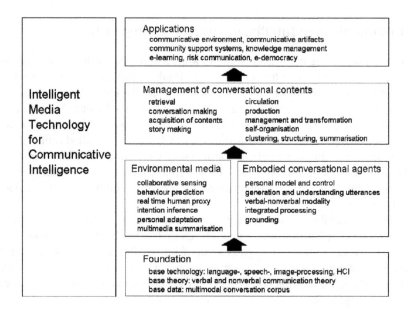

Fig. 1. The framework of Communicative Intelligence

ing of the subject. We believe that making conversation-rich community contributes a lot to resolve the understanding and communication bottlenecks.

We investigate Intelligent Media Technology for analysing and augmenting conversational knowledge process, comprising embodied conversational agents that can be embedded in the human society, environmental media that help social actors to interact with each other, and intelligent contents that can adapt themselves in the communication context. Intelligent Medial Technology is built on top of existing technologies such as language-, speech-, and image-processing, or human computer interaction, as well as existing theories such as the verbal and nonverbal communication theory and corpus (Fig. 1).

The significant portion of Intelligent Medial Technology overlaps Social Intelligence Design, which is a field of research on harmonising people and artifacts by focusing on social intelligence, defined as the ability of actors and agents to learn and to solve problems as a function of social structure and to manage their relationships with each other [1]. Social Intelligence Design as a field of study aims to integrate understanding and designing social intelligence. Engineering aspects of Social Intelligence Design involve design and implementation of systems and environments, ranging from group collaboration support systems that facilitate common ground building, goal-oriented interaction among participants, to community support systems that support a large-scale online discussions. Scientific aspects involve cognitive and social psychological understanding of social intelligence, attempting to provide a means for predicting and evaluating the effect of a given communication medium on the nature of discussions, interaction dynamics, and conclusions.

2   Intelligent Media Technology as Engineering Approach to Communicative Intelligence

A five-year research project "Intelligent Media Technology for Supporting Natural Communication between People" sponsored by Japan Society for the Promotion of Science (JSPS) addresses the realisation of Intelligent Media Technology for Communicative Intelligence. It consists of five technical subfields. The conversation measurement and analysis branch is concerned with the use of sensors and ubiquitous technologies to measure and analyse conversations. The conversational artifacts branch attempts to build artifacts that can make a reliable conversation with people in a natural fashion. The conversational environment design branch aims at designing an intelligent environment that allows effective communication among people and communicative artifacts. The conversational contents branch addresses building a suite of techniques for acquiring, editing, distributing, and utilising what is spoken or referred to in the conversations. The applied conversational systems branch seeks for conversations specialised in the application contexts. From theoretical points of view, our approach might be formalised as a framework called conversation quantization.

2.1   Conversation Quantization

Conversation Quantization is a technique of articulating a continuous flow of conversation by a series of objects called conversation quanta each of which represents a point of the discourse. Conceptually, it consists of extraction, accumulation, processing, and application of conversation quanta (Fig. 2). The extraction of conversation quantum results from identification and encoding of coherent segments of interactions in a conversational situation. The extracted conversation quanta are accumulated in a server, processed whenever necessary, and applied to other conversational situations. The application of a conversation quantum in a target situation involves production of conversational sequence or other form of presenting the content of information stored in the conversation quantum.

Conversation quantization allows for implementing a conversation system by reusing a collection of conversation quanta gathered from real/hypothetical conversation situations. Given a conversational situation, a conversation quantum that best matches it will be sought from the collection of conversation quanta, and one role of the participants of the retrieved conversation quantum can be replayed by an embodied conversational agent, and other roles will be mapped to the participants in the given conversational situation. Such an algorithm is relatively easy to implement and rather robust in nature.

The granularity and size of conversation quanta essentially depend on the context and background knowledge of the observer. Although the detailed investigation of the nature of conversation quantization is left for future, we conjecture, based on experiments made so far, that each conversation quantum roughly corresponds to a small talk often identified in the discourse of daily conversations.

The implementation of conversation quantization depends on the data structure for representing conversation quanta. One could use plain video clips as representation but its utility in retrieving and processing would be quite limited and a large cost would be required in retrieving, editing, and applying conversation quanta. Alternatively, a deep

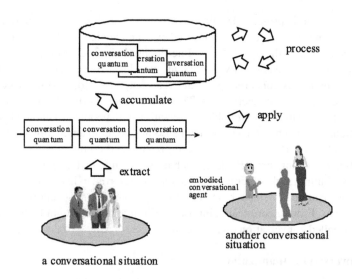

Fig. 2. Conversation quantization – the concept

semantic representation using logical formulas or case frames would not be ideal due to the expense and their limited capability of representing nonverbal information. A reasonable implementation appears to use annotated videos and images to represent a conversation quantum.

The current focus of our research is on acquisition, annotation, adaptation, and understanding of conversation quanta. The simplest method of acquiring conversation quanta is a manual input by an external observer. Alternatively, a more sophisticated method of extraction may involve automatic identification of a coherent segments of interactions from a conversational situation, and automatic annotation to the objects and events. Conversation quanta may well be generated from other media such as written documents using natural language processing techniques.

2.2   The Conversation Measurement and Analysis

Typical issue here is conversation corpus, which is important in investigating conversations in detail. The critical issue here is design of tags for conversation records. Den is designing an integrated tagging system for annotating verbal and nonverbal information.

Matsumura is investigating the structure of the individual's intention to participate in the community, in terms of the estimate of the community, the evaluation of tools, and the intention [2]. He proposed a causal model based on the statistic analysis of the test users' subjective evaluation. It suggests that in order to evaluate a communication tool for supporting a community, we should examine not only users' subjective evaluation of a communication tool but also their subjective evaluation of a community.

Content capturing motivates development of advanced techniques for conversation measurement, too. Sumi and his colleagues proposed a sophisticated method of capturing conversation quanta in the real world environment [3]. They implemented a smart room environment where conversational activities can be captured by environment sensors (such as video cameras, trackers and microphones ubiquitously set up around the room) and wearable sensors (such as video cameras, trackers, microphones, and physiological sensors). In order to supplement the limited capability of sensors, LED tags (ID tags with an infrared LED) and IR tracker (infrared signal tracking devices) are used to annotate the audio/video data with the positional information.

Events in the smart room are captured by analysing the behaviour of IR trackers and LED tags using knowledge about typical behaviours of the user, such as "stay", "coexist", "gaze", "attention", and "facing". For example, a temporal interval will be identified as a (joint) attention event when an LED tag attached to an object is simultaneously captured by IR trackers worn by two users, and the object in focus will be marked as a socially important object during the interval.

Research on the communication model of conversations aims at establishing a theoretical foundation of conversational content. We attempt at developing a unified model of verbal and nonverbal communication, a conversation corpus that accumulates conversation records with annotations to verbal and nonverbal events, and a method of analysing conversation behaviours. A typical subject in this vein is an analysis of the interactions of CMC. Matsumura proposed a model by applying the structural equation modelling to log data in 5748 message threads taken from a huge collection of message threads (2channel) with eight indices. It is suggested that the dynamism may be caused by three latent factors called specific expression, discussion type, and chitchat type [4]. Ueda and Komatsu have shown the possibility of meaning acquisition by mutual adaptation by investigating a communication environment only with prosodic information [5]. Den and Enomoto are investigating a conversation corpus with three participants to see how nonverbal cues are used to control conversation [6].

2.3   The Conversational Artifacts

Conversational artifacts make use of conversation quanta in order to produce services of various kind. Conversational artifacts make use of conversation quanta in order to produce a service.

The first topic in this vein is EgoChat which is a system for enabling an asynchronous conversational communication among community members [7]. EgoChat is based on the talking-virtualised-egos metaphor. A virtualised ego is a conversational agent that stores and maintains the user's personal memory, and talks on behalf of the user. It helps the user not only develop her/his personal memory but also better understand other members' interest, belief, opinion, knowledge, and way of thinking, which is valuable for building mutual understanding. EgoChat uses simple techniques to implement conversation quantization.

First, a primitive conversation quantum is implemented as a knowledge card consisting of a plain natural language text and a referenced object. One or more knowledge cards may be connected in series as a story to represent a complex conversation quantum.

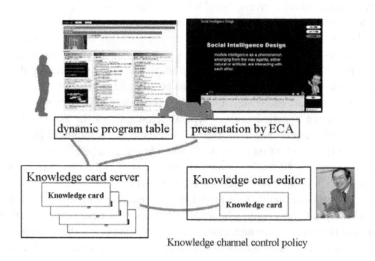

Fig. 3. The architecture of the EgoChat system [7]

Second, the awareness mechanism is employed to give the communication partners a sense of connectedness in an asynchronous communication environment using virtualised egos.

Third, we introduce the notion of knowledge channel for strategic delivery of content using a channel policy description language. Our channel policy description language allows both the sender and the recipient can specify channel policies. The content flow is determined by computing the negotiation of the channel policies for the sender and recipient, and will be visualised accordingly as a program table like this.

The entire framework is shown in Fig. 3. Knowledge cards are created at each user's terminal, uploaded and stored in servers, and distributed on demand. Embodied conversational agents (ECAs) are used to present knowledge cards. An ECA is a device for presenting stories in an interactive fashion. An ECA employs paralinguistic and nonlinguistic conversational means to control information flow in a conversation. In normal settings, each ECA stands for an existing real person so that the conversation partners can recognise who is represented by the ECA talking in front of them. This provides proper background information for interpreting messages from the ECA. Meanwhile, we might well employ anonymous ECAs in certain situations where we want to facilitate communication. A simple media conversion, such as Text-To-Speech conversion, is made at the time knowledge cards are presented, or made in advance and media data might be stored in the server.

SPOC, or Stream-oriented Public Opinion Channel, is a web-based multimedia environment that enables novice users to embody a story as multimedia content and distribute it on the Internet [8]. We developed a sophisticated presentation generation mechanism from the plain-text representation of conversation quanta specifying utterances of participants in the conversation. The system produces both digital camera work and agent animations according to linguistic information in a given natural language text. The animation generator called CAST implements the mechanism for determining appropriate agent behaviours according to the linguistic information contained in a Japanese text. The user can make a SPOC story from a static image and a movie. A digital camera work helps effectively display a static image. Even a scientifically advanced content originally created by an expert in the domain can be effectively presented like a scientific TV program. SPOC significantly reduces the cost for the production and presentation of such contents.

IPOC, or Immersive Public Opinion Channel, is a successor of SPOC [9]. IPOC allows for expanding conversation quanta in a virtual immersive environment. Users can interact with conversational agents in a story-space, which is a panoramic picture background and stories are embedded in the background. The embedded stories are presented on demand by the user or spontaneously according to the discourse. Stories are used to represent a discourse structure consisting of more than one conversation quantum. IPOC allows the user to create the vide-game level sense of reality. IPOC allows even non video-game programmers to create such contents.

In addition to those software agents, we are working on real world agents using hardware robots as well. The goal of research is to investigate basic communication capability that artifacts should embody in order to exchange rich information with humans.

Conversational robots can communicate with humans not only by verbal communication modalities but also nonverbal modalities such as eye gaze or gesture. We are developing socially intelligent robots that can facilitate conversations among people.

The autonomous mobile chair project aims at realising an autonomous robot chair that can align its behaviour with people [10]. The autonomous chair provides affordance or a clue that permits the user to sit. People react differently and align their behaviours to the novel artifacts to satisfy their goal.

The sociable sweeper robots projects addresses theoretical aspects of mutual adaptation between human and sweeper robots [11]. We introduce the entrainment mechanism consisting of synchronisation and modulation as a basic communication mechanism that permits the user to control the massive behaviour of multiple sweepers with a simple interaction principles. Currently, we are working with simulated robots. The collective behaviour of multiple sweeper robots is conducted by the user's non-symbolic gestures. The domain has a complex feature such as the carpet, as illustrated the red region, where the sweeper robots have to clean from two orientations specified in advance. Comparing with existing automatic sweeping algorithms and a manual control with a remote controller, the total time that the proposed system spent on completing the task is shorter than that of other automatic algorithms. Although it is longer than that of the time manually operated by the human user, humans had to attend all the time.

Currently, we combine probabilistic reasoning and the entrainment mechanism to realise a more sophisticated communicative robot that can listen and record human's explanation (Fig. 4, [12]).

Fig. 4. A conversational robot that can listen and record human's explanation [12]

2.4   The Conversational Environment Design

The goal of conversational environment design is to realise the socially intelligent environments technology, based on the "making-computers-invisible" approach, aiming at embedding computers into the everyday environment so that they can assist people in pursuit for their goals without enforcing them to pay special attention to computer operations. It addresses cooperative intelligent activity sensors, automatic analysis of nonverbal communication with high-resolution scene analysis, personalisation of environment medium, and intelligent editing of audio-visual streams.

Minoh and Kakusho developed a robust method for automatically recognising communicative events in a real class room by integrating audio and visual information processing [13]. Rutkowski studied a method for monitoring and estimating efficiency of the human-human communication based on recorded audio and video by computing correlation between sender activities and receiver responses [14]. Taniguchi and Arita used computer vision techniques to realise the notion of real time human proxy to virtually create a classroom for distributed learning environments [15]. The work by Sumi and his colleagues described in Section 2.2 falls in this category, too.

2.5 Conversational Contents

A typical subject on the environmental medium technology is semi-automated annotation to videos using real time computer vision. Kurohashi and Shibata integrate robust natural language processing techniques and computer vision to automatically annotate videos with closed caption [16]. Nakamura developed an intelligent video production system that can compute the best matching between the given index-scenario and video stream captured by camera to produce an annotated video [17]. The basic algorithm is scenario-speech matching where DP is used to calculate the best match between the given scenario and the utterances captured by a speech recognition system. The system also uses computer vision techniques to match the speech and motion cues for capturing basic behaviours such as pointing, holding out, manipulation, and illustration. The motion clue of pointing and holding-out is detected when the speaker's arm is stretched beyond the threshold. In contrast, there is no fixed pattern of manipulation or illustration. Currently, they are detected in a heuristic fashion by checking if the both hands are on or above the desk. In the vision system, information from various types of cameras is integrated to figure out the most plausible interpretation. For example, hand region is the intersection of the in-volume region, the moving region, the skin-temperature region and the skin-colour region, while held-object region is the intersection of in-volume region, moving region, but not in the hand region. Babaguchi and his colleagues developed a personalised video editing and summarization system based on the log data of user behaviours [18].

2.6 Applied Conversational Systems

Risk communication and E-learning are good application areas of Intelligent Media Technology. A persistent memory system is an approach to the resolution of the understanding bottleneck. By establishing a long-term relationship with a persistent memory that can coevolve as the user's biological memory evolves, the user, as we believe, will be able to understand what is given in the context of the accumulated experiences by not only her/himself but also by other members of the community to which s/he belongs.

Nishida, Kubota, and Huang are developing a system called the Sustainable Knowledge Globe (SKG, Fig. 5) that permits the user to build her/his own intellectual world by spatially arranging information [19,20]. SKG allows the user to build a customised intellectual world consisting of knowledge items on the surface of a globe.

The user can move around on the surface of the globe in search for interesting items and create/reconfigure landmarks consisting of a visual image and a text or an icon

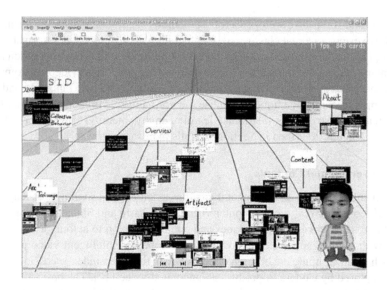

Fig. 5. A screenshot of Sustainable Knowledge Globe [20]

of an presentation by ECA that allows for interactive presentation about the subject represented by the icon.

Presentation by ECA is a temporal representation of knowledge in the sense that the major axis behind the representation is a temporal evolution of a story. In contrast, the configuration of knowledge items on the surface of the globe is a spatial representation. SKG allows the user to switch between temporal representation that allows for in-depth causal understanding of the issue and spatial representation that facilitates global and geometric understanding of the subjects.

SKG provides a number of novel features for overcoming subtleties of knowledge creation. Firstly, it permits the user to organise knowledge as spatial configuration. Secondly, it enables the user to establish a link and verbal annotations to keep information in logical forms, which is considered a more durable way of keeping information than merely preserving configuration or proximity of memory items.

3   Concluding Remarks

In this paper, I have addressed the understanding and communication bottlenecks against the knowledge society. I have focused on conversational communications, for conversation is the most natural means for communication. I have introduced Communicative Intelligence as a field of research aiming at investigating human conversational behaviours as well as designing conversational artifacts that can interact with people in a conversational fashion. Intelligent Media Technology highlights engineering aspects of Conversational Intelligence, aiming at inventing communicative artifacts that allow people and artifacts to interact with each other in a natural fashion and thereby enable conversation-rich knowledge society. It consists of five subfields: the conversation measurement and analysis subfield that is concerned with the use of sensors and ubiquitous technologies to measure and analyse conversations; the conversational artifacts subfield whose goal is to build artifacts that can make a reliable conversation with people in a natural fashion; the conversational environment design subfield that aims at designing an intelligent environment that allows effective communication among people and communicative artifacts; the conversational contents subfield that addresses building a suite of techniques for acquiring, editing, distributing, and utilising what is spoken or referred to in the conversations; and the applied conversational systems subfield that seeks for conversations specialised in the application contexts. I have overviewed major results obtained in each subfield.

References

1. Nishida, T.: Social Intelligence Design for Web Intelligence, Special Issue on Web Intelligence, IEEE Computer, Vol. 35, No. 11, pp. 37–41, November, 2002
2. Matsumura, K.: The Measures for the Evaluation of Communication Tools: the causality between the intention and users' subjective estimation of community, Proceedings of the 3rd Workshop on Social Intelligence Design, Enschede, The Netherlands, 5–7 July, pp. 85–90, 2004
3. Sumi,Y., Matsuguchi,T., Ito.S., Fels,S. and Mase,K.: Collaborative capturing of interactions by multiple sensors, Ubicomp 2003 Adjunct Proceedings, pp. 193–194, Oct. 2003
4. Komatsu, T., Utsunomiya, A., Suzuki, K., Ueda, K., Hiraki, K., and Oka, N.: Toward a Mutual Adaptive Interface: An interface induces a user's adaptation and utilizes this induced adaptation, and vice versa, In Proceedings of the 25th Annual Meeting of the Cognitive Science Society (CogSci2003), pp. 687–692, 2003
5. Matsumura, N., Miura, A., Shibanai, Y., Ohsawa, Y. and Nishida, T.: The Dynamism of 2channel, SID-2003:Social Intelligence Design, Royal Holloway University of London at Egham, Surrey, July 6–8, 2003 (an extended version will appear from AI & Society journal)
6. Enomoto, M., Den, Y.: Analysis of Nonverbal Behavior concerning the Alteration of Participatory Role in Conversation involving Three-Participants, SIG-SLUD-A301, JSAI, pp. 25–30 (in Japanese)
7. Kubota, H. and Nishida, T.: Channel Design for Strategic Knowledge Interaction, in Proc. Int. Conf. Knowledge-Based Intelligent Information & Engineering Systems (KES2003), pp. 1037–1043, 2003
8. Nakano, Y. I., Murayama, T., Kawahara, D., Kurohashi, S., and Nishida, T.: "Embodied Conversational Agents for Presenting Intellectual Multimedia Contents" in Proc. Int. Conf. Knowledge-Based Intelligent Information & Engineering Systems (KES2003), 2003.
9. Nakano, Y., Murayama, T. and Nishida, T.: Engagement In Situated Communication by Conversational Agents, in C. Danilowicz (ed.): Multimedia and Network Information Systems (vol. 2), Oficyna Wydawnicza Politechniki Wrocławskiej, Wrocław, Poland, pp. 95–101, 2004
10. Terada, K., Nishida, T.: Active Artifacts: for New Embodiment Relation between Human and Artifacts, In Proceedings of The 7th International Conference on Intelligent Autonomous Systems (IAS-7), Marina del Rey, California, USA March 25–27, 2002
11. Tajima, T., Xu, Y., Nishida, T.: Entrainment Based Tacit Intention Communication between Human and Agent, to be presented at The 2004 IEEE Conference on Robotics, Automation and Mechatronics (RAM), Traders Hotel, Singapore, December 1–3, 2004
12. Ogasawara, Y, Tajima, T., Hatakeyama, M, and Nishida, T.: Human-Robot Communication of Tacit Information based on Entrainment, The 18th Annual Conference of the Japanese Society for Artificial Intelligence, JSAI, 2B3-05, 2004 (in Japanese)

13. Minoh, S. N.: "Environmental Media - In the Case of Lecture Archiving System", Proc. Int. Conf. Knowledge-Based Intelligent Information & Engineering Systems (KES2003), Vol.II, pp. 1070–1076 (2003)
14. Rutkowski, M., Seki, S., Yamakata, Y., Kakusho, K., and Minoh, M.: Toward the Human Communication Efficiendy Monitoring from Captured Audio and Video Media in Real Environment, Proc. Int. Conf. Knowledge-Based Intelligent Information & Engineering Systems (KES2003), Vol.II, pp. 1093–1100 (2003)
15. Arita, D. and Taniguchi, R.: Non-verbal Human Communication Using Avatars in a Virtual Space, in Proc. Int. Conf. Knowledge-Based Intelligent Information & Engineering Systems (KES2003), pp. 1077–1084, Sep. 2003
16. Ozeki, M., Izuno, H., Itoh, M., Nakamura, Y., and Ohta, Y.: Object Tracking and Task Recognition for Producing Intaractive Video Content – Semi-automatic indexing for QUE-VICO, in Proc. Int. Conf. Knowledge-Based Intelligent Information & Engineering Systems (KES2003), pp. 1044–1053, 2003
17. Babaguchi, N., Kawai, Y., Ogura, T. and Kitahashi, T.: Personalized Abstraction of Broadcasted American Football Video by Highlight Selection, IEEE Trans. Multimedia (in press)
18. Shibata, T., Kawahara, D., Okamoto, M., Kurohashi, S., and Nishida, T.: Structural Analysis of Instruction Utterances, in Proceedings KES 2003, pp. 1054–1061, 2003
19. Nishida, T.: Social Intelligence Design and Communicative Intelligence for Knowledgeable Community, Invited Talk, International Symposium on Digital Libraries and Knowledge Communities in Networked Information Society DLKC'04, Kasuga Campus, University of Tsukuba, March 2–5, 2004
20. Nishida, T., Sumi, Y., Kubota, H., and Huang, H.: A Computational Model of Conversational Knowledge Process, in C. Danilowicz (ed.): Multimedia and Network Information Systems (vol. 2), Oficyna Wydawnicza Politechniki Wrocławskiej, Wrocław, Poland, pp. 103–112, 2004

Toward Enhancing User Involvement via Empathy Channel in Human-Computer Interface Design

Masashi Okamoto[1], Yukiko I. Nakano[2], and Toyoaki Nishida[3]

[1] Graduate School of Information Science and Technology, The University of Tokyo,
7-3-1 Hongo, Bunkyo-ku, Tokyo, 113-8656, Japan
`okamoto@kc.t.u-tokyo.ac.jp`
[2] Research Institute of Science and Technology for Society,
Japan Science and Technology Agency, Atago Green Hills MORI Tower 18F,
2-5-1 Atago, Minato-ku, Tokyo, 105-6218, Japan
`nakano@kc.t.u-tokyo.ac.jp`
[3] Graduate School of Informatics, Kyoto University, Yoshida-Honmachi,
Sakyo-ku, Kyoto, 606-8501, Japan
`nishida@i.kyoto-u.ac.jp`

Abstract. This paper reports our research toward enhancing the 'User Involvement' in human-computer interaction, which is introduced to grasp the idealised state in which a natural communication between a computer and its user should be established. Moreover, we also introduce a new idea of 'Empathy Channel', through which humans can interact with virtual agents and objects on computers with more sense of reality. The main issue of this paper is to clarify various methods for establishing an Empathy Channel in building a human-computer interface. We believe a good design of human-computer interface with an Empathy Channel is one of the best methods to enhance the User Involvement.

1 Introduction

This paper reports our research toward enhancing the "User Involvement" in human-computer interaction. As we describe in Section 2, the notion of the User Involvement is introduced to grasp the idealised state in which natural interaction between a computer and its user should be established. Moreover, we also introduce a new idea of 'Empathy Channel', through which humans can interact with virtual agents and objects on a computer screen with more sense of reality. The main issue of this paper is to clarify various methods for establishing an Empathy Channel in designing a human-computer interface. We believe a good design of human-computer interface with an Empathy Channel is one of the best methods to enhance the User Involvement.

In the following sections, first, we describe the requirements for establishing the User Involvement. Then, we insist that empathy is the key notion to comprehend cognitive abilities of a human to step into another world different from the real world he actually lives in. Secondly, we show some related works supporting our ideas. Thirdly, we introduce the reference-point ability to formulate the essential aspects of the User Involvement precisely, and then we discuss the possible designs of Empathy Channel in the human-agent communication environment. Finally, our future work on experiments to prove our ideas is shown.

L. Bolc et al. (Eds.): IMTCI 2004, LNAI 3490, pp. 111–121, 2005.

2   User Involvement in Human-Computer Interaction

To establish a natural communication between humans and computers, the following issues have been discussed recently:

- The human-to-computer interaction should/could be equated to that of human-to-human. [1]
- Though many children nowadays have been deep into computer games, most of non-entertainment computer services have not attracted people as much as games have done.
- Non-verbal information must be taken into consideration since verbal information alone is not sufficient for establishing human-computer communication.

Behind these discussions there exists a strong belief that the attributes of human-to-human communication, where a huge variety of complicated information is conveyed in a natural way, can be equally applied to human-to-computer interaction. However, there is no persuasive theoretical frameworks yet which describe how a human as a cognitive subject can communicate with computers as 'real' partners.

In order to comprehend such issues appropriately, we introduce the notion of 'User Involvement' here. User Involvement is the cognitive way humans willingly engage in the interaction with computers, or the way in which humans are, on the contrary, forced to be involved in a virtual world which computers display or in a human-to-robot communication. We believe that designing a human-to-computer communication environment mainly concerns the management of the User Involvement.

2.1   Requirements of User Involvement

The main requirements to establish the User Involvement are considered as follows:

- **Cognitive/Communicative reality is achieved:** The user should feel the virtual world or the human-to-computer interaction as 'real'.
- **Two (or more) cognitive spaces are linked:** When the user sees and steps into another world, there need to be at least two cognitive spaces, that is, his/her viewpoint (here) and what he/she sees (there) [2]. Moreover, there must be some link among those multiple cognitive spaces.

'Reality' is a difficult concept to define precisely. In a traditional philosophical context, reality refers to everything that actually exists and contrasted to non-existence or possibility. In our approach we use the term as it means "perceptions, senses, beliefs, and attitudes toward reality, that is, people's ways of seeing reality", as usually used in cognitive psychology, anthropology, or sociology. Then reality is classified into the following three dimensions:

- **Cognitive reality:** The way of seeing objects, events and their relations in the real/virtual world as real.
- **Communicative reality:** The sense of reality that is achieved through communication with others.
- **Social reality:** The collective and intersubjective sense of reality based on sharing thoughts or opinions with one another.

As social reality is concerned with a real or virtual community, we discuss cognitive and communicative reality in this paper.

When we feel the world 'real', we are not living in a single space. It is because we not only exist in an external world but also can 'think' in an internal world, namely in our mind. Seeing things, animals and other people outside, we often employ our thoughts on each of them inside. We are living in and cognitively shuttle between both of these two cognitive spaces, when our body is a vehicle or a channel to connect them. Moreover, if we can also find reality in a virtual world, it might be said that we already have stepped into another different space. This is why two or more cognitive spaces should be linked for the User Involvement to be established.

2.2   Multiple Modes of Involvement

When the User Involvement is considered as such, the way for users to interact with computers might be dual or multiple in itself. Norman [3] points out two types of cognitive involvement for humans to interact with the world: 'experiential cognition' and 'reflective cognition'. The former is the data-driven information processing with reactivation of information patterns in human memory, while the latter concept-driven processing in deep reasoning such as decision-making or planning. People use each cognitive mode appropriately in the human-to-computer interaction.

On the other hand, Laurel [4][5] also made it clear that users engage in the human-computer interaction in two ways, that is, a 'first-person' engagement (as active participant), and a 'third-person' engagement (as a passive observer)[1]. The former is seen in such activities as walking through woods, writing a letter and so on. Meanwhile, the latter engagement is observed in watching movies or reading novels, when the viewer or reader is outside the action and describes the events in the movies or novels using third-person pronouns. She insisted that first-personness is enhanced by an interface that enables inputs and outputs that are more nearly like their real-world referents, and predicted that the conventional menu- or command-based system will be replaced with systems that employ the natural language in ways that are mimetic of real-world activities.

The multiplex of involvement suggests that a human is usually involved not in a sole activity, either cognitive or behavioural, but in multiple cognitive spaces where he can smoothly switch his mode of involvement. Therefore, our research is focused on what factors enable a human to smoothly switch such multiple modes of involvement.

In the next section, we will show that 'Empathy Channel' becomes one of the links between cognitive spaces to enhance the User Involvement.

---

[1] Note that Laurel also mentioned *second-person* experiences, which frequently occur in operating a computer. However, it is not clear what characterises the second-person engagement, while the relation between the first-person and the third-person experiences might be compared to the binary opposition between 'subjective' and 'objective'. We thus excluded the second-person engagement from our discussion here.

3   Empathy Channel

In the human interaction, a human not only interacts with others but also reflects on his own interaction. Therefore, a human has two viewpoints when interacting with others; one is an 'object-level view, the other a 'meta-level view". The two viewpoints are tightly linked through the self-identification of 'ego' (reflective subject) and 'self' (experiential subject)[2] On the contrary, in observing others interaction at a distance, such duality is not established in general. However, if the observer can empathise with one participant in that interaction, he can also acquire the virtual object-level view, so that he can experience the interaction as if it were his own. This dual viewpoint via empathy shows how the 'first-person' engagement can be achieved (See Fig. 1).

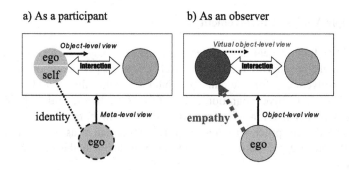

Fig. 1. The Empathy Channel: (a) involvement as participant in interaction, (b) involvement as observer outside interaction

In other words, empathising with others enables us to cross over two cognitive spaces (i.e. *here* and *there*), and enhances the psychological involvement with interaction in another world, which leads us to feel the world "real". Since empathising with characters or objects in a virtual world in particular functions as a channel to connect the real and the virtual world, we call it 'Empathy Channel' here. As suggested in subsection 2.1, it is one of the conditions that maintain our cognitive and communicative reality, which will enhance the User Involvement in human-computer interaction.

3.1   Empathy Channels in Computer Games

The good examples in which the Empathy Channel does effectively function are computer games (Fig.2).

In the early stages of computer games, the bird's-eye view is commonly used (seen in Fig. 2a). But, although such view excels in looking over the world where the user is involved, it has a disadvantage in feeling involved in the game playing itself. Later, in simulation games in particular, the first-person view was adopted in order to enhance

---

[2] This duality was originally provoked by G. H. Mead [6]. He distinguished Me and 'I' in that the former refers to the social aspect of self and the latter to the subjective aspect. In this paper, the 'ego-self' distinction roughly corresponds to the 'I-Me' distinction of Mead.

(a) Bird's-eye view
- Low engagement
- High overview

(b) 1st person view
- High engagement
- Low overview

(c) Fusional view (back image)
- High engagement
- High overview

Fig. 2. The transition of user's view in computer games: (a) old-fashioned games with bird's-eye view, (b) simulation-type games with 1st person view, (c) popular games with fusional view

the User Involvement (Fig. 2b). However, it in turn loses an overview of playing fields. After that, most of today's popular games have adopted the fusional view using the back image of the player's vehicle or virtual ego (Fig. 2c). In our opinion, it is a typical example of establishing the User Involvement via Empathy Channel. Through an empathised object (which is a back image of user's vehicle here) a user can smoothly step into the virtual world and go back to the real world to comprehend what he is doing.

3.2 Related Works

The effect of establishing an Empathy Channel in the user involvement has been proved in some empirical researches.

For example, Miyazaki [7] examined the emphatic effects of a back image on readers. When the experimenter presented a juvenile story to subjects, half of the subjects were presented a storybook with pictures drawn from the observer view, while the rest was presented the same story with pictures from the fusional view featuring a back image of the protagonist. After the presentation, all the subjects were asked about the feelings of the protagonist and the contents of the story. As a result, those subjects presented with the back images could comprehend more precisely what the protagonist in the story is feeling and were more strongly involved in the story. In brief, the back images helped the readers to experience the virtual world as if it were their own.

On the other hand, Morikawa, et al. [8] reported that using the HyperMirror system, which was built by them in order to enable the users in different places to be present virtually on the same computer screen, established a smooth communication among them. In this experiment, the users strongly felt as if they had stepped into the Hyper-Mirror space together without any eye contact. Compared with the video conferences or TV phones, it is noteworthy that lack of eye-contact does not prevent the communicative reality of the users. We assume that this experiment is an example of the Empathy Channel through which the self-image in a virtual world is naturally identified with the actual self of the user.

4   Empathy Channel as Reference Point

Toward building an effective and attractive human-computer interface it should be discussed how to establish an Empathy Channel to enhance the User Involvement. Take a human-agent communication environment for example. In such an environment which enables the user to communicate with virtual agents, he must be able to effortlessly step into the virtual world in advance. However, the virtual world on a computer screen feels not real for the user unless the screen is huge enough to surround him. It is thus necessary for either cognitive or communicative reality to be achieved.

In order to explore the candidates of Empathy Channel, we adopt the idea of the 'reference-point ability', which was originally provoked by Ronald W. Langacker [9], a cognitive linguist. This idea is also developed to formulate the model of the User Involvement in this section.

4.1   Reference-Point Ability

Imagine that you are asked by someone on a street about the location of the nearest post office. Then you would explain to her in the following way: "Can you see a traffic signal over there? Go there and turn left, then you'll reach the post office soon". In such an occasion, we cannot always access the target directly, so we use something that is easily accessible in our cognitive environment instead. Langacker [9] calls the clue for accessing the target as a 'reference point', and suggests that the reference-point phenomenon is so fundamental and ubiquitous that we often forget its effect. In our verbal activities it is often through some reference point we reach the target.

Langacker describes the essential aspects of the reference-point ability as shown in Fig. 3. The circle labelled C represents the *conceptualiser*, that is, a human as the cognitive subject. R is the *reference point* and T is the *target*, with which the conceptualiser establishes a mental contact using the reference point. The dashed arrows indicate the mental path which the conceptualiser follows in reaching the target, while the ellipse D represents an abstract entity, named the *dominion*, which can be defined as the class of potential targets. It is important that the reference point has a certain cognitive salience.

4.2   Reference Points in User Involvement

We believe that the reference-point ability also works in our non-verbal activities and can be applied to the User Involvement in a human-computer interaction as well. As

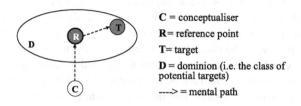

C = conceptualiser
R = reference point
T = target
D = dominion (i.e. the class of potential targets)
----> = mental path

Fig. 3. The essential aspects of the reference-point ability (Langacker, 1993)

described in Section 3, the user of a computer steps into the virtual world via some Empathy Channel that links his living space and the virtual space. From the point of view of the reference-point ability, the Empathy Channel is established by something that is cognitively accessible and can be empathised by the user. Therefore, it is a reference point for accessing the objects or characters in the virtual world as a target. Moreover, as suggested in Section 2, we conceive the real world or its entities via ourselves, which lie both in the internal space (i.e. the mind) and in the external space (i.e. the real world). Thus it can be said that we use ourselves as a reference point to conceptualise the entities in the real world.

Some of the aspects of the User Involvement in the view of the reference-point ability are illustrated in Fig.4.

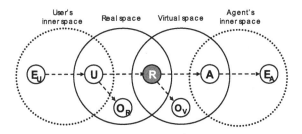

Fig. 4. The astigmatic model of User Involvement in human-to-computer interaction

In this model[3], $\mathbf{U}$ represents a user or his self/body, $\mathbf{E}_U$ is the ego of the user or the cognitive subject, and $\mathbf{O}_R$ refers to an object/entity in the real space. $\mathbf{A}$ represents a virtual agent, $\mathbf{E}_A$ is the ego of the agent, $\mathbf{O}_V$ refers to an object in the virtual space, and $\mathbf{R}$ represents the empathised object as a reference point (i.e. the Empathy Channel).

In conceptualising something ($\mathbf{O}_R$), a human uses his self/body ($\mathbf{U}$) as a reference point in our everyday lives. If the user recognises the reality of the $\mathbf{O}_V$ in human- computer interaction environment, his reality is achieved through some Empathy Channel ($\mathbf{R}$) as a reference point to access $\mathbf{O}_V$. Additionally, if the virtual agent on a computer screen is animated or lively, and thus felt to be real for the user, he will assume the existence of something like the agent's intention or belief (in EA) even though it is just an affectation.

5   What Is Needed for Establishing an Empathy Channel?

Our main goal is to clarify the conditions and the candidates for the Empathy Channel to be established in the design of a human-computer interface. The astigmatic model of the User Involvement suggests what will be required in the Empathy Channel:

---

[3] We call the model as the *Astigmatic Model* because the overlapping among the cognitive spaces is essential for the user involvement to be established with each reference point. In our hypothesis, one reality is always constructed on those overlapped cognitive spaces like seeing an object with astigmatic eyes.

(1) The high accessibility in the real space
(2) The consistent functioning in the virtual space
(3) The continuous correspondence of behaviours in both the real and the virtual
    spaces

The reason for (1) is that the empathised object should be highly accessible to the user in the real space to function as the reference point. Additionally, since the empathised object also lies in the virtual space, it should consistently function as a member of the virtual space to maintain the reality of the world, and it is the reason for (2). Moreover, the empathised object connects two cognitive spaces simultaneously. If its behaviours in each space are not corresponding to each other, the connection will be broken.

5.1   Empathy Channel for Human-Computer Interfaces

When we first think about a human-computer interface, a mouse or a keyboard is easily evoked. According to the astigmatic model of the User Involvement, a good human-computer interface should be (1) easily accessible or operational by the user in the real world, and (2) consistently functioning in the monitor, and should (3) maintain the coordination of each behaviour of the device in both worlds. From that view, the mouse and the keyboard are not so good in that using such devices contains no natural behaviours in our everyday lives, and that the correspondence of the user's action in the real space and the device's response in the virtual space is frequently broken. Therefore, many researchers are now trying to create a new interface device using our natural behaviours or movements to replace the mouse and the keyboard with. We believe that such a new interface should be an appropriate one to the User Involvement.

Similarly, a good human-computer interface in a human-agent communication environment should follow the theory of the User Involvement. Different from a mouse or a keyboard, the interface in the human-agent communication environment consists of a virtual world and virtual agents that resemble our real world and its habitants. Then, establishing a cognitive or communicative reality is necessary for the user to be smoothly and deeply involved in the virtual world.

5.2   Empathy Channel for Cognitive/Communicative Reality

The candidates for an Empathy Channel in a human-agent communication environment are shown as follows:

– Establishing cognitive reality
  - Self-image of the user in the virtual space
  - Matching age/sex/ethnicity
  - Smooth viewpoint switching

– Establishing communicative reality
  - Exchanging verbal information
  - Eye contact
  - Appropriate reactions of a virtual agent
  - Joint attention

Though we do not insist that all the possible candidates are fully cited above, these are considered to function well as establishing an Empathy Channel.

In order to achieve the cognitive reality, as shown in Section 3, self-images of the user in the virtual space work as an Empathy Channel. Not a full image but a partial body image of the user will be an Empathy Channel, like the image of a hand or a face of the user. In empathising with an agent in a monitor, the correspondence of sex, gender or ethnicity between the user and the agent will surely enhance the empathising effect. Furthermore, in movie-like contents, there needs to be a smooth viewpoint switching that would reduce the cognitive burden of the user experiencing the virtual world.

On the other hand, a user should feel the communication with the virtual agents as real. Since the prototype of the natural human-computer communication is a human-to-human communication, the characteristics of the human communication can be also applied to the human-agent communication environment, such as exchanging verbal information, an occasional eye contact, appropriate reactions or responses corresponding to the precedent actions, and joint attention. However, it is difficult for the current technologies to realise as sufficient communicative behaviours of the virtual agents as in a human-to-human communication. For instance, exchanging verbal information between a user and a computer requires highly intellectual technologies of natural language processing, speech synthesis, speech recognition and so on. Moreover, lack of eye contact between a user and an agent often makes the agent and the computer look like just a mock figure and a vacant box. Again, needless to say, the range of possible reactions that perfectly correspond to the user's actions is very limited. Those characteristics will surely work as the Empathy Channel for communicative reality if they are sufficiently realised, but we have to consider what is possible and effective in the limited actions the current computers can perform.

5.3   The Visual Settings Using Empathy Channel

Lastly we describe the possible settings of the human-agent communication environment using the Empathy Channel. See Fig.5 below.

A typical setting of the virtual agent is like (a), which features a conversational agent that faces up to the user and talks to him. In such a setting, the user gets less satisfied with the agent as its appearance becomes more human-like, because the user places more expectations on the agent. In particular, lack of eye contact will betray the expectations. That is why cartoonish agents are often used instead in interactive contents.

Fig. 5. The possible settings of human-computer communication environment: (a) the setting featuring an agent facing the user, (b) the setting featuring a back image as Empathy Channel, (c) the setting featuring joint attention as Empathy Channel

Fig. 6. The shot transition motivated by the agent's attention behaviour

Therefore, we suggest that using such a facing-up agent setting should be kept to the necessary minimum. Instead, the back image setting or the joint attention setting should be more used. As shown in (b), the user can easily empathise with the agent through its back image as an Empathy Channel. Presenting the landscape with the back image will enhance the User Involvement more than presenting the landscape alone. It is because the correspondence between the viewpoint of the agent and that of the user produces the sense of involvement as if the user were actually standing in the landscape.

The joint attention setting (c) evokes the attention of the user toward a target which the agent is watching. The difference between the back image setting and the joint attention setting is that the former makes the user empathise with the agent and share a mutual viewpoint while the latter does not. Instead, the joint attention setting makes the user and the agent virtually share the communicative environment including the target. Furthermore, not only the static visual settings but also the dynamic transition settings can enhance the User Involvement. See the following Fig. 6.

In movie-like contents featuring the human-agent communication, the shot or scene transition is very important for the User Involvement to be established. If some irrelevant shot is inserted in movie contents, the viewer will be embarrassed and will have to process the cognitive burden that the irrelevant shot lays on. Therefore, the smooth switching of the shots should be considered in constructing any movie-like contents. We suggest that one of the smooth shot transition types with less cognitive burden for the viewer is that which is motivated by the attention behaviours of the agent. The attention behaviours, such as turning a gaze, pointing by hand, and a verbal reference toward the target, will enable the viewer to smoothly accept the shot transition from an agent shot to a target shot. Once such an Empathy Channel as described here is established, the user will be inclined to communicate with conversational agents even in a small computer monitor.

6   Conclusion and Future Work

In this paper, we have presented our theory of the User Involvement. The main issues described so far were as follows:

- As well as in our everyday experiences, the user should also creatively use multi-involvement in a human-computer interaction.
- To enhance the User Involvement, it should be considered how to establish an Empathy Channel between the real world and the virtual world.
- Empathy Channel works as a reference point for the user to step into a virtual world.

Furthermore, we discussed the requirements of establishing an Empathy Channel in human-computer interfaces, and then the effective and empathetic visual settings of a human-agent communication environment were described in both static and dynamic settings in the view of the User Involvement.

We thus conclude that establishing an Empathy Channel will surely enhance the User Involvement in a human-to-computer interaction. However, the theory should be attested by building systems based on the User Involvement with the subsequent experiments on the psychological effects toward the users.

Now we are constructing the following two types of human-computer interaction environment based on the User Involvement theory. One of the ongoing researches is building a supporting system for the immersive CG contents creation, which is based on the analysis of the shot transition in actual TV programme. The other is establishing the natural human-robot communication environment using a listener robot, which can establish the joint attention. The reports of these ongoing researches will be done in the near future.

References

1. Reeves, B., Nass, C.: *The Media Equation: how people treat computers, television, and new media like real people and places*, CSLI (1996)
2. Miyazaki, K., Ueno, N.: *Viewpoint (in Japanese)*. University of Tokyo Press (1985)
3. Norman, D. A.: *Things That Make Us Smart: Defending Human Attributes in the Age of the Machine*, Addison-Wesley (1993)
4. Laurel, B.: Interface as mimesis, In: Norman, D. A. & Draper, S. (eds.): *User Centered System Design: New Perspectives on Human-Computer Interaction*. Lawrence Erlbaum (1986)
5. Laurel, B.: *Computers as Theatre*, Addison-Wesley (1991)
6. Mead, G. H. *Mind, Self, and Society: from the standpoint of a social behaviorist*. The University of Chicago Press (1934)
7. Miyazaki, K.: The Effects of Human Back-image as a Mooring Point in Empathetic Comprehension through Visual Images *(in Japanese)*. *Japan Educational Psychology Association Proceedings* (1993) 35
8. Morikawa, O., Hashimoto, R., Yamashita, J.: Self Reflection Can Substitute Eye Contact. *CHI2003 Extended Abstracts* (2003) 944–945
9. Langacker, R. W.: Reference-Point Constructions. *Cognitive Linguistics 4* (1993) 1–38

Named-Entity Recognition for Polish with SProUT

Jakub Piskorski

DFKI GmbH, Stuhlsatzenhausweg 3, 66123 Saarbrücken, Germany
piskorsk@dfki.de

Abstract. Although considerable work on named-entity recognition for few major languages exists, research on this topic in the context of Slavonic languages has been almost neglected. This paper presents a rule-based named-entity recognition system for Polish built on top of SProUT, a novel multi-lingual NLP platform. We pinpoint the encountered difficulties and present some promising evaluation results.

1 Introduction

Named entities (NE) constitute a significant part of natural language texts and are widely exploited in various NLP applications. In particular, their proper recognition is crucial for intelligent content extraction systems. Although considerable work on named-entity recognition (NER) for English and few other major languages exists, research on this topic in the context of Slavonic languages has been almost neglected. Some NER systems for Bulgarian and Russian have been constructed by adapting the famous IE platform GATE [5], and were presented at a recent IESL workshop [2]. This paper presents a NER engine for Polish, built on top of SProUT [8], a novel general purpose multi-lingual NLP platform. Polish is a West Slavonic language, and analogously to other languages in the group, it exhibits a highly inflectional character (e.g., nouns and adjectives decline in seven cases) and has a relatively-free word order (e.g., adjectives may either precede a noun, or they can follow a noun) [14]. Due to these specifics and general lack of linguistic resources for Polish, construction of a NER system for Polish is an intriguing and challenging task.

The rest of the paper is organised as follows. Firstly, in Section 2, we introduce SProUT and its particularities. Section 3 takes an insight into setting up and fine-tuning SProUT to the processing of Polish. The NE-grammar development is described in Section 4. The next section focuses on evaluation. Finally, we finish off with some conclusions in Section 6.

2 SProUT

Analogously to the widely-known GATE system, SProUT[1] is equipped with a set of reusable Unicode-capable online processing components for basic linguistic operations, including tokenisation, sentence splitting, morphological analysis, gazetteer lookup,

---

[1] SProUT – Shallow Text Processing with Unification and Typed Feature Structures.

L. Bolc et al. (Eds.): IMTCI 2004, LNAI 3490, pp. 122–133, 2005.

and partial reference matching. Typed feature structures (TFS) constitute a uniform data structure for representing all linguistic objects in the system and as a consequence they are used for I/O specification purposes. Therefore, the processing components can be flexibly combined into a pipeline that generates several streams of linguistically annotated structures, which serve as an input for the shallow grammar interpreter, applied at the next stage. The backbone architecture of SProUT is depicted in Figure 1.

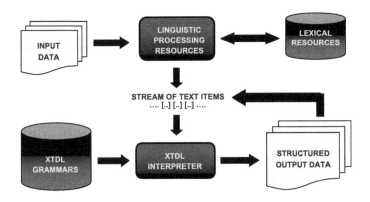

Fig. 1. The backbone Architecture of SProUT

The grammar formalism in SProUT, called *XTDL*, is a blend of very efficient finite-state techniques and unification-based formalisms which are known to guarantee expressiveness and transparency. To be more precise, a grammar in SProUT consists of the so called pattern/action rules, where the LHS of a rule is a regular expression over TFSs, representing the recognition pattern, and the RHS of a rule is a TFS specification of the output structure. Additionally, functional operators and coreferences may be used on both sides of the rules. Coreferences express structural identity, create dynamic value assignments, and serve as means of information transport into the output descriptions. Generally, variables can be assigned arbitrarily complex TFSs as their values. All necessary types are arranged system's type hierarchy, which is maintained by the user. Furthermore, grammar rules can be recursively embedded, which in fact provides grammarians with a context-free formalism. Functional operators provide a gateway to the outside world, and they are primarily utilised for forming the output of a rule (e.g., concatenation of strings, converting complex number expressions into their corresponding numeric values, or lemmatisation of small-scale structures) and for introducing complex constraints in the rules, i.e., they can act as predicates that produce Boolean values. Current version of SProUT comes with circa 20 predefined functional operators, which can be easily extended by the user. The following rule for the recognition of prepositional phrases gives an idea of the syntax of the grammar formalism [8]:

```
pp :>   morph & [ POS Prep,
                   SURFACE #prep,
                   INFL [ CASE #c ] ]
    (morph & [ POS Det,
               INFL [ CASE #c,
                      NUMBER #n,
                      GENDER #g ]] ) ?
    (morph & [ POS Adjective,
               INFL [ CASE #c,
                      NUMBER #n,
                      GENDER #g ] ] ) *
    (morph & [ POS Noun, SURFACE #noun,
               INFL [ CASE #c,
                      NUMBER #n,
                      GENDER #g ] ] )

-> phrase & [ CAT pp, PREP #prep,
              AGR agr & [ CASE #c,
                          NUMBER #n,
                          GENDER #g]
                          CORE_NP #core_np]],
      where #core_np=Append(#det,'' ``,#noun).
```

The first TFS matches a preposition. Then one or zero determiners are matched. It is followed by zero or more adjectives. Finally, a noun item is consumed. The variables #c, #n, #g establish coreferences expressing the agreement in case, number, and gender for all matched items (except for the initial preposition item which solely agrees in case with the other items). The RHS of the rule triggers the creation of a TFS of type phrase, where the surface form of the matched preposition is transported into the corresponding slot via the variable #prep. A value for the attribute core_np is created through a concatenation of the matched determiner and noun (variables #det and #noun). This is realised via a call to a functional operator called Append.

Grammars consisting of such rules are compiled into extended finite-state networks with rich label descriptions (TFSs). Consequently, the grammar interpreter uses a unifiability operation on TFS as the equality test while traversing such networks, whereas the construction of fully-fledged output structures is carried out through unification of the TFSs representing the matched items with a TFS-representation of the appropriate rule [2]. Since fully specified TFSs usually do not allow for minimisation and efficient processing of such networks, a handful of methods going beyond standard finite-state techniques (e.g., sorting all outgoing transitions of a given state via a computation of a transition hierarchy under subsumption, which potentially reduces the number of time-consuming unification operations) have been deployed to alleviate this problem [11].

SProUTs' shallow grammar interpreter comes with some additional functionalities, including rule prioritisation, output merging mechanism [3], and a reference matching tool, which can be activated on demand. The first tool allows for defining a total order on a subset or grammar rules, which is used to filter out the output structures. The second mechanism offers several techniques for merging the output structures, e.g., via a sequence of unification operations, which can be seen as local template merging. The reference matching tool takes as input the output structures generated by the interpreter, potentially containing user-defined information on variants of the recognised entities for certain NE classes, and performs an additional pass through the text, in order to discover mentions of previously recognised entities. The variant specification is done explicitly by defining additional attributes, e.g., variant, on the RHS of grammar rules, which contain a list of all variant forms (e.g., obtained by concatenating some of the constituents of the full name).

3   Adopting SProUT to the Processing of Polish

Since SProUT provides linguistic resources for the processing components for Germanic and Roman languages, they could be exploited to some extent for fine-tuning SProUT to processing Polish w.r.t. NER.

3.1   Tokenisation and Sentence Splitting

The tokeniser in SProUT is Unicode compatible and allows for fine-grained token classification. There are circa 30 main token types, which have been designed in order to meet the needs of processing Indoeuropean languages (e.g., *currency sign*, *email*, *words containing both lowercase and uppercase characters*, *complex structures including hyphens* etc.). All tokens which cannot be assigned any of the main token types, undergo postsegmentation, i.e., they are split into a sequence of strings and separators, where each of such strings belongs to one of the predefined main token classes. The provided tokeniser resources could be easily adopted by extending the character set with some specific Polish characters and slightly adjusting some of circa 30 predefined token classes. For instance, the class *word-with-apostrophe* for Polish defines all strings containing at least one apostrophe, whereas its counterpart for English or French are restricted to a proper subset for appropriate handling of contractions like *it's*. Since the main design criteria for developing SProUT focus on strong decomposition of the linguistic analysis into clear-cut components, the context information is disregarded during token classification. Consequently, sentence splitting constitutes a stand-alone module. The aforementioned component relies on a list of potential sentence boundary markers, a list of sentence non-final items, and a list of sentence non-initial items.

3.2   Morphological Analysis

Subsequently, Morfeusz, a morphological analyser for Polish which uses a rich tagset based on both morphological and syntactic criteria (Przepiórkowski and Woliński, 2003) has been integrated. It is capable of recognising circa 1,800,000 Polish contemporary word forms. Some work has been accomplished in order to infer additional implicit information (e.g., tense) hidden in the tags generated by *Morfeusz*. The following TFS exemplifies the result produced by the morphology component for the word *urzędzie* (office – locative and vocative form).

```
[ SURFACE urzędzie
    STEM urząd
    POS noun
    INFL[ CASE_NOUN loc_voc,
          NUMBER_NOUN singular,
          GENDER_NOUN masc3 ] ]
```

3.3 Gazetteer

The task of the gazetteer is the recognition of full names (e.g., locations, organisations) and keywords (e.g., company designators, titles) based on static lexica. The gazetteer entries may be associated with a list of arbitrary attribute-value pairs which strongly supports text normalisation. Due to the highly inflectional nature of Polish (e.g., complex declension paradigm), this specific feature of the gazetteer comes particularly in handy. Apart from adapting a subset of circa 50,000 gazetteer entries for Germanic languages (mainly first names, locations, organisations, and titles), which appear in Polish texts as well, additional language-specific resources from various Web sources were acquired. Furthermore, we semi-automatically produced all orthographic and morphological variants for the subset of the acquired resources. For instance, we implemented and applied a brute-force algorithm which generates full declension of first names. In the ensuing phase, they were manually validated. Finally, the created entries were additionally enriched with semantic tags and some basic morphological information, e.g., for the word form '*Argentyny*' (genitive form for *Argentyna*) the following gazetteer entry has been created:

```
Argentyny  |  GTYPE:gaz_country
           |  G_CASE:gen
           |  CONCEPT:Argentyna
           |  full-name:Republika Argentyńska
```

The current status of the additional language-specific resources collected and created so far is depicted in the table in Figure 2.

Type	Amount
large companies	1211
federal government organisations	164
higher schools	68
Cities	2482
Countries	1727
Geographical regions	420
first names	1804

Fig. 2. Language-specific gazetteer resources

Since producing all variant forms is a laborious job, and because the process of creating new names is very productive, a further way of establishing a better interplay between the gazetteer and the morphology module was achieved through an extension of the gazetteer processing module so as to accept lemmatised tokens as input. This is beneficial in case of single-word NEs covered by the *Morfeusz*, but becomes less important in the context of multi-word NEs due to the complex declension, and the fact that frequently some of the words they comprise are unknown. Finally, we boosted the gazetteer by exploiting SProUT itself for the generation of diverse variants of the same NEs from the available text corpora.

3.4 Lemmatisation

Proper construction of name variants is crucial for the coreference resolution component, in order to successfully discover other mentions of previously recognised entities. The essential information for creation of name variants comes from the correct lemmatisation of proper names, which is a challenging task with regard to Polish. For instance, a variant of a person name could be the base form of the last name, or a combination of the title or position and the base form of the last name. The main difficulty w.r.t. Polish arises from the fact that, in general, both first name and surname undergo declension.

Lemmatisation of first names is handled by the gazetteer which provides the main forms (at least for the frequently used Polish first names), whereas lemmatisation of surnames is a far more complex task. Firstly, we have implemented a range of rough sure-fire rules, e.g., rules that convert suffixes like *-skiego, -skim, -skiemu* into the main-form suffix *-ski*, which covers a significant part of the surnames. Secondly, for surnames which do not match any such rules, slightly more sophisticated rules are applied that take into account several factors, including the part-of-speech/gender of the surname (in case it is provided by the morphology), and contextual information, such as the gender of the preceding first name. For instance, if the gender of the first name is feminine (e.g., *Stanisława*), and the surname is a masculine noun (e.g., *Grzyb 'mushroom'*), then the surname does not undergo declension (e.g. main form: *Stanisława Grzyb* vs. accusative form: *Stanisławę Grzyb*). If in the same context the first name is masculine (e.g., *Stanisław*), then the surname undergoes declension (e.g. nom: *Stanisław Grzyb* vs. acc: *Stanisława Grzyba*). On the other hand, if the surname is an adjective it always declines. No later than now, can we witness how useful the inflectional information for the first names provided by the gazetteer is. A maze of similar lemmatisation rules was derived from the bizarre proper name declension paradigm presented in [10].

In some contexts, e.g., in the phrase *Powiadomiono wczoraj wieczorem G. Busha o ataku* ([They have informed] [yesterday] [evening] [G. Bush] [about] [the attack]), correctly inferring the main form of the surname *Busha* would at least involve a subcategorisation frame for the verb *powiadomić* (*to inform* – takes accusative NP as argument). Since subcategorisation lexica are not provided, such cases are not covered at the moment.

The lemmatisation component is integrated in SProUT simply via a functional operator. Consequently, any extensions or adaptations to processing other languages w.r.t. lemmatisation are straightforward. Lemmatisation of organisation names is done implicitly in the grammar rules as we will see in the next section.

4 NE-Grammar for Polish

Within the declarative grammar paradigm of SProUT, we have developed grammars
for recognition of MUC-like NE types [4], including persons, locations, organisations,
etc. This task was accomplished with the visual grammar development environment
provided by SProUT (see figure 3). Fore each NE type, fine-grained template structures
were defined. Figure 4 shows the template for person names. As a matter of fact, our
recognition task resembles more the Template Element (TE) extraction task [1] rather
than the simpler NE-boundary recognition problem.

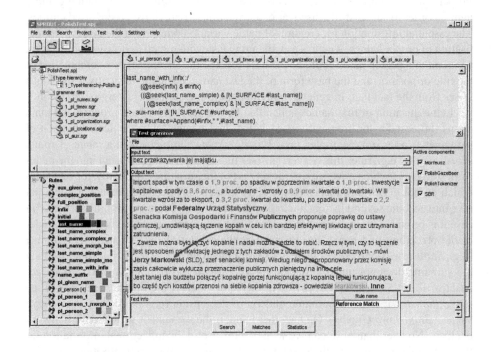

Fig. 3. The SProUT Integrated Development environment

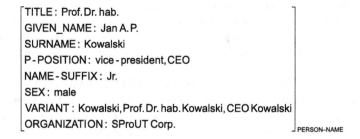

Fig. 4. The template for person names

In the first step, to avoid starting from scratch, we recycled some of the existing NE-grammars for German and English via simply substituting crucial keywords with their Polish counterparts. As NEs mainly consists of nouns and adjectives, major changes focused on replacing the occurrences of the attribute SURFACE with the attribute STEM (main form) and specifying some additional constraints to control the inflection. Contrary to German and English, the role of morphological analysis in the process of NER for Polish is essential, as the following rule for identifying time spans illustrates.

```
time_span_pl :>   token & [  SURFACE "od"]
                  (@seek(pl_month) & [ STEM #start,
                                       INFL [ CASE_NOUN gen,
                                       NUMBER_NOUN sg]])
                  token & [SURFACE "do"]
                  (@seek(pl_month) & [ STEM #end,
                                       INFL [ CASE_NOUN gen,
                                       NUMBER_NOUN sg]])
                  gazetteer & [ GTYPE gaz_year,
                                CONCEPT #year]
 -> timex & [ FROM [ MONTH #start,
                     YEAR #year],
              TO [ MONTH #end,
                   YEAR #year]].
```

This rule matches expressions like *od stycznia do lutego 2003* (from January till February 2003), where genitive forms of month names are required. Please note, that this rule calls a sub-grammar for recognition of month names (seek statement).

Lemmatisation of some named entities is directly encoded in the grammars, which is exemplified in our next sample rule for recognition of organisation names. Due to the fact that organisation names are frequently built up of noun phrases, their lemmatisation relies on proper recognition of their internal structure.

```
org :> (morph & [ SURFACE #key,
                  STEM ``urząd'' & #stem,
                  INFL #infl]) |
       (morph & [  SURFACE #key,
              STEM ``komitet'' & #stem,
              INFL #infl])
          @seek(pl_np_gen) & [ SURFACE #rest]
  -> enamex & [ SURFACE #surf,
                TYPE organisation,
                SUBTYPE #stem,
                CONCEPT #conc,
                INFL #infl],
  where  #surf=ConcWithBlanks(#key,#rest),
         #conc=ConcWithBlanks(#stem,#rest).
```

This rule identifies diverse morphological forms of keywords, such as *urząd* (office), or *komitet* (comitee) followed by a genitive NP (realized by the seek statement). The RHS of the rule generates a named-entity object, where the functional operator

`ConcWithBlanks` simply concatenates all its arguments and inserts blanks between them. For instance, the above rule matches all variants of the phrase *Urząd Ubezpieczeń Zdrowotnych* (Health Insurance Office). It is important to notice that in this particular type of constructions, only the keyword undergoes declension (*urząd*), whereas the rest remains unchanged. Hence, the main form is reconstructed via concatenating the stem of the keyword and the surface forms of the remaining constituents (`CONCEPT` attribute).

Actually, as soon as we had addressed the issue of lemmatisation, the major part of the rules created so far for the particular NE classes had to be broken down into several rules, where each new rule covers different lemmatisation phenomenon. The following fragment of the lemmatisation schema for organisation names visualises the idea.

[A]   [N-key] NP_{gen}
(e.g., [*Naczelną*]   [*Izbą*]   *Kontrolii*)
supreme$_{ins}$ chamber$_{ins}$ audit$_{gen}$

[A]   [N-key]   [A] NP_{gen}
(e.g., [*Okręgowemu*] [*Komitetowi*] [*Organizacyjnemu*] *Budowy Autostrady*)
local$_{acc}$ committee$_{acc}$ organising$_{acc}$ building-the-highway$_{gen}$

`N-key` represents nominal keywords. The constituents which undergo declension are bracketed. For each rule in such schema a corresponding NER rule has been defined. However, the task can become more challenging, since NEs may have potentially more than one internal syntactical structure, which is typical for Polish, since adjectives may either stand before a noun, or they can follow a noun. For instance, the phrase *Biblioteki Głównej Wyższej Szkoły Handlowej* has at least three possible segmentations:

(1) [*Biblioteki Głównej*] [*Wyższej Szkoły Handlowej*]
    [of the main library] [of the Higher School of Economics],

(2) [*Biblioteki Głównej Wyższej*] [*Szkoły Handlowej*]
    [of the main higher library] [of the School of Economics],

(3) [*Biblioteki*] [*Głównej Wyższej Szkoły Handlowej*]
    [of the library (of the libraries)] [of the Main Higher School of Economics]

In order to tackle such complicacies, an introduction of collocations (e.g., '*Biblioteka Główna*' in the example above) reduced the number of ambiguities.

Last but not least, there exists another issue which complicates lemmatisation of proper names in SProUT. We might easily identify the structure of organisation names such as *Komisji Europejskiej Praw Człowieka* (of the European Commission for Human Rights), but the part which undergoes declension, namely *Komisji Europejskiej* (of the European Commission) can not be simply lemmatised via a concatenation of the main forms of these two words. This is because *Morfeusz* returns the nominal masculine form as the main form for an adjective, which generally differs in the ending from the corresponding feminine form (masc: *Europejski* vs. fem: *Europejska*), whereas the word *Komisja* is a feminine noun. Once again, functional operators were utilized to find a rough workaround and minimise the problem.

Ultimately, somewhat 'more relaxed' rules have been introduced in order to capture entities which could not have been captured by the ones based on morphological features and those which perform lemmatisation. Such rules cover sequences of capitalised words, conjunctions and some keywords. Consequently, SProUT's mechanism for rule prioritisation has been deployed in order to give higher preference to rules capable of performing lemmatisation and rules which potentially instantiate higher number of slots in the output structures. The current grammar consists of 143 rules.

In an additional pass through the text, mentions of previously recognised entities (persons, organisations, and locations) are discovered, based on the variants in the output structures returned by the grammar interpreter. Since the VARIANT slots in the output structures solely include main forms (and no morphological generation functionality is available at this time), only nominative mentions could be identified. On the other hand, the major part of name mentions in our test corpus appeared to be nominative.

5   Evaluation

A corpus consisting of 100 financial news articles from an online version of *Rzecz-pospolita*, a leading Polish newspaper, has been selected for analysis and evaluation purposes. The precision-recall metrics are depicted in the table in Figure 5.

NE TYPE	PRECISION	RECALL
TIME	81.3	85.9
PERCENTAGE	100.0	100.0
MONEY	97.8	93.8
ORGANISATIONS	87.9	56.6
LOCATIONS	88.4	43.4
PERSONS	90.6	85.3

Fig. 5. Precision-recall metrics

Somewhat worse results were obtained for persons, locations, and organisations due to the problems outlined in the previous sections. We also evaluated the quality of lemmatisation. 79.6of the detected NEs were lemmatised correctly. From all extracted NEs, 13 % were recognised via the application of the partial coreference resolution mechanism. The analysis of erroneously recognised NEs revealed that major problem concerned the classical morphological ambiguity. Let us consider the following text fragment.

... Dane Federalnego Urzędu Statystycznego w Wiesbaden ...
[data$_{nom}$] [federal$_{gen}$] [office$_{gen}$] [statistical$_{gen}$] [in] [Wiesbaden$_{nom}$]

SProUT recognises *Dane Federalnego* as a person name since *Dane* is a gazetteer entry representing an English first name. Consequently, the text fragment *Federalnego Urzędu Statystycznego w Wiesbaden* could not be recognised as an organisation name. Potentially, an introduction of heuristic techniques for solving such NE overlapping collisions would improve the precision. Further investigations showed that occasionally coordinated structures are not handled properly. We expect to gain recall via providing additional gazetteer resources and improvement of the lemmatisation of unknown multi-words. Although the recall values are still far away from the state-of-the-art results obtained for the more studied languages, the initial results are promising.

6   Conclusions

We have presented a preliminary attempt towards constructing a grammar-based NER system for Polish via fine-tuning SProUT, a flexible multi-lingual NLP platform, and by introducing some language-specific components which could be easily integrated via functional operators. The peculiarities of Polish pinpointed in this article reveal the indispensability of integrating additional language-specific resources and components including lemmatiser for unknown multi-words [9], subcategorisation dictionary [12], morphosyntactic tagger [7], and a morphological generation module in order to gain recall and improve the overall performance of the presented approach, which is probably among the pioneering studies in the context of automatic NER for Polish. While proximate work will concentrate on improving the overall system, in a parallel line of research an investigation of applying serious machine learning techniques to NER for Polish is envisaged. In particular, corpus annotation work is in the foreground.

Acknowledgements

I am greatly indebted to Witold Drożdżyński, Petr Homola, Marcin Woliński, Adam Przepiórkowski, Anna Drożdżyńska, and Marcin Rzepa for their contribution to the task of adapting SProUT to Polish and acquisition of language specific resources. The work reported here was supported by the EU-funded project MEMPHIS under grant no. IST-2000-25045 and by additional non-financed personal effort of the author and aforementioned persons.

References

1. Appelt, D., Israel, D.: *An introduction to information extraction technology.* A Tutorial prepared for IJCAI-99 Conference, (1999)
2. Becker, M., Drożdżyński, W., Krieger, H.-U., Piskorski, J. Schäfer, U., Xu, F.: *SProUT – Shallow Processing with Typed Feature Structures and Unification.* In Proceedings of ICON 2002, Mumbai, India, (2002)
3. Busemann, S., Krieger, H.-U.: *Resources and Techniques for Multilingual Information Extraction.* In Proceedings of International Conference on Language Resources an Evaluation– LREC 2004, Lissabon, Portugal, (2004)
4. Chinchor, N., Robinson, P.: *MUC-7 Named Entity Task Definition (version 3.5).* Proceedings of the MUC-7, Fairfax, Virginia, USA, (1998)
5. Cunningham, H., Paskaleva, E., Bontcheva, K., Angelova, G.: *Proceedings of the Workshop IESL – Information Extraction for Slavonic Languages*, Borovets, Bulgaria, (2003)
6. Cunningham, H., Maynard, D., Bontcheva K., Tablan V.: *GATE: A Framework and Graphical Development Environment for Robust NLP Tools and Applications.* In Proceedings of the ACL'02, Philadelphia, USA, (2002)

7. Dębowski, Ł.: *Trigram morphosyntactic tagger for Polish*. In Proceedings of IIS 2004, Zakopane, Poland, (2004)
8. Drożdżyński, W., Krieger, H.-U., Piskorski, J., Schäfer, U., Xu F.: *Shallow Processing with Unification and Typed Feature Structures – Foundations and Applications*. In German AI Journal KI-Zeitschrift, Vol. 01/04, Gesellschaft für Informatik e.V., (2004)
9. Erjavec, T., Džeroski, S.: *Lemmatising Unknown Words in Highly Inflective Languages*. In Proceedings of the IESL 2003, Borovets, Bulgaria, (2003)
10. Grzenia, J.: *Słownik nazw własnych – ortografia, wymowa, słowotwórstwo i odmiana*. Published by PWN, Seria: Słowniki Języka Polskiego, ISBN: 83-01-12500-4, (1998)
11. Krieger, H.-U., Drożdżyński, W., Piskorski, J., Schäfer, U, Xu F.: *A Bag of Usefull Techniques for Unification-Based Finite-State Transducers*. In Proceedings of KONVENS 2004, Vienna, Austria, (2004)
12. Przepiórkowski, A.: *Towards the design of a Syntactico-Semantic Lexicon for Polish*. In Proceedings of IIS 2004, Zakopane, Poland, (2004)
13. Przepiórkowski, A., Woliński, M.: *A flexemic tagset for Polish*. Proceedings of Morph logical Processing of Slavic Languages, EACL-2003, Budapest, Hungary, (2003)
14. Świdziński, M., Saloni, Z.: *Składnia współczesnego języka polskiego*. Publisher: PWN, ISBN: 83-01-12712-0, (1998)

A Survey of Recent Results on Spatial Reasoning via Rough Inclusions*

Lech Polkowski

Polish-Japanese Institute of Information Technology,
ul. Koszykowa 86, 02-008 Warsaw, Poland
polkow@pjwstk.edu.pl

Abstract. The term *rough inclusion* was introduced as a generic term by Polkowski and Skowron in the seminal paper that laid foundations for Rough Mereology – a paradigm for Approximate Reasoning that combines ideas of Mereology – a set theory based on the notion of a part – with ideas of Rough Set Theory and Fuzzy Set Theory; in particular, its basic predicate of rough inclusion is a rendering of the notion of being a part to a degree. Rough Mereology is an approach towards constructing reasoning schemes that take into account uncertainty of either knowledge or concepts used in reasoning. This abstract reasoning methodology is therefore a constituent of the vast field of Cognitive Technologies (styled also Artificial Intelligence).

It is well–known that mereological theories of objects have been applied in Spatial Reasoning – reasoning about uncertainty in spatial contexts. The majority of theories based on mereology and applied in reasoning about spatial objects stem from the idea of A. N. Whitehead, viz., Mereology Theory based on the predicate of being connected.

In this article, we give a survey of the current state of the art in spatial reasoning based on constructs of Rough Mereology. We include here theoretical results – some of them already shown in earlier works – that witness applicability of constructs based on rough inclusions in spatial reasoning as well as we mention recent works on practical applications to real–world robot navigation.

Keywords: Rough mereology, spatial reasoning, mereo–topology, mereo–geometry, mobile robotics.

1 Introduction

Approximate Reasoning deals with cases of problems where complexity of a problem and/or uncertainty resulting from either the data acquisition technique or data nature lead to necessity of ascertaining the truth of statements, produced in the process of reasoning, to a degree.

Symbolically, one may express this peculiarity of reasoning with the help of well–known figures of reasoning: *Modus Ponens* and *Modus Tollens*. Modus Ponens is a deduction mood based on the following scheme:

---

* This article is based on the keynote lecture by the author at IMTCI (Intelligent Media Technology for Communicative Intelligence) International Workshop, Polish–Japanese Institute of Information Technology, Warsaw, September 2004.

L. Bolc et al. (Eds.): IMTCI 2004, LNAI 3490, pp. 134–146, 2005.

$$\frac{p \Rightarrow q; p}{q}, \tag{1}$$

whereas Modus Tollens is described by the following figure,

$$\frac{p \Rightarrow q; \neg q}{\neg p}. \tag{2}$$

Both Modus Ponens and Modus Tollens are used in deduction and induction schemes based on classical logics when truth values of statements are exactly known.

Counterparts of these two figures of reasoning used in approximate reasoning would look like this,

$$\frac{(p \Rightarrow q, r); (p, s)}{(q, t)}, \tag{3}$$

respectively,

$$\frac{(p \Rightarrow q, r); (q, s)}{(p, t)}, \tag{4}$$

where (p, r) means that p is satisfied to degree r.

Let us observe that – although we try to describe validity of p approximately – yet we are compelled to precisely describe the degree r to which p is valid. This is the case, e.g., with Fuzzy Set Theory proposed by Zadeh [32], in which one has to ascertain the degree of membership of an object in the given concept; that task is done by a subjective choice of standards departure from which is a measure of degree of membership.

Approximate reasoning, in its various shapes and guises, is fundamental to Communicative Intelligence (cf. the article by Professor Nishida in this Volume). Interactions of humans and artifacts, by their very nature require some forms of dealing with uncertainty, and one of the most important aspects of these interactions is related to spatial considerations (loc. cit.). It is therefore inferred that approximate approach to spatial reasoning is vital to the field of Communicative Intelligence.

We present here theoretical foundations of spatial reasoning based on rough inclusions – predicates basic to Rough Mereology. In the theoretical aspect, we demonstrate that the notion of connection may be derived in a canonical way in this framework. We also introduce some predicates of Mereogeometry induced from rough inclusions.

We demonstrate a theoretical analysis of possibility to employ the mereogemetric notions in mobile robot's localisation and navigation. We also include some results of real–world experiments with a mobile robot done in the Robotics Laboratory at the Polish–Japanese Institute of Information Technology in which these mereogeometric concepts were implemented and tested[1].

2   The Paradigm of Mereology

Mereological theories of sets are in a sense higher–level set theories. We refer here to two mainstream theories of Mereology viz. Mereology due to Stanisław Leśniewski [11], and Mereology based on Connection [4], [31], [5].

---

[1] The author is indebted to Dr Eng. A. Szmigielski for providing these results that constitute a part of his PhD Dissertation [25] supervised by the author at the Institute of Automation and Applied Computer Science of the Warsaw University of Technology, May 2004.

To introduce the basic idea, let us consider sets in the usual sense along with the containment (proper subset) relation $\subset$. In case $X \subset Y$, for sets X, Y, one can say that *the set X is a part of the set Y*, e.g., in the sentence *the unit circle is a part of the unit closed disc*. One may feel intuitively that this theory of sets is suited well for discussions on geometric properties of bodies like solids, figures, etc., etc.

Abstracting from the above example, Mereology proposed by Leśniewski (op. cit.) starts with the basic predicate *part* of to be a part of.

2.1   Mereology Based on Parts

We denote with π the relation of *to be a part of* that is subject to the following requirements; u, v, w are individual entities (not any collections).

(P1) $u\pi v \wedge v\pi w \Longrightarrow u\pi w$ (transitivity);
(P2) $\neg(u\pi u)$ (non–reflexivity).

On the basis of the notion of a part, we define the notion of an *element* (i.e., an improper, possibly, part; called originally by Leśniewski an *ingredient*) as a predicate el, defined as follows,

$$u\,el\,v \Longleftrightarrow u\pi v \vee u = v. \tag{5}$$

The remaining axioms of mereology are related to the class functor Cls which converts distributive classes (general names) into individual entities.

Invoking the example of $\subset$ as the relation of a part, one obtains, as the related class operator, the operation of converting a family of sets into a set by means of the union of sets operation.

We may now introduce the notion of a (collective) class in general via the class functor Cls that is defined as follows, for a collective property Y,

(C1) $u \in Y \Rightarrow u\,el\,Cls(Y)$;
(C2) $u\,el\,Cls(Y) \Rightarrow \exists v, w.v\,el\,u, v\,el\,w, w \in Y$.

Thus, the class operator pastes together individuals in Y by means of their common elements.

One may prove, [11], the following inference rule that is essential in manipulating the class notion,

$$\textbf{(INF)}\ [\forall w.(w\,el\,u \Rightarrow \exists t.(t\,el\,w \wedge t\,elv))] \Rightarrow u\,el\,v.$$

The rule INF says, that in order to verify the claim that $u\,elv$, it is sufficient to check that each element of u is an element of an element of v.

2.2   Mereology Based on Connections

This approach [4], [31] is based on the functor C of *being connected* that satisfies the following,

(CN1) uCu;
(CN2) $uCv \implies vCu$;
(CN3) $[\forall w.(wCu \iff wCv)] \implies (u = v)$.

From C, other functors are derived; we recall them now,

(DC) [disconnected] $uDCv \iff \neg(uCv)$;
(El) [C–element] $uel_C v \iff \forall w.(wCu \implies wCv)$;
(Pt) [C–part] $upt_C v \iff uel_C v \land \neg(vel_C u;)$
(O) [overlap] $uOv \iff \exists w.(wel_C u \land wel_C v)$;
(EC) [externally connected] $uECv \iff uCv \land \neg(uOv)$;
(TP) [tangential part] $uTPv \iff upt_C v \land \exists w.(wECu \land wECv)$;
(NTP) [non–tangential part] $uNTPv \iff upt_C v \land \neg(uTPv)$.

These notions altogether offer a rich variety of predicates with which to describe fairly complex relations among spatial objects, see [5].

Of the two theories, Mereology based on Connection offers a richer variety of mereo–topological functors; yet, as Mereology of Leśniewski is based on the notion of *part*, it offers a formalism of which the formalism of Rough Mereology may be – under a suitable choice of primitive expressions – a direct extension and generalisation. This is actually the case: Rough Mereology was proposed [19], to contain Mereology of Leśniewski as the theory of the predicate μ_1 and this feature is preserved in the formalisation proposed here.

2.3 Rough Mereology

Rough Mereology is an extension of Mereology based on the predicate of *being a part of to a degree*; this predicate is rendered here as a family μ_r parameterised by a real parameter $r \in [0,1]$ with the intent that $u\mu_r v$ reads "*u is a part of v to a degree at least r*".

We assume a predicate el of an element satisfying Mereology axiom system given; around this, we develop a system of axioms for Rough Mereology.

The Axiom System. The following is the list of basic postulates.

(RM1) $u\mu_1 v \iff uelv$;
(RM2) $u\mu_1 v \implies \forall w.(w\mu_r u \implies w\mu_r v)$;
(RM3) $u\mu_r v \land s \leq r \implies u\mu_s v$.

It follows that the predicate μ_1 coincides with the given predicate el establishing a link between Rough Mereology and Mereology while predicates μ_r with $r < 1$ diffuse el to a graded family of predicates expressing being an element (or, part) in various degrees.

Mereology may be applied in exact schemes of reasoning (similarly to logic on which exact schemes of reasoning are based) related to objects whose structure (in terms of their decomposition into parts) is well–known; however, when our reasoning is applied to situations where our knowledge is uncertain, incomplete, etc., we may outline a decomposition scheme only approximately, i.e., we may evaluate only that our object in question is composed of some other objects as parts up to a certain degree. In consequence, other constructs used in spatial reasoning like a neighbourhood, an interior, etc., are defined approximately only, the degree of approximation determined by degrees of being a part in an intricate way.

3   Rough Mereology in Information Systems

Information systems are defined as pairs of the form (U, A), where U is the set of objects described by means of attributes in the set A; each attribute $a \in A$ is a mapping $a : U \to V$ of the set U into the set V of *values*. Information systems are one of basic frameworks for Rough Set Theory [15], whose ideas has led the author to the idea of rough mereology.

We propose a method for inducing in information systems of a variety of rough inclusions based on properties of t–norms, familiar from fuzzy set theory.

We recall that a t–norm T is *archimedean* if in addition to common properties[2], it is continuous and $T(x, x) < x$ for each $x \in (0, 1)$. It is well known (see, e.g., [17]) that any archimedean t–norm T, can be represented in the form,

$$T(x, y) = g(f(x) + f(y)), \tag{6}$$

where $f : [0, 1] \to [0, 1]$ is continuous decreasing and g is the pseudo–inverse to f.[3]

For an information system (U, A) about which we assume that given objects $x \neq y$ there is an attribute $a \in A$ such that $a(x) \neq a(y)$, we consider for each pair $x, y \in U$ of objects, the set $DIS(x, y) = \{a \in A : a(x) \neq a(y)\} \subseteq A$.

For an archimedean t–norm, T, we define a relation μ_T by letting,

$$\mu_T(x, y, r) \text{ holds if and only if } g(\frac{|DIS(x, y)|}{|A|}) \geq r. \tag{7}$$

Then, μ_T is a rough inclusion that satisfies the transitivity rule,

$$\frac{\mu_T(x, y, r), \mu_T(y, z, s)}{\mu_T(x, z, T(r, s))}. \tag{8}$$

Particular examples of rough inclusions are the *Menger rough inclusion*, and the Łukasiewicz rough inclusion, corresponding, respectively, to the product t–norm $T_M(x, y) = x \cdot y$, and the Łukasiewicz tensor product $T_L(x, y) = max\{0, x + y - 1\} = \otimes(x, y)$.

The Menger Rough Inclusion. For the t–norm T_M, the *generating function* $f(x) = -lnx$ whereas $g(y) = e^{-y}$ is the pseudo–inverse to f. According to (7), the rough inclusion μ_{T_M} is given by the formula,

$$\mu_{T_M}(x, y, r) \Leftrightarrow e^{-\frac{|DIS(x,y)|}{|A|}} \geq r. \tag{9}$$

---

[2] Meaning: T is increasing, symmetric, associative, and $T(0, x) = 0$.

[3] This means that $g(x) = 1$ for $x \in [0, f(1)]$, $g(x) = 0$ for $x \in [f(0), 1]$, and $g(x) = f^{-1}(x)$ for $x \in [f(1), f(0)]$.

The Łukasiewicz Rough Inclusion. For t–norm T_L, the generating function $f(x) = 1 - x$ and $g = f$ is the pseudo–inverse to f. Therefore,

$$\mu_{T_L}(x, y, r) \text{ if and only if } 1 - \frac{|DIS(x, y)|}{|A|} \geq r. \tag{10}$$

Let us show a simple example of an information system $\mathcal{A}$ in Table 1.

Table 1. The information system $\mathcal{A}$

U	a_1	a_2	a_3	a_4
x_1	1	1	1	2
x_2	1	0	1	0
x_3	2	0	1	1
x_4	3	2	1	0
x_5	3	1	1	0
x_6	3	2	1	2
x_7	1	2	0	1
x_8	2	0	0	2

For the information system $\mathcal{A}$ of Table 1, we calculate values of μ_{T_L}, shown in Table 2; as μ_{T_L} is symmetric, we show only the upper triangle of values.

Table 2. μ_{T_L} for Table 1

U	x_1	x_2	x_3	x_4	x_5	x_6	x_7	x_8
x_1	1	0.5	0.25	0.25	0.5	0.5	0.25	0.25
x_2	-	1	0.5	0.5	0.5	0.25	0.25	0.25
x_3	-	-	1	0.25	0.25	0.25	0.25	0.5
x_4	-	-	-	1	0.75	0.75	0.25	0
x_5	-	-	-	-	1	0.5	0	0
x_6	-	-	-	-	-	1	0.25	0.25
x_7	-	-	-	-	-	-	1	0.25
x_8	-	-	-	-	-	-	-	1

In similar vein, we may define rough inclusions on finite subsets of a given universe U, by letting,

$$\mu(X, Y, r) \text{ if and only if } g(\frac{|X \setminus Y|}{|X|}) \geq r, \tag{11}$$

where $|X|$ stands for the cardinality of the set X.

As an example, let us notice that (11) in case of the rough inclusion μ_{T_L} takes the form,

$$\mu_{T_L}(X, Y, r) \text{ if and only if } \frac{|X \cap Y|}{|X|} \geq r, \tag{12}$$

becoming a well–known formula employed in Machine Learning (see, e.g., association rules of Agrawal et al. [1]).

4   Introduction to Qualitative Spatial Reasoning

Qualitative Reasoning aims at studying concepts and calculi on them that arise often at early stages of problem analysis when one is refraining from qualitative or metric details cf. [5]; as such it has close relations to the design as well as planning stages of the model synthesis process. Classical formal approaches to spatial reasoning, i.e., to representing spatial entities (points, surfaces, solids etc.) and their features (dimensionality, shape, connectedness degree etc.) rely on Geometry or Topology, i.e., on formal theories whose models are spaces (universes) constructed as sets of points; contrary to this approach, qualitative reasoning about space often exploits pieces of space (regions, boundaries, walls, membranes, etc.) and argues in terms of relations abstracted from a commonsense perception (like *connected, discrete from, adjacent, intersecting*). In this approach, points appear as ideal objects (e.g., ultrafilters of regions/solids [10], [27]). Qualitative Spatial Reasoning has a wide variety of applications, among them, to mention only a few, representation of knowledge, cognitive maps and navigation tasks in robotics (e.g., [9]), Geographical Information Systems and spatial databases including *Naive Geography* (e.g., [6]), high–level Computer Vision (e.g., [30]), studies in semantics of orientational lexemes and in semantics of movement (e.g., [2]). Spatial Reasoning establishes a link between Computer Science and Cognitive Sciences (e.g., [8]), and it has close and deep relationships with philosophical and logical theories of space and time (e.g. [23], [3]). A more complete perspective on Spatial Reasoning and its variety of themes and techniques may be acquired by visiting one of the following sites: [24], [29], [13].

We address here a basic approach to spatial reasoning that has been based on the notion of connection (see works quoted).

5   Connections from Rough Inclusions

In this section we investigate some methods for inducing connections from rough inclusions, including results in [18].

5.1   Granulation of the Universe

We assume a rough inclusion μ on a mereological universe (U, el) with a part relation π. For given $r < 1$ and $x \in U$, we let,

$$g_r(x) = Cls(\Psi_r), \tag{13}$$

where

$$\Psi_r(y) \Leftrightarrow y\mu_r x. \tag{14}$$

The class $g_r(x)$ collects all atomic objects satisfying the class definition with the concept Ψ_r.

We will call the class $g_r(x)$ the r–*granule* about x; it may be interpreted as a neighbourhood of x of radius r. We may also regard the formula $y\mu_r x$ as stating *similarity* of y to x (to degree r). We do not discuss here the problem of representation of granules; in general, one may apply sets or lists as the underlying representation structure.

5.2 From Graded Connections to Connections

We begin with a definition of an individual $Bd_r u$ as the class $Cls(\mu_r^+ u)$, where $v\mu_r^+ u \iff v\mu_r u \land \neg(\exists s \geq r.v\mu_s u)$.

We introduce a *graded (r, s)–connection* $C(r, s)$ $(r, s < 1)$ via,

$$uC(r, s)v \iff \exists w.wel(Bd_r u) \land wel(Bd_s v). \tag{15}$$

We have then, (i) $uC(1, 1)u$; (ii) $uC(r, s)v \implies vC(s, r)u$.

Concerning the property (CN3), we adopt here a new approach. It is valid from theoretical point of view to assume that we may have "infinitesimal" parts i.e. objects as "small" as desired.[4]

Infinitesimal Parts Model. We adopt a new axiom of infinitesimal parts,

(IP) $\neg(uelv) \implies \forall r > 0.\exists w, s, r, 1.welu, s < r, w\mu_s^+ v.$

Our rendering of the property (CN3) under (IP) is as follows:

$$\neg(uelv) \implies \forall r > 0.\exists w, s \geq r.wC(1, 1)u \land wC(1, s)v. \tag{16}$$

Connections from Graded Connections. Our notion of a connection will depend on a threshold, α, set according to the needs of the context of reasoning. Given $0 < \alpha < 1$, we define,

$$uC_\alpha v \iff \exists r, s \geq \alpha.uC(r, s)v. \tag{17}$$

Then C_α has all the properties (CN1)–(CN3) of a connection.

For instance, applying the above formula to data in Table 2 (and ignoring for the example sake the fact that (IP) is not satisfied in this table), we may find that the relation $C_{0.75}$ is satisfied for pairs $(x_4, x_5), (x_4, x_6)$ and all pairs of the form (x_i, x_i) with $i = 1, 2, \ldots, 8$.

Let us also notice that this form of the predicate of being connected may be applied in any case when knowledge is represented as a data table in the above form of an information system.

6 Mereogeometry

Predicates μ_r may be regarded as weak distance functions also in the context of geometry. From this point of view, we may apply μ in order to define basic notions of rough mereological geometry, see [20].

In the language of this geometry, we may approximately describe and approach geometry of objects described by data tables; a usage for this geometry may be found, e.g., in navigation and control tasks of mobile robotics, [30].

It is well-known (cf. [3], [28]) that geometry of Euclidean spaces may be based on some postulates about the basic notions of a point and the ternary equi–distance functor.

---

[4] Cf. an analogous assumption in mereology based on connection [12]).

In [28] postulates for Euclidean geometry over a real–closed field were given based on the functor of betweenness and the quaternary equi–distance functor. Similarly, in [3], a set of postulates aimed at rendering general geometric features of finite–dimensional spaces over reals was discussed, the primitive notion there being that of nearness.

We first introduce a notion of distance κ_r in our rough mereological universe by letting

$$\kappa_r(u, v) \Longleftrightarrow r = \min\{u, w : u\varepsilon\mu_u^+ v \wedge v\mu_w^+ u\}.$$

We now introduce the notion of betweenness, $Btw(u, v)$,

$$wBtw(u, v) \Longleftrightarrow \forall z.\kappa_r(z, w) \wedge \kappa_s(u, z) \wedge \kappa_t(v, w) \Longrightarrow s \le r \le t \vee t \le r \le s. \quad (18)$$

A straight line $Line$ contains a triple u, v, w of regions if and only if the following holds,

$$u\, Btw(u, w) \ \vee\ vBtw(u, w) \ \vee\ wBtw(u, v). \quad (19)$$

We may also apply κ to define in our context the functor $Near$ of nearness proposed in [3],

$$wNear(u, v) \Longleftrightarrow (\kappa_r(w, u) \wedge \kappa_s(u, v) \Longrightarrow s < r). \quad (20)$$

Here, nearness means that w is closer to u than to v.

We now may introduce the notion of equi–distance $Eq(u, v)$,

$$wEq(u, v) \Longleftrightarrow \neg(uNear(w, v)) \wedge \neg(vNear(w, u)). \quad (21)$$

For instance, the notion of a straight line, $Line$, may be defined by requiring that for each of its three points, one lies between the two other.

These constructs may be applied in mobile robot localisation and navigation, of which we give a concise example.

7   Applications to Mobile Robotics

In the recent PhD Thesis [25],[26] supervised by this Author, a scheme for robot navigation was proposed based on the notions proposed above. The robot was equipped with an omnidirectional sonar, allowing for finding the radius of the collision–free region, and a sonar emitter that was conversing with a sonar GPS system in the environment, setting around the current receiver a receiver region. This configuration is shown in Fig. 1. Here the disk $\mathbf{D}$ centered at O – the receiver is the receiver region, the disk $\mathbf{R}$ centered at S–the robot is the collision–free region. The rough inclusion selected for implementations of the predicates Btw, $Near$, etc., is,

$$\mu(\mathbf{D}, \mathbf{R}, r) \text{ if and only if } \frac{|\mathbf{D} \cap \mathbf{R}|}{|\mathbf{D}|} \ge r, \quad (22)$$

where $|A|$ is the area of the region A.

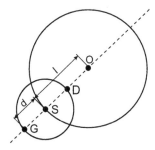

Fig. 1. Configuration of non-collision region and receiver region

7.1   Examples of Robot Tasks

For region configuration presented in Fig. 1, both regions have the smallest *mereo-distance* (equal to $\frac{2}{3} - \frac{\sqrt{3}}{2\pi} \approx 0,391$) if and only if they have the same radii and centers of each lie on the boundary of the other. From a control point of view, every region, included in the *non-collision region* is also a *non-collision region*. If there exists a non-collision region x, whose distance to a receiver region y is minimal, then the *non-collision region x is near* to the receiver region y, in symbols x near y. The intention of movement,

– GOAL OF CONTROL:
  move the robot near to the receiver region

can be replaced by a formula

– MEREOLOGICAL DESCRIPTION:
  x near y.

We denote with the symbols $\kappa(o, j), \kappa(o, s), \kappa(o, p)$, respectively, mereo–distances between regions (disks) of radii d centered, respectively at points G, S, D in Fig. 1, and the receiver region at O.

Clearly, $\kappa(o, j) < \kappa(o, s) < \kappa(o, p)$. The symbol κ will denote the distance between the non–collision and the receiver regions after the movement is made.

Table 3 presents basic rules determining the rotation angle α of the robot as a function of the distance κ.

Table 3. Rotation angle as a function of mereo–distance

mereo–distance	center distance	angle of rotation
$\kappa(o, p)$	1-d	0
$\kappa(o, s)$	1	$\frac{\pi}{2}$
$\kappa(o, j)$	1+d	π

The form of the function $\kappa \to \alpha$ of which Table 3 is an approximation, is set as,

$$\alpha = \arctan((\kappa(o, p) - \kappa(o, j)) \cdot \frac{\kappa(o, s) - \kappa}{(\kappa - \kappa(o, j)) \cdot (\kappa(o, p) - \kappa)}) + \frac{\pi}{2}. \qquad (23)$$

The direction of rotation is set by the decision rule,

$$\text{if } \alpha_{present} > \alpha_{previous} \text{ then change the direction of rotation,} \qquad (24)$$

where $\alpha_{present}$, $\alpha_{previous}$ denote the current, respectively, previous, value of the rotation angle.

Driving Robot in Straight Line. The intention of movement: GOAL OF CONTROL: *move the robot in the straight line*, can be replaced by a mereological formula MEREO-LOGICAL DESCRIPTION:$x\pi Eql$, where Eql is the *straight line* according to (19).

Turning the Robot. Turning the robot can be executed in three stages: 1. to go straight, 2. to reach the point of changing the navigated pair of receivers, 3. to go following the new navigating points.

An exemplary task of managing the corner is shown in Fig. 2 (see [25]).

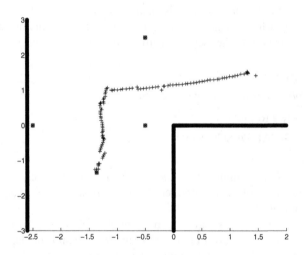

Fig. 2. The trajectory of the robot around the corner

Let us observe that mereological formalisation presented above allows for natural language usage, a most important feature to Communicative Intelligence: in the surface structure, commands are in natural language, like "go in the straight line defined by a and b"; in the deep structure this command is rendered as:$x\pi Eql$, i.e., as a formula of mereology, transformed in turn into actions of a robot.

Acknowledgements. The author thanks Dr Adam Szmigielski for granting his results of implementations of the author's mereological theory, quoted in this paper. In real world experiments Pioneer P2DX robot, produced by *Activmedia Corporation* was used.

References

1. Agrawal, R., et al.: Fast discovery of association rules, in: U.M.Fayyad et al., eds., Advances in Knowledge Discovery and Data Mining, The AAAI Press/The MIT Press 1996, pp. 307–328

2. Aurnague, M., Vieu, L.: A theory of space-time for natural language semantics, in: K. Korta and J. M. Larrazábal, eds., Semantics and Pragmatics of Natural Language: Logical and Computational Aspects, ILCLI Series I, Univ. Pais Vasco, San Sebastian, 1995, pp. 69–126

3. vanBentham, J.: The Logic of Time, Reidel, Dordrecht, 1983

4. Clarke, B.L.: A calculus of individuals based on connection, Notre Dame Journal of Formal Logic 22(2), 1981, pp. 204–218

5. Cohn, A.G.: Calculi for qualitative spatial reasoning, in: J. Calmet, J. A. Campbell, J. Pfalzgraf (eds.), Artificial Intelligence and Symbolic Mathematical Computation, Lecture Notes in Computer Science vol. 1138, Springer Verlag, Berlin, 1996, pp. 124–143

6. Egenhofer, M.J., Golledge, R.G. (eds.): Spatial and Temporal Reasoning in Geographic Information Systems, Oxford U. Press, Oxford, 1997

7. Freksa, C., Mark, D.M. (eds.): Spatial Information Theory. Cognitive and Computational Foundations of Geographic Information Science. Proceedings COSIT'99, Lecture Notes in Computer Science vol. 1661, Springer Verlag, Berlin, 1999

8. Freksa, C., Habel, C.: Repraesentation und Verarbeitung raeumlichen Wissens, Informatik-Fachberichte, Springer Verlag, Berlin, 1990

9. Kuipers, B.: Qualitative Reasoning: Modeling and Simulation with Incomplete Knowledge, MIT Press, Cambridge MA, 1994

10. De Laguna, T.: Point, line, surface as sets of solids, J. Philosophy 19, 1922, pp. 449–461

11. Leśniewski, St.: On the foundations of mathematics, Topoi 2, 1982, pp. 7–52

12. Masolo, C., Vieu, L.: Atomicity vs. infinite divisibility of space, in: C. Freksa, D. M. Mark (eds.), Spatial Information Theory. Cognitive and Computational Foundations of Geographic Information Science, Lecture Notes in Computer Science vol. 1661, Springer Verlag, Berlin, 1999, pp. 235–250

13. http://www.cs.albany.edu/'amit

14. Pal, S.K., Polkowski, L., Skowron, A.: *Rough–Neural Computing. Techniques for Computing with Words*, Springer Verlag, Berlin, 2004

15. Pawlak, Z.: Rough Sets: Theoretical Aspects of Reasoning about Data, Kluwer, Dordrecht, 1992

16. Pawlak, Z., Skowron, A.: Rough membership functions, in: R. R. Yager, M. Fedrizzi, J. Kacprzyk (eds.), Advances in the Dempster-Schafer Theory of Evidence, John Wiley and Sons, New York, 1994, pp. 251–271

17. Polkowski, L.: *Rough Sets. Mathematical Foundations*, Physica–Verlag, Heidelberg, 2002

18. Polkowski, L.: On connection synthesis via rough mereology, Fundamenta Informaticae 46 (1/2), 2001, pp. 83–96

19. Polkowski, L., Skowron, A.: Rough mereology: a new paradigm for approximate reasoning, International Journal of Approximate Reasoning 15(4), 1997, pp. 333–365

20. Polkowski, L., Skowron, A.: Rough mereology in information systems with applications to qualitative spatial reasoning, Fundamenta Informaticae, 43(1–4), 2000, pp. 291–320

21. Polkowski, L., Skowron, A. (eds.): Rough Sets in Knowledge Discovery. Methodology and Applications,in: J. Kacprzyk, ed., Studies in Fuzziness and Soft Computing, vol. 18, Physica Verlag/Springer Verlag, Heidelberg, 1998

22. Polkowski, L., Skowron, A. (eds.): Rough Sets in Knowledge Discovery. Applications,Case Studies and Software Systems in: J. Kacprzyk, ed., Studies in Fuzziness and Soft Computing, vol. 19, Physica Verlag/Springer Verlag, Heidelberg, 1998

23. Reichenbach, H.: The Philosophy of Space and Time (repr.), Dover, New York, 1957
24. http:/agora.leeds.ac.uk/spacenet/spacenet.html
25. Szmigielski, A.: *Using a System of Sonars for Description of Working Environment of a Mobile Robot by Means of Mereology*, PhD Thesis, Institute of Automation and Computer Science, Warsaw University of Technology, L. Polkowski, supervisor, May 2004
26. Szmigielski, A., Polkowski, L.: Computing from words via rough mereology in mobile robot navigation, in: Proveedings IEEE/JRS International Conference on Intelligent Robots and Systems IROS2003, Las Vegas, NV, US, October 2003, 3498–3503
27. Tarski, A.: Les fondements de la géométrie des corps, in: Księga Pamiątkowa I Polskiego Zjazdu Matematycznego (Memorial Book of the 1st Polish Mathematical Congress), a supplement to Annales de la Sociéte Polonaise de Mathématique, Cracow, 1929, pp. 29–33
28. Tarski, A.: What is elementary geometry?, in: L. Henkin, P. Suppes, A. Tarski (eds.), The Axiomatic Method with Special Reference to Geometry and Physics, Studies in Logic and Foundations of Mathematics, North-Holland, Amsterdam, 1959, pp. 16–29
29. http://www.cs.utexas.edu/users/qr/
30. http://www.cs.utexas.edu/users/qr/robotics/argus
31. Whitehead, A.N.: Process and Reality. An Essay in Cosmology, Macmillan, New York, 1929 (corr. ed. : D. R. Griffin, D. W. Sherbourne (eds.), 1978)
32. Zadeh, L.A.: 1996, Fuzzy logic = computing with words, *IEEE Trans. on Fuzzy Systems*, 4, pp. 103–111

Smart Sensor Mesh: Intelligent Sensor Clusters Configuration and Location Discovery for Collaborative Information Processing

Tomasz M. Rutkowski, Yoko Yamakata, Koh Kakusho, and Michihiko Minoh

Academic Center for Computing and Media Studies,
Kyoto University, Kyoto, Japan
tomek@mm.media.kyoto-u.ac.jp

Abstract. This paper discusses a concept of an intelligent self-configuration of sensors' clusters in a grid network as an overlay on contemporary grid technologies for processing of the sensory information locally and collaboratively. An approach for information exchange among sensors with utilisation of sensor agents for later service discovery in sensor mesh is proposed. The main task of sensor agents is to localise themselves in information space from the point of view of captured sensory data and not only a geographical location, which is often unknown to the sensors. The experiments were conducted in a large scale lecture room, where several microphones and cameras were installed in order to capture students' audiovisual activities.

1 Introduction

The core of modern multimedia communications or virtual presence applications rests upon the clear and realistic capture of audiovisual media. In case of sound, an ideal solution should preserve the spatial hearing comfort, together with the robust reduction of environmental and other noise signals. The audio capture system should rely on the microphones which positions and capture capabilities guarantee a good quality with a possibly limited need for signal postprocessing in order to remove interference. Similar problem occurs in a visual domain, where in environments equipped with many cameras (e.g. the lecture room in Figure 1) a "proper camera" capturing a certain situation should be localised quickly. As in the nature, where insect swarms [1] live and build hierarchical communities to solve daily problems, networked sensors processing environmental information (i.e. a proposed *sensor mesh*) should have some communication possibilities in order to localise themselves among neighbours which physical proximity is unknown. Such neighbourhood discovery on environmental sensors level could lead to creation of local communities of small devices capable to capture similar information based on communicative intelligence principles [2].

In the presented approach we refer to the situations, where in the environment many sensors are installed without any special position calibration procedures or detailed prior knowledge of their technical specifications. The sensors – microphones and cameras, in the example presented in this paper – are connected together building a sensor network called the sensor mesh. The concept of an automatic configuration of

L. Bolc et al. (Eds.): IMTCI 2004, LNAI 3490, pp. 147–157, 2005.

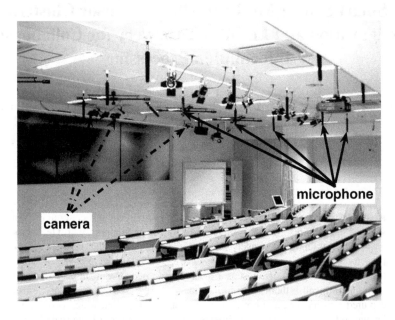

Fig. 1. The classroom designed for distance lectures equipped with microphones and cameras installed over the students area to capture their activity or the professor's lecture. The arrangements of microphones and cameras is unknown to the sensor mesh, so it is possible to test localisation and clustering procedures.

"ad-hoc" connected sets of sensors equipped with signal processing and networking capabilities is a subject of intensive research in computer networking related communities [3]. Traditional computer networks, used daily around the world, have a fixed topology and a known number of nodes. Their design is usually optimised for the maximum throughput rate of data. The sensor mesh networks, on the other hand, are designed for an environment discovery (service discovery) [4] and proper capture of the events there [5]. The purpose of a sensor mesh constructed based on many microphones and cameras is to detect, identify, localise, and track the audiovisual sources with utilisation of signal processing techniques, that reduce the impact of environmental interference. Such problems have several solutions for the fixed configurations of sensors, where their locations are known through the design process [6]. The problem arises, when the sensors are placed ad-hoc and the proximity is unknown. In this paper a concept of a sensor location self-discovery from the point of view of processed information is discussed. The purpose of presented research is to determine sensor-to-sensor information exchange procedures, that would allow a simple and efficient proximity evaluation of small devices without a sensor mesh overloading with randomly transferred data. It is important to stress that sensors have very limited computation resources, so it is important to design smart and efficient *insect style intelligence* procedures. The idea of our approach is based on a recently popular concept of *swarm intelligence* [7]. We propose, however, a little modified approach in which sensors initialise active communication advertising there knowledge about captured environment in order to create small-task-oriented communities based on similarities of captured data. In order to realise it, the concept of sensor agents is utilised together with collaborative information processing procedures, that lead to final sensor clusters organisation in information capture space. In the next section a concept of creation of communicative intelligence in sensor communities is proposed. After that two examples of real world data processing in microphone and camera sensor meshes are presented. Finally, discussion of obtained results is made and conclusions are drawn.

2   Sensor Agents and Individual/Communicative Intelligence

A sensor agent is a piece of software installed at every sensor that is responsible for communication with neighbouring sensors and with an application server, which sends requests for a certain data collection scenario. The agent contains also the information processing module which processes the raw sensory data before offering it to the network (i.e. audio signal conditioning in case of microphones and video for cameras). In the current approach we assume that the network layer of the sensor mesh network is built based on sensor network technology [3]. The adaptive data acquisition and later collaborative communication in the application layer is discussed here. From the point of view of the application server which is a higher level layer application requesting data acquisition from sensors, there are two critical expectations:

- there should be an easily accessible information about sensors which are able to deliver high quality information streams, including good candidates for neighbours;
- the sensors should configure themselves automatically, including simple signal conditioning operations, which do not require multisensory signal processing.

Such a two stage approach to self organisation in autonomous multi-agent environments was discussed in scope of *collective intelligence* approaches [8], where information processing was divided into two stages:

local/individual: where captured information is preprocessed (i.e. filtered or separated into useful and noise from application server's request point of view);
group/swarm: where captured information is evaluated based on similarity levels among members of a sensor group/cluster or such local sensor communities are built based on discovered similarities.

The swarm, in computer science applications, has been defined as a set of agents which are liable to communicate directly or indirectly with each other, and which collectively carry out a distributed environment discovery and/or problem solving. Swarm intelligence is a property of a system, built on several interacting and simple agents, whereby the collective behaviours cause coherent functional global patterns to emerge [7]. Such collective intelligence can provide thus a basis with which it is possible to explore environment collectively leading to a problem solving without centralised control or the provision of a global model. Communication is the most important part of any emergent group intelligence. Without communication between agents and between the environment and the agents, not much knowledge can be acquired. Ants, for example, communicate with each other through the use of pheromone [1], which is a chemical signal that they release into the environment for other ants to "read". In swarm intelligence applications a concept of pheromone evaporation is used, which helps to avoid suboptimal solutions. As a result of such communication, each agent interprets their local situation and adopts its neighbourhood information accordingly. The single agent, like a single ant or bee, is not concerned about the global situation of environment, but only with own sensory information and its similarity to other neighbours.

The concept of pheromone in our approach is modified to an exchange of pieces of captured environmental data which is first preprocessed locally by agents. Such local preprocessing which is referred to the individual intelligence of sensors, and it could be adopted by request from the application server, results in lower data traffic and more efficient information exchange for later cluster formation. The sensor agents are only interested in their own local environment and this is really where the power of swarm intelligence lies. The agents do not need to know anything beyond what impacts them and sensory information that they process and prepare for sending to a higher level application layer. This cuts down on communication costs, and also the memory and rules required for a single agent to operate. The important aspect of the communicative intelligence for such simple insect style agents is that not only do they read the communicative signals that circulate in networked environment, but they also broadcast their own signals as a response together with information about created clusters. As a result, groups of sensors are collected that are not only listening, but also broadcasting together their own signals, which can be processed efficiently by the application server without overloading the network with heavy traffic. This phenomenon is known as *stigmergy*, in which individual's behaviour modifies the environment (information space), which in turn modifies the behaviour of other individuals (e.g. information processing strategies, grouping of information sources). In other words, every sensor is impacted by every other sensor in a created cluster, and that sensor then has an impact on others.

2.1   Local Sensory Intelligence

Before sensors start to communicate in order to form clusters in the smart mesh, it is necessary to condition acquired data according to a higher level application request. Usually such a higher level application should send request to the sensors with processing recipes (i.e. program code). In the case of presented study, there is a preset assumption, that sensor mesh should localise speaking persons and form sensors in groups of three members capturing voiced waveforms. Such task includes mostly the local interference removal techniques as discussed in [6], where an adaptive normalised least mean square algorithm (NLMS) can be utilised. Such adaptive filtering is performed locally without a need to communicate among sensors, since usually sources of noise in large rooms are distributed randomly [9]. Every sensor in presented example is conducting the following adaptive filtering procedure, which is a combination of linear adaptive prediction, together with a coefficient update ($\mathbf{w}_i(k)$) given by

$$e_i(k) = s_i(k) - x_i(k), \tag{1}$$

$$x_i(k) = \sum_{j=1}^{N} s_i(k-i)w_i(k) = \mathbf{s}_i^T(k)\mathbf{w}_i(k), \tag{2}$$

$$\mathbf{w}_i(k+1) = \mathbf{w}_i(k) + \mu(k)e_i(k)\mathbf{s}_i(k), \tag{3}$$

$$\mu(k) = \frac{\lambda_w(k)}{\|\mathbf{s}_i(k)\|_2^2}, \tag{4}$$

where $e_i(k)$ is a prediction error, $s_i(k)$ signal's sample and $x_i(k)$ its predicted value. The learning rate adaptation, $\mu(k)$, is obtained with utilisation of a dynamical parameter $\lambda_w(k)$, which is the critical variable toward catering for the unknown dynamics of the recorded signals. The exemplary sensor mesh application is to identify the speech occurrences in captured waveforms and to remove non-speech related interference. For local interference reduction, we employ speech identification from noisy recordings with the adaptive step size for NLMS $\lambda_w(k)$, proposed in equation (4), which is obtained from a *cepstral* voice activity detector. Speech and noise are assumed to be mutually statistically independent, therefore the spectrum of the enhanced speech signal $\left|\tilde{S}(\omega)\right|$ can be obtained from the noisy version $|X(\omega)|$, after subtracting the noise spectrum estimate $|N(\omega)|$, calculated from regions labeled as noise [10]. The spectrum of such a signal with noise subtracted can be expressed as

$$\left|\tilde{S}(\omega)\right|^2 = \begin{cases} |X(\omega)|^2 - |N(\omega)|^2, & \text{if } |X(\omega)|^2 > |N(\omega)|^2, \\ 0, & \text{otherwise} \end{cases} \tag{5}$$

In order to remove "stationary-in-time" and local to every sensor interference (stable noise) from a time window at time k, the power of the subtracted signal E_{cs} can now be evaluated over the time window and compared with the total (with noise) power E_{total} to update the the the value of $\lambda_w(k)$, as

$$\lambda_w(k) = \begin{cases} S_{cs}(k)/S_{total}(k), & S_{cs}(k) \geqslant \nu_{room}, \\ const, & S_{cs}(k) < \nu_{room}, \end{cases} \tag{6}$$

In the above equation, $S_{cs}(k)$ is the cepstrally subtracted short time signal power and $S_{total}(k)$ is the total short time power at time k [10]. Value ν_{room} reflects the background room noise and its average is calculated in longer time windows.

At this stage there is no need to transmit raw data from the sensor to the higher level in the network application hierarchy, since the signal detection and preprocessing is performed locally by the agent. Once the proper data is obtained, sensor agents can start advertising captured signal features for later negotiants with neighbours in a network layer. In order to limit traffic generated by "talking sensors", only speech features are exchanged in the form of *Mel cepstrum cepstral coefficients* [11] [12].

2.2   Group Sensory Communicative Intelligence

In order to prevent the sensor mesh overload, a behavioural technique based on *look-around-principle* is applied to sensor agents, which starts the search for neighbours based on comparison of captured information features (similarities). In the presented example, the data requested from application server should contain audio streams from microphones, which capture speaking persons in a lecture room in order to automatically create a small microphone array (e.g. blind beamformer [5]). In presented examples, clusters of three microphones capturing speech were sought. For such an application it is important for microphones to build local clusters capturing similar sound (same

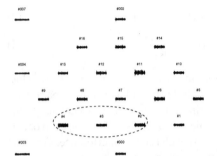

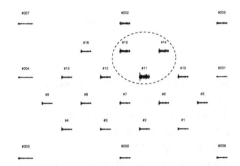

Fig. 2. The original recordings from 24 micro-phones located on the ceiling of a classroom as in Figure 1. Excessive environmental noise caused proper localisation of even single person talking not possible (compare result in Figure 3).

Fig. 3. The properly preprocessed sound waves from 24 microphones as in Figure 2. Now a cluster of three microphones capturing the best quality speech was formed (dashed line ellipsoid). The obtained position was similar to physical position of a speaker.

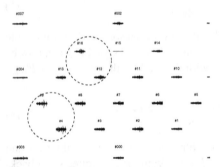

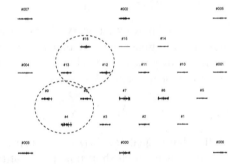

Fig. 4. Sound waves of two persons talking at once and located close to each other (a 24 microphone layout as in Figure 1). Noise and small distance between talking people made the proper three sensors clusters construction not possible.

Fig. 5. Sound waves of persons talking at once and located close to each other (a 24 microphone layout as in Figure 1). Proper signal conditioning by the sensors made the information exchange for cluster construction more efficient.

level of signal-to-noise ratios or speech related features comparison), so the higher level application could process it saving time on search.

Search for neighbours capturing similar sensory information can progress, once the captured signals by sensor agents are preprocessed and their features are advertised on the network, the grouping of neighbours can be started. Sensor agents utilise the networked infrastructure of the sensor mesh built in the network layer [3]. Since every agent advertises its media capture capabilities, network nodes can easily identify compatible sensors. The pair of sensors negotiate communication links and exchange portions of captured data for a similarity check. This is the second step in the sensor

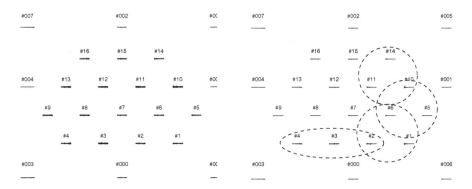

Fig. 6. Sound waves of a walking person in a noisy environment. Higher level of noise and a faster walking person is not possible to localise without signal preprocessing. The 24 microphones were located on the ceiling of a classroom as in Figure 1.

Fig. 7. Sound waves of a walking person. In this experiment the level of noise was much higher and a faster walking person was not possible to localise without proper signal conditioning by the sensors (see Figure 6).

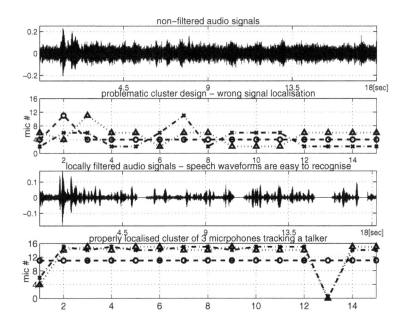

Fig. 8. Sound signal preprocessing by the sensor agents in order to remove local interference. The upper two panels present a situation where local interferences in a captured signal made a proper cluster localisation impossible. The lower two panels present a proper and stable cluster localisation and speech signals are easy to distinguish.

cluster forming, where the exchanged data let the sensors confirm, that they capture a similar content. In case of sound capture, there are two main approaches for similarity

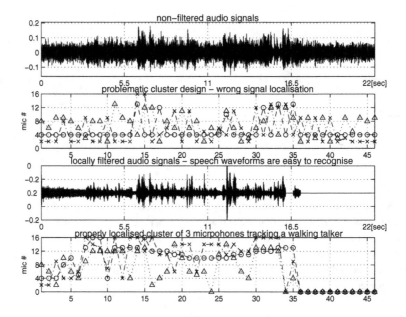

Fig. 9. Example with a walking person. In this experiment a shorter analysis window was chosen in order to capture position changes. Also here audio signal preprocessing was necessary in order to localise properly speakers position (compare microphones clusters-proximity-in second and bottom panels in the above figure).

measurers. The first one is based on a correlation calculated between sensory data and it requires the proper time synchronisation between the nodes. The second measure is based on comparison of the perceptual power for the captured sound. In the presented approach the second method is utilised to avoid the data capture synchronisation problems. The sensors compare the communicated data in pairs in order to find the best neighbours. The order of search is decided by the broadcasted features by other sensors and the similarity to the own calculated features. Every sensor updates its own neighbourhood table with evaporating pheromone like features [1] indicating possible necessity for an information update (sensor-to-sensor feature exchange). For security reasons the neighbourhood list is longer in order to have a possibility to find a probable replacement, in case former neighbourhood's sensor would stop responding or captured information would change. Once a pair negotiate the neighbourhood, the next one from the list is communicated with information that already a pair is configured (the cluster extension by looking for the next one approach). In the presented application, the cluster sizes were limited to three neighbours in a 24 microphone array – a local sound capture matrix size required by the higher level application.

2.3 Experiments in Audio Domain

The first experiment with a three microphone cluster design is presented in Figure 2, where original recordings from 24 microphones located on the ceiling of a classroom

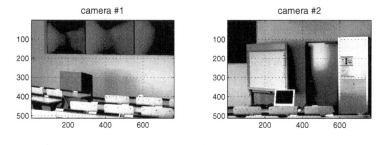

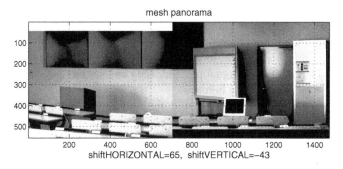

Fig. 10. An application of neighbourhood discovery in overlapping video streams based on growing edges comparison principle. An simple approach to compare neighbouring regions leads to efficient information about video regions proximity and a proper panorama image design.

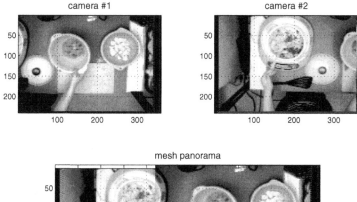

Fig. 11. Second example of neighbourhood discovery in overlapping video streams based on growing edges comparison principle. It this case it is shown, that there is no need to know a proper order of cameras in order to create the proper panoramic image.

as in Figure 1 did not allow to build a properly localised cluster due to excessive environmental noise, which misled the speech search, even if only a single person was talking. The cluster was designed easily after local conditioning of signals and sensors' communication as shown in Figure 3.

The second experiment shown in Figures 4 and 5 was conducted with two persons talking at once and located close to each other (a 24 microphone layout as in Figure 1). Environmental noise and closeness between talking people made the proper three sensors clusters construction not possible due to mixing of two speeches in microphones on the border between two speakers. Here again a proper local sound waves conditioning allow better clusters design.

The third experiment shown in Figures 6 and 7 presents similar results with a walking person in the same environment as above. Here, additionally, the movement of a talking subject caused additional localisation problems (see Figure 6 where clusters were not built) but after local signal preprocessing and sensors negotiations, the clusters were built sequentially as in Figure 7.

The results in Figures 8 and 9 show dynamical cluster changes over time, since a talking person in the lecture room was moving around. The upper three panels in both figures present the situation, in which the local information conditioning by sensor agents was switched off and the stable cluster forming in time was not achieved resulting in wrong localisation of a talking person. The three lower panels present the situation, where three stable neighbours could be configured together and their proximity remained stable and accurate, comparing to a known speaker's physical location.

2.4   Experiments in Visual Domain

Similar experiments as for speech capture using multiple microphones were conducted using cameras. In this case we were trying to build a panoramic image asking camera sensors to compare images there in order to find neighbours. The camera proximity in a visual information space domain was estimated based on sensor-to-sensor overlapping regions comparison for later panoramic scene "mosaicing" based on search for image regions building a continuous visual scene with detected and removed overlapping regions. Images captured by the cameras scattered in an environment can be exchanged only partially (borders) in order to find similarities and possible overlapping regions as shown in Figures 10 and 11, where for two different situations captured by two cameras a panoramic image could be built based only on search of similarities (linear combinations and shift detection) of neighbouring areas, advertised by sensors which do it to evaluate there proximity in captured visual media.

3   Conclusions

The concept of intelligent sensor clusters configuration and location discovery for collaborative information processing presented in this paper allows for the localisation of sensors neighbourhoods in the ad-hoc organised sensor mesh. The two stages information processing approach in computationally limited sensors allows for necessary signal conditioning locally and after that simple communication among them to find neighbourhood in information spaces. The presented example of sound capturing mesh allowed us to localise three best microphones capturing the speaking person, without necessity of sensors location knowledge. Since sound propagation in large rooms is very difficult to model due to unknown sound waves reflection paths [9], a dynamic search for best microphones is a best solution as shown in this paper. In the presented approach, the microphones/sensors were doing that job only later reporting cluster configurations to the application layer. Similar experiments in visual domain show that the strategy based on local information conditioning and later feature exchange in order to find neighbourhood works well despite of nature of the processed data. The next step will be a cross-modal communication between sensors from different domains.

References

1. Bonabeau, E., Dorigo, M., Theraulaz, G.: Swarm Intelligence – From Natural to Artificial Systems. Santa Fe Institute Studies in Sciences of Complexity. Oxford University Press, Inc. (1999)
2. Nishida, T.: Towards intelligent media technology for communicative intelligence. In Bolc, L., ed.: Proceedings of International Workshop of Intelligent Media Technology for Communicative Intelligence, PJIIT Warsaw, Poland, PJIIT Publishing House (2004) 1–7
3. Traversatm, B., Arora, A., Abdelaziz, M., Duigou, M., Haywood, C., Hugly, J.C., Pouyoul, E., Bernard, B.: Project jxta 2.0 super-peer virtual network. Technical report, Sun Microsystems, Inc. (2003)
4. Meguerdichian, S., Slijepcevic, S., Karayan, V., Potkonjak, M.: Localized algorithms in wireless ad-hoc networks: Location discovery and sensor exposure. In: Proceedings of MobiHOC2001. (2001) 106–116
5. Lim, A.: Distributed services for information dissemination in self-organizing sensor networks, in: Special issue on distributed sensor networks for real-time systems with adaptive reconfiguration. Journal of Franklin Institute 338 (2001) 707–727
6. Rutkowski, T.M., Yokoo, M., Mandic, D., Yagi, K., Kameda, Y., Kakusho, K., Minoh, M.: Identification and tracking of active speaker's position in noisy environments. In: Proceedings of International Workshop on Acoustic Echo and Noise Control (IWAENC2003), Kyoto, Japan (2003) 283–286
7. Bonabeau, E., Dorigo, M., Theraulaz, G.: Inspiration for optimization from social insect behaviour. Nature 406 (2000) 39–42
8. Hoen, P.J., Bohte, S.M.: Collective intelligence with sequences of actions coordinating actions in multi-agent systems. In Lavrac, N., Gamberger, D., Todorovski, L., eds.: Lecture Notes in Computer Science: Proceedings of 14th European Conference on Machine Learning (ECML2003), Cavtat-Dubrovnik, Croatia, Heidelberg, Springer-Verlag (2003) 181–192
9. Everest, F.A.: Master Handbook of Acoustics. 4th edn. McGraw-Hill (2001)
10. Gustafsson, H., Nordholm, S.E., Claesson, I.: Spectral subtraction using reduced delay convolution and adaptive averaging. IEEE Transactions on Speech and Audio Processing 9 (2001) 799–807
11. Becchetti, C., Ricotti, L.P.: Speech Recognition. John Wiley & Sons, Inc., Great Britain (1999)
12. Furui, S.: Digital Speech Processing, Synthesis, and Recognition – Second Edition, Revised and Expanded. 2nd edn. Signal Processing and Communications Series. Marcell Dekker, Inc., New York, Basel (2001)

Towards 3D Face Model from 2D View

Władysław Skarbek[1], Krystian Ignasiak[1], Marcin Morgoś[1],
and Michał Tomaszewski[1,2]

[1] Warsaw University of Technology, Institute of Radioelectronics,
ul. Nowowiejska 15/19, 00-665 Warsaw, Poland
{W.Skarbek, K.Ignasiak, M.Morgos, M.Tomaszewski}@ire.pw.edu.pl
[2] Polish-Japanese Institute of Information Technology,
ul. Koszykowa 86, 02-008 Warsaw, Poland

Abstract. In the context of intelligent communication for distance learning, the paper describes the 3D face modelling framework based on advanced face recognition descriptor for a 2D facial image and on a 3D eigenfaces concept.

1 Introduction

Distance learning-based systems which use multimedia tools for more realistic tele-presence, require mutual visibility of teachers and students. This requirement now excludes the use of cheap Internet transmission for e-learning with performance of traditional learning.

In this paper we describe a face modelling framework in which sending only a small number of parameters per second can animate a realistic three-dimensional (3D) face model, provided that the client has downloaded a PCA model for faces. This kind of

Fig. 1. Face and eyes detection before facial image normalisation

L. Bolc et al. (Eds.): IMTCI 2004, LNAI 3490, pp. 158–162, 2005.

object model-based communication exhibits features which we can link to intelligent communication.

The 3D face modelling framework is based on the correspondence between 2D face descriptions and 3D shape and colour facial PCA coefficients.

We report in this paper the advanced state of research on the framework including a 2D face descriptor extraction and 3D eigenfaces design. The paper is concluded by sketching the procedure which finds 2D-3D correspondences.

In order to extract a 2D face descriptor a normalisation of facial image is performed which scales face images to fixed resolution (46×56 pixels) with fixed eye centers. To this end face localisation and eye localisation procedure are used. Both of them are based on the AdaBoost approach [7] in which analysis windows in a range of resolutions are sliding over the whole image or its predefined part. To get precise eye centre positions texture fitting is performed in a low dimensional mesh shape space (cf. fig. 1).

A 2D face description is the output of a Dual LDA (DLDA) cascade. It is a novel approach related to an MPEG-7 Advanced Face Recognition Descriptor [5].

Our Face Recognition framework forms a three-stage cascade of operators with the DLDA playing the main role as a tool providing a compact set of features of great discriminative power. The cascade is a kind of complex feature extractor returning for the every input facial image its corresponding descriptor.

Each input of the cascade refers to the particular part of the original image. There are six image parts: the whole image, its upper half, its lower half, the central part of image (32×32), its upper half, and its lower half. Each of six parts is independently

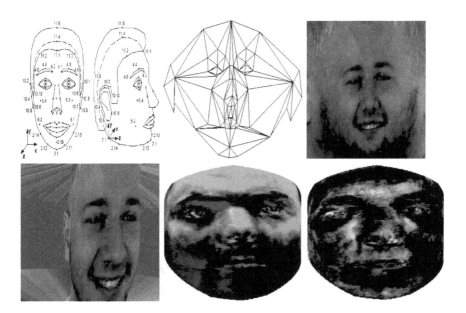

Fig. 2. Facial Action Points, FAP mesh, FAP points on texture, on 3D facial image, and two selected 3D eigenfaces

transformed by 2D Fourier transform, then some Fourier channels are selected and their real, imaginary and amplitude components are combined before passing to the DLDA discriminative transformation.

The 2D facial image descriptor is used in our system to find 3D PCA coefficients. The linear combination of 3D PCA coefficients with 3D eigenfaces gives us the 3D face model on the basis of a single 2D face image.

2 Design of 3D Eigenfaces

To design 3D eigenfaces we use 3D laser scans by Cyberware machinery. We have now 150 scans of different human heads, but we plan to add at least 50 scans more.

The registration of scans is performed via MPEG-4 mesh of Facial Action Points [4] depicted manually and barycentric coordinates concept (cf. fig. 2) implemented automatically.

3D laser scans of human heads enable representation of faces as a *cloud of N points* together with associated colour information. Typically such spatial set contains more than 10^5 points in 3D space ($N > 10^5$) and it is too complex as a 3D model for face recognition and face animation.

It appears that the collection of *head clouds,* obtained for a large group of L persons ($L > 50$), and considered as a set of points in a high N dimensional space can be approximated by a hyperplane (subspace) of relatively low dimension M (typically $M \approx 50$). One of possible linear algebraic bases spanning this hyperplane is obtained by Principal Component Analysis (PCA – cf. [3]) as eigenvectors of covariance matrix for the given training set of points.

In case of 2D facial images PCA eigenvectors are called eigenfaces [6] and by the analogy for 3D facial cloud of points, PCA eigenvectors are recognised as 3D eigenfaces [1] (cf. fig. 2). Having M 3D eigenfaces $F_1, \ldots, F_M$ and average face F_0, any 3D face F can be approximated by a linear combination of 3D eigenfaces where coefficients α_i are appropriate dot products (cf. fig. 3):

$$F \approx F_0 + \sum_{i=1}^{M} \alpha_i F_i, \quad \alpha_i \triangleq (F - F_0)^t F_i$$

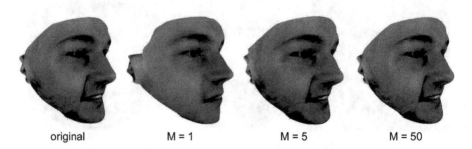

original   M = 1   M = 5   M = 50

Fig. 3. 2D views from reconstructed 3D model

3D eigenfaces are built by Singular Value Approximation [2] (SVA) what allows to avoid building prohibitively large covariance matrices. In the current experiments each 3D eigenface consists like other original 3D scan of the depth and the colour maps which are next used to compute *color cloud of points*.

3   Analysis Synthesis Loop for Face Modelling

Finally, the shape and the texture PCA coefficients are to be obtained by analysis-synthesis loop (cf. fig. 4, 5) which refers to nonlinear relationship between 2D and 3D face descriptions considering face pose and illumination changes, too.

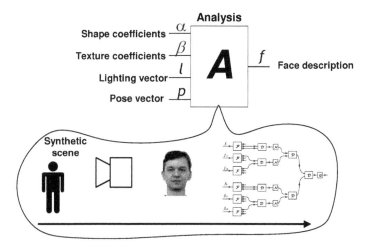

Fig. 4. Analysis of synthetic images

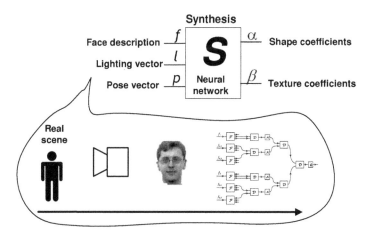

Fig. 5. Synthesis of shape and texture model for real images

The unknown shape and texture coefficients α, β are estimated on the basis of extracted 2D descriptor f and the predicted pose and illumination vectors p, l. This is performed in a synthesis phase S. The prediction is improved by optimisation of error defined as the difference between the actual descriptor f and the descriptor obtained by the analysis phase:

$$\begin{bmatrix} \alpha \\ \beta \end{bmatrix} = S(f, l, p) \qquad \begin{bmatrix} \alpha^* \\ \beta^* \end{bmatrix} = \arg\min_{l,p} \| A(\alpha, \beta, l, p) - f \|$$

Acknowledgment. The work presented was developed within VISNET, a European Network of Excellence (http://www.visnet-noe.org), funded under the European Commission IST FP6 programme.

References

1. Blanz, V., Romdhani, S., Vetter, T.: *Face Identification across Different Poses and Illumination with a 3D Morphable Model*, Proc. FG'02, pp. 202–207, 2002
2. Golub, G., Van Loan, C.: *Matrix Computations*, Johns Hopkins University Press, Baltimore, 1996
3. Jolliffe, I.T.: *Principal Component Analysis, Second Edition*, Springer, 2002
4. Ostermann, J.: *Animation of synthetic faces in MPEG-4*, Computer Animation, June:49–51, 1998
5. Skarbek, W., Kucharski, K., Bober, M.: *Dual Linear Discriminant Analysis for Face Recognition*, Fundamenta Informaticae, 61(3-4), May 2004
6. Turk, M., Pentland, A.: *Eigenfaces for Recognition*, Journal of Cognitive Neuroscience, 3(1): 71–86, 1991
7. Viola, P., Jones, M.: *Rapid Object Detection using a Boosted Cascade of Simple Features*, Conference on Computer Vision and Pattern Recognition, 2001

Intelligent Content Production for a Virtual Speaker

Karlo Smid[1], Igor S. Pandzic[2], and Viktorija Radman[1]

[1] Ericsson Nikola Tesla, Krapinska 45, p.p. 93, HR-10 002 Zagreb
{karlo.smid, viktorija.radman}@ericsson.com
[2] Faculty of electrical engineering and computing, Zagreb University,
Unska 3, HR-10 000 Zagreb
Igor.Pandzic@fer.hr

Abstract. We present a graphically embodied animated agent (a virtual speaker) capable of reading a plain English text and rendering it in a form of speech accompanied by the appropriate facial gestures. Our system uses a lexical analysis of an English text and statistical models of facial gestures in order to automatically generate the gestures related to the spoken text. It is intended for the automatic creation of the realistically animated virtual speakers, such as newscasters and storytellers and incorporates the characteristics of such speakers captured from the training video clips. Our system is based on a visual text-to-speech system which generates a lip movement synchronised with the generated speech. This is extended to include eye blinks, head and eyebrow motion, and a simple gaze following behaviour. The result is a full face animation produced automatically from the plain English text.

1 Introduction

Our intelligent content production system is an extension of the Visual Text-to-Speech (VTTS) system. A classical VTTS system [1], [2], [3], [4] produces lip movements synchronised with the synthesised speech based on timed phonemes generated by speech synthesis. Normally, it also solves the coarticulation problem [5], [6], [7]. A face that only moves the lips, looks extremely unnatural because natural speech always involves facial gestures. However, a VTTS system can only obtain phonetic information from speech synthesis and has no basis for generating realistic gestures. Very often this problem is solved by introducing some partially random gestures triggered by a set of rules [8]. Another solution is recording one or more sequences of facial gestures from real speakers and then playing those tracks during a speech [9]. These methods produce better visual results than a static talking face, but the movements are generally too simplistic. Yet another approach is to manually insert tags or bookmarks into a text from which the facial gestures or expressions are generated [16]. Obviously, this is time consuming and unsuitable for the fully automatic applications. The Eyes Alive system [10] introduces a full statistical model of eye movement based on the known theory of eye movement during speech, as well as precise recordings of eye motion during speech. The system reproduces eye movements that are dynamically correct at the level of each movement and that are globally also statistically correct in terms of frequency of movements, intervals between them and their amplitudes. However, the movements are still

L. Bolc et al. (Eds.): IMTCI 2004, LNAI 3490, pp. 163–174, 2005.

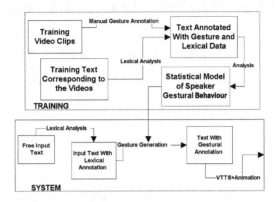

Fig. 1. Training and content production processes

unrelated to the underlying speech content, punctuation, accents etc. In natural speech, most gestures are directly related to the lexical structure of speech and have distinct functions [11], [12], [13], [14]. The BEAT system [15] uses linguistic and contextual information contained in a text to control the movements of hands, arms and a face, and the intonation of a voice. The mapping from a text to the facial, intonational and body gestures is contained in a set of rules derived from a state of the art research in nonverbal conversational behaviour. That mapping also depends on the knowledge base of an ECA environment. That knowledge base is populated by a user who animates the ECA so the production of the facial gestures is not automatic. Furthermore, the system does not introduce a full statistical model for the supported gestures so occurrences of the supported nonverbal features could be too predictive. Also, in the current set of supported nonverbal behaviours, head nods and eyes blinks must be included.

We propose a new approach that combines the lexical analysis of input text with the statistical model describing frequencies and amplitudes of facial gestures. The statistical model is obtained by analysing a training data set consisting of several speakers recorded on video and stenographs of their speech. A lexical analysis of the stenograph texts allowed to correlate the lexical characteristics of a text with the corresponding facial gestures and to incorporate this correlation into a statistical model. Using a lexical analysis of input text to trigger this statistical model, a virtual speaker can perform gestures that are not only dynamically correct, but also correspond to the underlying text. Fig. 1. depicts training and content production processes.

2   Background

A conversation consists of two domains: verbal and nonverbal. These two domains are highly synchronised because they are driven by the same forces: the prosody and lexical structure of the uttered text as well as the emotions and personality of a person that is involved in a conversation [18]. The verbal domain deals with a human voice, while body and facial gestures (head, eyes and eyebrows movement) are part of the nonverbal domain. In this article, our focus is on facial gestures and how they are synchronised

Table 1. The specification of facial gestures

Head	Nod	^ v < >	An abrupt swing of a head with a similarly abrupt motion back. We have four nod directions: up and down (^), down and up (v), left and right (<) and right and left (>).
	Overshoot nod	~	Nod with an overshoot at the return, i.e. the pattern looks like an 'S' lying on its side.
	Swing	u d L R diag	An abrupt swing of a head without a back motion. Sometimes rotation moves slowly, barely visible, back to the original pose, sometimes it is followed by an abrupt motion back after some delay. Five directions: up (u), down (d), left (l), right (R) and diagonal (diag).
	Reset	reset	Sometimes follows swing movement. Returns head in central position.
Eyes	Movement in various directions		The eyes are always moving. Parameters are: gaze direction, points of fixation, the percentage of eye contact over gaze avoidance, duration of eye contact.
	Blink		Periodic blinks keep the eyes wet. Voluntary blinks support conversational signals and punctuators.
Eyebr ows	Raise	^^	Eyebrows go up and down.
	Frown	^^	Eyebrows go up and down.

and driven by the prosody and lexical structure of uttered text. Facial gestures are driven by [19]:

☐ **interactional function of speech**: we unconsciously use facial gestures to regulate the flow of speech, accent word or segments, and punctuate speech pauses.
☐ **emotions**: they are usually expressed with facial gestures.
☐ **personality**: it can often be read through facial gestures.
☐ **performatives**: for example, advice and order are two different performatives and they are accompanied with different facial gestures.

In this article we deal with the interactional function of speech. In this context, facial gestures can have several different roles, usually called determinants [1]. These determinants are:

☐ **conversational signals**: they correspond to the facial gestures that clarify and support what is being said [20].
☐ **punctuators**: they correspond to the facial gestures that support pauses [13].
☐ **manipulators**: they correspond to the biological needs of a face, such as blinking to wet the eyes or random head nods because being completely still is unnatural for humans.
☐ **regulators**: they control the flow of a conversation [21].

Since we are currently concentrating on Autonomous Speaker Agent, which is not involved in a conversation but performs a presentation, this work focuses on conversational signals, punctuators and manipulators. All these functions are supported by a fairly broad repertoire of facial gestures. We distinguish three main classes of facial gestures [1]: head movement, eyes movement and eyebrows movement. Within each class we distinguish specific gestures, each characterised by their particular parameters. The parameters that are important for head and eyebrow movements are amplitude and velocity. Those two parameters are in inverted proportion. A movement with a big amplitude is rather slow. shows the types of facial gestures as identified during our data analysis (Section 4). This is an extension of the classification proposed in [22]. We introduce symbols incorporating both a gesture type and a movement direction.

3   Lexical Analysis of an English Text

The speech analysis module [23] performs the linguistic and contextual analysis of a text written in English language with a goal of enabling the nonverbal (gestures) and verbal (prosody) behaviour assignment and scheduling.

Starting from a plain English text, it produces an XML document annotated with tags for each word. These tags allow us to distinguish between the newly introduced words, words known from a previous text and punctuation marks. Based on this knowledge, the process, described in Section 5, assigns and schedules the gestures.

The input text is first phrase-parsed because the module needs to know the morphological, syntactic and part-of-speech information. In order to get the morphologic data about the words in a sentence, we have developed a module that classifies words according to the English grammar rules. In the first release we used the Connexor's Machinese Phrase Tagger[1] (MPT). MPT is a commercial tool, its public interface is changing from version to version, and it has much more functionality that we needed. So we have made the simplified version of the morphologic and semantic analyser extending WordNet 2.0 database. In order to determine the correct word type based on the output queried from the extended WordNet 2.0 database, we must pass multiple times through the whole sentence and apply various English grammatical rules. WordNet 2.0 database contains nouns, verbs, adverbs and adjectives, so for other English word types we made our own database using the MySQL engine. Our database contains auxiliary verbs, determiners, pronouns, prepositions and conjunctions. Besides that, one additional table has been created. This table was dynamically filled with new data each time some particular word was not found either in WordNet 2.0 or in our database. After passing through numerous examples, we concluded that 99% of these words were nouns. We can say that our module is learning based on the examples that passed through it. For every query to WordNet 2.0 and our database, we got more than one word type for a particular word. In order to get correct type of a word, we must pass multiple times through the whole text and apply various grammatical rules to it. Here are some of the rules:

1. Every determiner (a, an, the) is followed by an adjective or a noun.
2. Every personal pronoun (I, he, you, ...) is followed by a verb, an adverb, or an auxiliary verb.
3. Every possessive pronoun (my, your, hers, ...) is followed by a noun or an adjective.

---

[1] http://www.connexor.com/

In the second step we break the paragraphs (UTTERANCE) into clauses (CLAUSE). The largest unit is UTTERANCE, which represents an entire paragraph of input. The next, smaller, unit is CLAUSE, which is held to represent a proposition. In order to detect clauses in an utterance, the module is searching for the punctuation marks and a placement of verb inside a phrase.

The smallest unit is a word with its **new** attribute. To determine the newness of each word, we keep track of all previously mentioned words in an utterance. We also use WordNet 2.0.[2] database to identify sets of synonyms. We tagged each noun, verb, adverb or adjective as **new** if they or their synonyms had not been seen in an utterance before. Other word classes are not considered for the new parameter. Since pronouns need to be tagged as **new** and WordNet 2.0 does not process them at all, an algorithm is proposed to deal with the pronouns. The logic for this algorithm is based on knowledge and intuition, but that, of course, does not lead us to the universal solution. After going through many Connexor analysing examples and studying all the pronouns found in them, the following conclusion has been made: every pronoun, substituting a noun that appears after it, or a noun that does not appear in a text at all, needs to be tagged as **new**. The algorithm is as follows:

Every pronoun, that is not preceded by a noun in a sentence, and is part of the following set: ("any", "anything", "anyone", "anybody", "some", "somebody", "someone", "something", "no", "nobody", "no-one", "nothing", "every", "everybody", "everyone", "everything", "each", "either", "neither", "both", "all", "this", "more", "what", "who", "which", "whom", "whose")

or any pronoun that is a part of the following set: ("I", "you", "he", "she", "it", "we", "they"), gets the **new** tag assigned. All other pronouns, which do not fulfill the above-stated requirements, are not tagged with **new**.

4 Statistical Model of Gestures

In this section we present the statistical model of facial gestures and the methods, tools and datasets used in order to build it.

As a training set for our analysis, we chose Ericsson's 5minutes video clips. Those clips are published by LM Ericsson for internal usage and offer occasional in-depth interviews and reports on major events, news or hot topics from the Telecom industry. They are presented by professional newscasters. We used a footage showing the newscasters (Fig. 2.). We investigated three female and two male Swedish newscasters.

First, using a video editing tool, we extracted the news casting extracts from the video, according to their stenographs. Then we grouped those news extracts for every observed speaker. Observing those news casting clips, we marked the starting and ending frames for every eye blink, eyebrow raise and head movement (Fig. 2.). Analysing those frames, the speakers Mouth-Nose Separation unit (MNS0) value, facial gesture amplitude value, facial gesture type and direction were determined. We used the following algorithm for amplitude values: the values represent the difference between the speaker's nose top position at the end and the beginning of a facial gesture (an eyebrow raise or head movement).

---

[2] http://www.cogsci.princeton.edu/ wn/

Fig. 2. Tonya's nod with overshoot[3]

Data values, that were gathered from the video clips, were statistically processed using Microsoft Excel and MatLab 5.3. That means that a number of pie charts (Fig. 3.) were produced by simply calculating how many times were facial gestures triggered/not triggered by words. Every gesture type has a corresponding pie chart. Amplitude values probabilities (Fig. 4.) were calculated using the histogram statistical function.

Table 2. An example of the data set gathered during the analysis

word	52		Three	arraignments
eyes	3		blink::cs	
head		|up;A=2	|d to n |d A=0.25	Id A =0.5
eyebrows	2		raise::cs A=1/4	
pitch	13		+	
lexical	44		new	new
			cs – conversational signal	
			p – punctuator	
			m – manipulator	
		~nod::A1=2:A2=0.5::cs		

The **word** row contains an analysed news extract separated word-by-word. The **eyes**, **head** and **eyebrows** rows hold data about facial motion that occurred on the corresponding word (separated with the :: symbol), the type of motion and its direction, amplitude value (A stands for amplitude) and determinant code values (cs, p, m summarised in Table 2). The head basic motions are mapped to head movements as described in the last column of . We replayed the newscaster footage to determine the facial gestures type, direction and duration parameters. The last row in Table 2 contains the head movement facial gesture parameters.

The **pitch** row indicates which words were emphasised by voice intonation. The **lexical** row holds information about word's newness in the text context (Section 3). The second column in Table 2 represents the number of occurrences of a particular facial gesture and pitch accents, the number of words in the current news extract and the number of words that are new in the text context.

A determinant value for a particular facial motion is determined as follows. If a facial motion occurred on a punctuator mark, then a determinant for that motion was

---

[3] Published with permission of LM Ericsson.

the punctuator (p). If a facial motion accompanied a word that is new in the context of uttered text, then a determinant was the conversational signal (cs). Otherwise, a determinant of a facial motion was the manipulator (m). The raw data tables were populated by manual analysis and measurement. All amplitude values were normalised to MNS0 for the particular speaker. MNS0 is a Facial Animation Parameter Unit (FAPU) in the MPEG-4 Face and Body Animation (FBA) standard [16]. Using MNS0 FAPU our model could be applied to every 3D model of a speaker. In our model, the basic unit which triggers facial gestures is a word. We chose not to subdivide further into syllables or phonemes for simplicity reasons. Since some facial gestures last through two or more words, this level of subdivision seems appropriate.

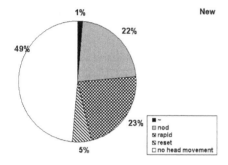

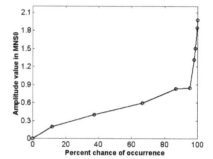

Fig. 3. Statistical data for head gestures occurrences in the context of a new word

Fig. 4. The linear approximation of the cumulative histogram for the amplitude of a rapid head movement

The raw data (Table 2) for the complete training set was statistically processed in order to build a statistical model of speaker behaviour. A statistical model consists of a number of components, each describing the statistical properties for a particular gesture type in a specific speech context. A speech context can be an old word, a new word or a punctuator. The statistical properties for a gesture type include the probability of occurrence of particular gestures and histograms of amplitude and duration values for each gesture. Fig. 3. shows an example of a statistical data component for head gestures in the context of a new word. It is visible that in 51% of occurrences, we have some kind of head movement. For example, the probability of occurrence for rapid head movements is 22%. Further, we have five directions: up (u), down (d), left (L), right (R) and diagonal (diag). In the end, we must determine the amplitude for a rapid movement. Fig. 4. shows a linear approximation of the cumulative histogram for the amplitude of a rapid head movement.

Such statistics exist for each gesture type and for each speech context we treated. They are built into the decision tree (Fig. 5.) that triggers gestures. The process is described in the following section. Note that, in the context of punctuators, only eyes gestures are used, because the statistics show that other gestures do not occur on punctuators.

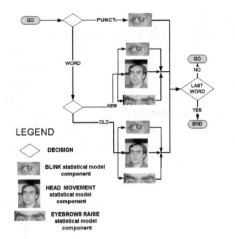
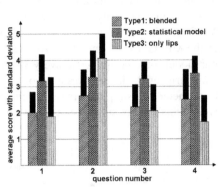

Fig. 5. Decision tree with components of the statistical model

Fig. 6. Results of subjective evaluations. Average score and standard deviation

5   The System

Fig. 7. shows the complete Autonomous Speaker Agent system. The input to the system is plain English text. It is processed by lexical analysis (Section 3) which converts it into an XML format with lexical tags (currently describing new/old words and punctuators). The facial gesture module is the core of the system – it actually inserts appropriate gestures into text in the form of special bookmark tags. These bookmark tags are read by the TTS/MPEG-4 Encoding module. While the Microsoft Speech API (SAPI) Text To Speech (TTS)[4] engine generates an audio stream, the SAPI notification mechanism is used to catch the timing of phonemes and bookmarks containing gesture information. Based on this information, an MPEG-4 FBA bitstream is encoded with the appropriate viseme and facial gestures animation. For MPEG-4 FBA bitstream generation, we are using Visage SDK API[5] that uses SAPI 4.0 or 5.1. Visage SDK API uses information provided by the SAPI notification mechanism.

The facial gesture module is built upon the statistical model described in the previous section. The statistical model is built into the decision tree illustrated in Fig. 5. Let us follow the decision tree. The first branch point classifies the current context as either a word or a punctuation mark. Our data analysis showed that only eye blink facial gesture had occurred on the punctuation marks. Therefore only the blink component of the statistical model is implemented in this context.

The words could be new or old (Section 3) in the context of uttered text – this is the second branch point. All facial gestures occurred in both cases but with different probabilities. Because of that, in each case we have different components for facial gestures parameters. From Fig. 5., it is obvious that a word could be accompanied by all

---

[4] Microsoft speech technologies http://www.microsoft.com/speech/ 29/03/2004.

[5] Visage Technologies AB http://www.visagetechnologies.com/ 29/03/2004.

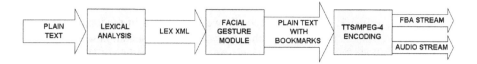

Fig. 7. The data flow through the Autonomous Speaker Agent system

three types of facial gestures at the same time. The facial gesture signals (eye blink, head movement, eyebrow raise) are generated separately, based on their statistical component data. They will be blended later in the TTS/MPEG-4 encoding component. The output from the facial gesture module is plain English text accompanied by bookmark pairs for facial gestures.

Every facial gesture has a corresponding pair of bookmarks: one bookmark marks the starting moment of a facial gesture and the other marks the ending moment. The head and eyebrows movement bookmark values not only define the type of facial gesture, but also contain the amplitude data of a facial movement. For example, bookmark value 2300 defines the rapid head movement to the left (symbol L) of amplitude 1 MNS0 (Bmk_code for this facial gesture is 2200). The function for amplitudes of facial gestures is:

$$A = ((Bmk\_value - Bmk\_code)/100) \tag{1}$$

The interval for bookmark values for L is $[2200, 2500 >$ because the statistical model showed that the maximal amplitude value for facial gesture L was 2.2 MNS0. Head nods and eyebrow raises could last through two or more words. Statistics have shown that the maximum duration of a nod is five words, an eyebrow raise could last through eleven words and the maximal duration for a nod with an overshoot is eight words. We code a nod with an overshoot as two nods: a nod up immediately followed by a nod down. Every nod has its own amplitude distribution.

TTS/MPEG-4 encoding module, using the bookmark information, encodes an MPEG-4 FBA bitstream with an appropriate viseme and gestures animation. The animation model for head and eyebrow movement facial gestures is based on the trigonometry sine function. That means that our Autonomous Speaker Agent nods his head following the sine function trajectory.

We have implemented a simple model of gaze following, meaning that the eyes of our Autonomous Speaker Agent are moving in the opposite direction of a head movement. This gives an impression of an eye contact with the Autonomous Speaker Agent.

6   Results

We conducted a subjective test in order to compare our proposed statistical model to simpler techniques. We synthesised facial animation on our face model using three different methods. In the first (Type 1), head and eye movements were produced playing animation sequence that was recorded by tracking movements of a real professional speaker. In the second (Type 2), we produced a facial animation using the system described in this paper. In the third (Type 3), only the character's lips were animated.

We conducted a subjective test to evaluate the three types of facial animation. The three characters (Type 1, Type 2 and Type 3) were presented in random order to 29 subjects. All three characters presented the same text. The presentation was conducted in the Ericsson Nikola Tesla[6] and all subjects were computer specialists. However, most of the subjects were not familiar with virtual characters, and none of the subjects were authors of the study. The subjects were asked the following questions:

☐ Q1: Did the character on the screen appear interested in (5) or indifferent (1) to you?
☐ Q2: Did the character appear engaged (5) or distracted (1) during the conversation?
☐ Q3: Did the personality of the character look friendly (5) or not (1)?
☐ Q4: Did the face of the character look lively (5) or deadpan (1)?
☐ Q5: In general, how would you describe the character?

Note that higher scores correspond to more positive attributes in a speaker. For questions 1 to 4, the score was graded on a scale of 5 to 1. Fig. 6. summarizes the average score and standard deviation (marked with a black color) for the first four questions. From the figure, we can see that the character of type 2 was graded with the highest average grade for all questions except for the Q2. The reason for that is because type 3 character only moves its lips and its head is static. This gave the audience the impression of engagement in the presentation. A Kruskal-Wallis ANOVA indicated that the three character types had significantly different scores (p = 0.0000). According to general remarks in Q5, the subjects tended to believe the following:

1. Type 1 looked boring and uninteresting, it seemed to have cold personality. Also, implemented facial gestures were not related to the spoken text.
2. Type 2 had a more natural facial gesturing and facial gestures were coarticulated to some extend. Head movements and eye blinks are related to the spoken text. However, eyebrow movements were with unnatural amplitudes and were not related to the spoken text.
3. Type 3 looked irritating, stern and stony. However, it appeared to be concentrated and its lips animation was the best.

7   Conclusion and Future Work

According to feedback that we have received from the audience, we can conclude that our statistical model of facial gestures can be used in a system that implements a fairly convincing Autonomous Speaker Agent. Furthermore, the implemented decision tree produces better animation than previous techniques. The problem with eyebrow amplitudes can be easily solved by changing some of the parameters in the TTS/MPEG-4 encoding module. Also, with statistical data that we have gathered during our work, we have confirmed some of the conclusions of other papers. We confirmed that, on average, the amplitude of a faster head nod is lesser than the amplitude of a slower nod. Furthermore, we concluded that words, that bring something new in the utterance context, are very often accompanied by some facial gesture.

---

[6] http://www.ericsson.com/hr 26/09/2004.

However, our system is not ready yet for the Turing test. An extension to Embodied Conversational Characters is the logical item for future work, extending the system to support the natural gesturing during a conversation and not only for independent speakers. This will include adapting and extending the statistical model to include more complicated gesturing modes and speech prosody that occur in a conversation. Also, new statistical data should be calculated based on the existing training set data. In this calculation, it must be taken into consideration that words form two higher logical groups: OBJECT and ACTION. Because those groups are labelled with new and old tags, this fact results in new statistical data for facial gestures. Also, coarticulation of facial display occurrences must be taken into consideration during the production of this new statistical model.

Modifying speech prosody ([24], [25], [26]) of input text according to statistical prosody data of professional speakers would produce a much more convincing Autonomous Speaker Agent. In order to get more natural head movements, the velocity dynamics [27] of those movements must be implemented in the TTS/MPEG-4 encoding module. New Visage SDK API5 works with Microsoft SAPI 5.0 engine. That engine uses XML notation for user defined bookmarks and, because of that, output of the Facial Gesture Module should be adapted to this new notation.

References

1. Pelachaud, C., Badler, N., and Steedman, M.: 1996. Generating Facial Expressions for Speech, *Cognitive, Science*, 20(1), 1–46
2. Legoff, B. and Benoît, C.: 1997. A French speaking synthetic head. In *Proceedings of the ESCA Workshop on Audio-Visual Speech Processing* 1997, C. Benot, and R. Campbell, Eds., Rhodes, Greece, 145–148
3. Lewis, J.P., Parke, F.I.: 1987. Automated lipsynch and speech synthesis for character animation. In *Proceedings of Human Factors in Computing Systems and Graphics Interface 1987,* J. H. Caroll and P. Tanner (Eds.), 143–147
4. Smid, K., Pandzic, I.S.: 2002. A Conversational Virtual Character for the Web. In *Proceedings of Computer Animation* 2002, Geneva, Switzerland, 240–248
5. Beskow, J.: 1995. Rule-based visual speech synthesis. In *Proceedings of ESCA-EUROSPEECH 1995*. 4th European Conference on Speech Communication and Technology, Madrid. vol. 1, 299–302
6. Cohen, M.M., Massaro, D.W.: 1993. Modeling coarticulation in synthetic visual speech. In *Proceedings of Models and Techniques in Computer Animation*, M. Magnenat-Thalmann, and D. Thalmann, Eds., Springer-Verlag, Tokyo, 139–156
7. Lundeberg, M., Beskow, J.: 1999. Developing a 3D-agent for the August dialogue system. In *Proceedings from AVSP1999*, Santa Cruz, USA
8. Ostermann, J., and Millen, D.: 2000. Talking heads and synthetic speech: An architecture for supporting electronic commerce. In *Proceedings of* ICME 2000, 71–74
9. Pandzic, I.S.: 2002. Facial Animation Framework for the Web and Mobile Platforms. In *Proceedings of Web3D Symposium* 2002, Tempe, AZ, USA, 27–34
10. Lee, S.P., Badler, J.B., Badler, N.I.: 2002. Eyes Alive. In Proceedings of the 29th annual conference on Computer graphics and interactive techniques 2002, San Antonio, Texas, USA, ACM Press New York, NY, USA, 637–644
11. Cassell J., Sullivan J., Prevost S., Churchill E.: 2000. *Embodied Conversational Agents*. The MIT Press Cambridge, Massachusetts London, England

12. Argyle, M., Cook, M.: 1976. *Gaze and mutual gaze*. Cambridge University Press
13. Collier, G.: 1985. *Emotional expression*. Hillsdale, N.J.: Lawrence Erlbaum Associates
14. Chovil, N.: 1992. Discourse-oriented facial displays in conversation. *Research on Language and Social Interaction* 25:163–194
15. Cassell, J., Vilhjálmsson, H., and Bickmore, T.: 2001. BEAT: the Behavior Expression Animation Toolkit. In *Proceedings of SIGGRAPH 2001*, ACM Press / ACM SIGGRAPH, New York, E. Fiume, Ed., Computer Graphics Proceedings, Annual Conference Series, ACM, 477–486
16. Pandzic, I.S., and Forchheimer R.: 2002. MPEG-4 Facial Animation – The standard, implementations and applications. John Wiley & Sons
17. Hadar, U., Steiner, T., Grant, E., and Rose, F.C.: 1983. Kinematics of head movements accompanying speech during conversation. *Human Movement Science*, 2:35–46
18. Faigin, G.: 1990. *The artist's complete guide to facial expression*. Watson-Guptill Publications, New York
19. Ekman, P., Friesen, W.: 1969. The repertoire of nonverbal behavioral categories – Origins, usage, and coding. *Semiotica* 1:49–98
20. Ekman, P.: 1979. About brows: Emotional and conversational signals. *Human ethology: Claims and limits of a new discipline*, M. von Cranach, K. Foppa, W. Lepenies, and D. Ploog, eds., New York: Cambridge University Press. 169–249
21. Duncan, S.: 1972. Some signals and rules for taking speaking turns in conversations. *Journal of Personality and Social Psychology*, Oxford University Press , 23(2), 283–292
22. Graf, H.P., Cosatto, E., Strom, V., Huang, F.J.: 2002. Visual Prosody: Facial Movements Accompanying Speech. In *Proceedings of AFGR 2002*, 381–386
23. Radman, V., 2004. Leksička analiza teksta za automatsku proizvodnju pokreta lica. Graduate work no. 2472 on Faculty of Electrical Engineering and Computing, University of Zagreb
24. Hiyakumoto, L., Prevost, S., Cassell, J.: 1997. Semantic and Discourse Information for Text-to-Speech Intonation. In *Proceedings of ACL Workshop on Concept-to-Speech Generation 1997,* Madrid. 47-56
25. Parent, R., King, S., Fujimura, O.: 2002. Issues with Lip Synch Animation: Can You Read My Lips?, In *Proceedings of Computer Animation* 2002, Geneva, Switzerland, pp. 3–10
26. Silverman, K., Beckman, M., Pitrelli, J., Osterndorf, M., Wightman, C., Price, P., Pierrehumbert, J., Herschberg, J.: 1992. ToBI: A Standard for Labeling English Prosody. In Proceedings of Conference on Spoken Language, 1992, Banff, Canada, 867–870
27. Gratch, J.: 2000. Emile: Marshalling Passions in Training and Education. Proceedings of the Fourth International Conference on Autonomous Agents, ACM Press, 325–332

Facilitating Understanding for Children by Translating Web Contents into a Storybook

Kaoru Sumi[1] and Katsumi Tanaka[1,2]

[1] National Institute of Information and Communications Technology,
Interactive Communication Media and Contents Group,
3-5 Hikaridai, Seika-cho, Soraku-gun, Kyoto, 619-0289, Japan
Kaoru@nict.go.jp
http://www2.nict.go.jp/jt/a133/indexe.html
[2] Kyoto University, Graduate School of Informatics,
Yoshida Honmachi, Sakyo, Kyoto 606-8501, Japan
ktanaka@i.kyoto-u.ac.jp

Abstract. This paper describes a medium, called *Interactive e-Hon*, for helping children to understand contents from the Web. It works by transforming electronic contents into an easily understandable "storybook world". In this world, easy-to-understand contents are created generated by creating 3D animations that include contents and metaphors, and by using a child-parent model with dialogue expression and a question-answering style comprehensible to children.

1   Introduction

We are awash in information flowing from the World Wide Web, newspapers, and other types of documents, yet the information is often hard to understand; laypeople, the elderly, and children find much of what is available incomprehensible. Thus far, most children have missed an opportunities to use such information, because it has been prepared by adults for adults. The volume of information specifically intended for children is extremely limited, and primarily it is still primarily adults who experience the globalising effects of the Web and other networks. The barriers for children include difficult expressions, prerequisite background knowledge, and so on. Our goal is to remove these barriers and build bridges to facilitate children's understanding and curiosity. In this research, we are presently considering the applicability of systems for facilitating understanding in children.

This paper describes a medium, called *Interactive e-Hon*, for helping children to understand difficult contents. It works by transforming electronic contents into an easily understandable "storybook world". *Interactive e-Hon* uses animations to help children understand contents. Visual data attract a child's interest, and the use of concrete examples like metaphors facilitates understanding, because each person learns according to his or her own unique mental model [1] [2], formed according to one's background. For example, if a user poses a question about something, a system that answers with a concrete example in accordance with the user's specialisation would be very helpful. For users who are children, an appropriate domain might be a storybook world. Our

L. Bolc et al. (Eds.): IMTCI 2004, LNAI 3490, pp. 175–184, 2005.

long-term goal is to help broaden children's intellectual curiosity [3] by broadening their world [1].

Attempts to transform natural language (NL) into animation began in the 1970s with SHRDLU [4], which represents a building -block world and shows the animations of adding or removing blocks. In the 1980s and 1990s, HOMER [5], and Put-that-there [6], AnimNL [7], and other applications, in which the users operate human agents or other animated entities derived from natural language understanding, appeared. Recently, there has been research on the natural behaviour of life-like agents in interactions between users and agents. This area includes research on the gestures of an agent [8], interactive drama [9], and the emotions of an agent [10]. The main theme in this line of inquiry is the question of how to make these agents close to humans in terms of dialogicality, believability, and reliability.

In contrast, our research aims to make contents easier for users to understand, regardless of agent humanity. Little or no attention has been paid to media translation from contents with the goal of improving users' understanding.

2   Interactive e-Hon

Figure 1 shows the system framework for Interactive e-Hon. In this storybook world, easy-to-understand contents are created by paraphrasing the original contents with a colloquial style, by creating animations that include contents and metaphors, and by using a child-parent model with dialogue expression and a question-answering style comprehensible to children.

Fig. 1. Interactive e-Hon: This system transforms electronic contents into a storybook world by using animation and multidimensional QA (MQA), which includes ontologies and a thesaurus

Interactive e-Hon transforms electronic contents into a storybook world that uses dialogues to answer questions and explain concepts along with 3D animations derived from NL and based on conceptual metaphors. This system was originally designed for the Japanese language. It is based on a multidimensional question answering (MQA) system that includes ontologies and a thesaurus, and on text information with semantic tags following the Global Document Annotation (GDA) [2] tagging standard, with other, additional semantic tags.

MQA create a question-answering system automatically by using digital documents that might appear anywhere. Users can receive not just the normal answer to a question but also generalised or concretised answers to a given problem; this is accomplished by using ontologies and a thesaurus. Simultaneously, users can access multiple content domains, which can be limited to a peculiar domain or not limited at all. Thus, in addition to a simple answer, a user can receive generalised or concretised answers to a given problem with the chosen domain configuration. MQA aims to transform a certain concept in a target field into a concrete example in another field.

Documents are tagged by using tags with several semantic meanings for every morpheme, such as "length", "weight", "organisation", etc. To tag electronic documents, we apply GDA, with which Internet authors can annotate their electronic documents with a common, standard tag set, allowing machines to automatically recognise the semantic and pragmatic structures of the documents[1]. To provide normal answers with MQA, the system searches for tags according to the meaning of a question. To provide generalised and concretised answers with MQA, after searching tags according to a question's meaning and obtaining one normal answer, the system then generalises/concretises the answer by using ontologies. Recently, the Semantic Web [2] and its associated activities have adopted tagged documentation. Tagging will be done in the next generation of Web documentation.

In the following sub-sections, we describe the key aspects of Interactive e-Hon: the information presentation model, the transformation of electronic contents into dialogue expressions, the transformation of electronic contents into animations, and the expression of conceptual metaphors by animations.

2.1   Content Presentation Model

Our system presents agents that mediate a user's understanding through intelligent information presentation. In the proposed model, a parent agent (mother or father) and a child agent have a conversation while watching a "movie" about the contents, and the user (or users in the case of a child and parent together) watches the agents. In this model, the child agent represents the child user, and the parent agent represents his or her parent (mother or father). For this purpose, the agents take the form of moving shadows of the parent and child. There are agents for both the user or users (avatars) and others (guides and actors), and the avatars are agentive, dialogical, and familiar [12]. Thus, we designed the system for child users to feel affinities with ages, helping them to deepen their understanding of contents.

According to the classification scheme of Thomas Rist et al. [13], a conversational setting for users and agents involves more cooperative interaction. This classification includes various style of conversation, e.g., non-interactive presentation, hyper-presentation/dialogue, presentation teams, and multi-party, multi-threaded conversation. With its agents for the users and for others, and with its process of media transformation from contents (e.g., question-answering, dialogue, and animation), Interactive

---

[1] http://i-content.org/GDA

e-Hon corresponds to between a multi-party, multi-threaded conversation and a presentation team. As for considering the grain size of Interaction between contents and agents, Interactive e-Hon has Morpheme level Interaction, because it has a close relationship with the contents being explained.

2.2   Transformation from Contents into Dialogue Expressions

For transforming contents into dialogues and animations, we first make a list which that includes subjects, objects, predicates, and modifiers from the text information of content. It also means to shorten and divide the long and complicated sentences.

Then, by collecting these words and connecting them in a friendly, colloquial style, conversational sentences are made. In addition, the system prepares repetition by the conversational partner by changing phrases to a thesaurus. It prepares explanations through abstraction and concretisation using based on ontologiesy, which that it adds explanations of background knowledge. For example, in the case of abstraction, "Antananarivo in Madagascar" can be changed into "the area of Antananarivo in the nation of Madagascar", which uses ontologiesy "Antananarivo is the an area" and "Madagascar is the a nation". Similarly, in the case of concretisation, "woodwind" can be changed into "woodwind; for example, a clarinet, saxophone, and or flute." these transformations make it is easy to understand the concepts.

In the case of abstraction, our semantic tag "person" adds the expression, "person whose name is"; "location" adds the expression "the area of" or "the nation of"; "organization" adds "the organization of". In the case of concretisation, if a target concept includes lower concepts, the system uses explanations of the lower concepts.

2.3   Transformation of Contents into Animations

Interactive e-Hon transforms contents into animations by using the list, which described in the previous sub-section. A subject is treated as a character, and a predicate is treated as the passive action in an animation. One animation and one dialogue are generated by each list, and these are then played at the same time.

Many characters and actions have been recorded in the our database. A character or an action is a one-to-many relationship. Various character names are linked to characters. Various action names are linked to actions, because often several different names indicate the same action. Actions can be shared among characters in order to prepare a commoditised skeleton of characters.

If there is a word correspondence between the name of a character and a subject or object in the list, the character is selected. If there is not a word correspondence, in the case of having a semantic tag of "person", the system selects a general person character by following an ontology of characters. When there is no semantic tag of "person", the system selects a general object by following an ontology of characters.

2.4   Searching and Transformation of Metaphors into Animations

If a user does not know the meaning of the term, "president", it would be helpful to show a dialogue explanation that "a president is similar to a king in the sense of being the person who governs a nation", together with an animation of a king. People understand unfamiliar concepts by transforming the concepts according to their own mental models [1][2]. The above example follows this process.

The explanation is shown according to the results of searching world-view databases. The process of searching is used in the explaining of the dialogue.

The system's world-view databases described the real world, storybooks (which children have in common), insects, flowers, stars, etc. Which world should be used depends on a user's curiosity, which is acquired from the user's input in the main menu. For example, there are "a company president controls a company" and "a bear attacks a man" in the common world-view database, and "a king reigns over the a country" and "a wolf attacked on Little Red Riding-Hood" in the world-view database for storybooks, which is the target database for the present research. The explanation of "a company president" is searched for the storybook world-view database by including the synonyms from a thesaurus. Then, the system searchesd for "king" and obtains the explanation, "A company president who governs a company is similar to a king who governs the a nation". In the same way, the explanation of the a bear, "A bear that attacks a man is similar to the wolf that attacked Little Red Riding-Hood", is accompanied by an animation of a wolf.

In terms of search priorities, the system uses the following order: (1) complete correspondence of an object and a predicate, (2) correspondencen of an object and a predicate including synonyms, (3) correspondence of a predicate, and (4) correspondence of a predicate including synonyms.

If there is a result of (1), it uses (1). If there is no (1), it uses (2). If there is no (1) and (2), it uses (3), and so on.

Commonsense computing [14] is related research on describing world-views by using NL. In that research, world-view are transformed it into networks with well-defined data, like semantic networks. A special feature of our research is that we use NL in conjunction with ontologiesy and a thesaurus.

3   Application to Web Contents

Web contents can easily be written by anybody and made available to the public. These contents differ from publications, which are written by professional writers and proofread, in that they are not always correct or easy to understand. Because these contents may include errors and unknown words (like newly coined words, slang, and locutions), they tend to be ill-defined. We thus discuss practical problems and solutions for transforming Web contents into a storybook world in this section.

For example, we might try to transform the actual contents of "the origin of the *teddy bear's* name" from the web into an animation and dialogue (Figure. 2).

In this case, e-Hon is explaining the concept of "president" by showing a king's animation. The mother and child agents talk about the contents.

3.1   Transformation of Web Contents into Dialogues

As described above, the system first makes a list of subjects, objects, predicates, and modifiers from the content's text information; it then divides sentences. For example, it makes some lines of the list from a the long sentence as below:

Fig. 2. A sample view from Interactive e-Hon. (adapted from the original Japanease version)

(Original sentence 1)

"It is said that a confectioner, who read it, made a stuffed bear, found the nickname "Teddy", and named it a "Teddy bear".

(List 1) MS; a modifier of a subject, S; a subject, MO; a modifier of an object, O; an object, MP; a modifier of a predicate, P; a predicate

– S: confectioner, MS: who read it, P: make, O: stuffed bear,

– S: confectioner, P: find, O: nickname "Teddy", MO: his

– S: confectioner, P: name, MP: "Teddy bear", name

– S: it, P: said

(Original sentence 2)

"But, the president refused to shoot the little bear, and helped it".

(List 2)

– S: President, P: shoot, O: little bear

– S: President, P: refuse, O: to shoot the little bear

– S: President, P: help, O: little bear

The system then generates a dialogue lines one by one, putting them in the order (in Japanese) of a modifier of a subject, a subject, a modifier of an object, an object, a modifier of a predicate, and a predicate, according to the line units of line in the list. To the characteristics of storytelling, the system uses past tense and speaks differently depending on whether the parent agent is a mother or a father.

Sometimes the original contents uses reverse conjunction, as with "but" or "however" in the following examples: "but... what do you think happens after that?"; "I can't guess. Tell me the story." In such cases, the parent and child agents speak by using questions and answers to spice up the dialogue. Also, at the ending of every scene, the system repeats the same meaning with different words by using synonyms.

3.2   Transformation of Web Contents into Animations

In the case of an animation, the system combines animations of a subject as a character, an object as a passive character, and a predicate as an action, according to the line units in the list.

For example, in the case of original sentence 2 shown above, first,

– president (character) shoot (action)

– little bear (character; passive) is shot (action; passive)

are selected. After that,

– president (character) refused (action)

is selected. Finally,

– president (character) help (action)

– little bear (character; passive) is helped (action; passive)

are selected.

This articulation of animation is used only for verbs with clear action. For example, the be-verb, and certain common expressions, such as "come from" and "said to be" in English, cannot be expressed. Because there are so many expressions like these, the system does not for register verbs for such expressions as potential candidates for animations.

3.3   Handling Errors and Unknown Words

One problem that Interactive e-Hon must handle is errors and unknown words from Web contents, such as a newly coined words, slang, locutions, and new manners of speaking. The text area in the system shows original sentences. Erroneousr words and unknown words are originally shown in the text area, but they are exempt from concept explanation by metaphor expression.

In generating dialogue expressions using such words, the resulting dialogues and animation may be generated strange because of misunderstood modification. In the case of a subject or predicate error, an animation cannot be generated. In this system, if an animation is not generated, the previous animation continues to loop, so errors may prevent the animation from changing to match the expressions in a dialogue. If both the animation and the dialogue work strangely, the text area helps the user to guess the original meaning and the reason. In addition, new unknown words can be registered in the NL dictionary, animation library, and ontologies.

In fact, our example of "the origin of the *teddy bear*'s name" from the Web may have some errors in Japanese, such as "Teodore Roosevelt" or "Othedore Roosevelt". In such cases, since the original text is shown in the system's text area, and most rephrasing words which mean "Roosevelt" are "the president", this was not a big problem.

4   Experiment Using Subjects

We conducted an experiment using real subjects for to examine whether Interactive e-Hon's expression of dialogue and animation was helpful for users. We again used the example of "the origin of the *teddy bear*'s name". Three types of contents were presented to users and evaluated by them: the original content read by a voice synthesiser (content 1), a dialogues generated by Interactive e-Hon and read by a voice synthesiser (content 2), and a dialogues with animation generated by Interactive e-Hon and read by a voice synthesiser (content 3). The subjects were Miss T and Miss S, both in their 20s,; child K, five years old; and child Y, three years old.

Both women understood content 2 as a dialogue but found content 1 easier to understand because of its compaction. They also thought content 3 was easier to understand than content 2 because of its animations. T, however, liked content 1 the best, while S favoured content 3. As T commented, "Content 1 is the easiest to understand, though content 3 is the most impressive". In contrast, S commented, "Content 3 is impressive even if I don't hear it in earnest. Content 1 is familiar to me like TV or radio". She also noted, "The animations are impressive. I think the dialogues are friendly and may be easy for children to understand."

K, who is five years old, said that he did not understand content 1. He first felt that he understood content 2 a little bit, but he did not express his own words about it. He found content 3, however, entirely different from the others, because he felt that he understood it, and he understood the difficult word *kobamu* in Japanese, which means "refuse" in English. Child Y, who is three years old, showed no recognition of contents 1 and 2, but he seemed to understand content 3 very well, as he can was able to give his thoughts on the content by asking (about President Roosevelt), "Is he kind?". In this experiment, we observed that there was a difference between the results for adults and children, despite the limited number and age range of the subjects. At first, we thought that all users will would find it easiest to understand content 3 and would like it and be attracted it. In fact, the results were different.

We assume that contents that are within a user's background knowledge are easier to understand by regular reading, as in the case of the adults in this experiment. In contrast, the contents outside a user's background knowledge, animations is expected to be very helpful for understanding, as in the case of the children. Further experiments may show that for a given user, difficult contents outside the user's background knowledge can be understood through animation, regardless of the user's age.

5   Evaluation

Interactive e-Hon's expressions of dialogue and animation are generated from NL processing of the Web contents. For dialogue expression, it generates a plausible, colloquial style that is easy to understand by shortening a long sentence and extracting a subject, objects, a predicate, and modifiers from it. For animation expression, the system generates a helpful animation by connecting selected animations for a subject, objects, and a predicate. The result is an expression of dialogue with animation that can support a child user's understanding, as demonstrated by the above experiment using real subjects.

In the process of registering character data and corresponding words, or an action and its corresponding words, which are one-to-many correspondences, certain groups of words that are like new synonyms are generated via the 3D contents. These groups of synonyms are different from NL synonyms, and new relationships between words can be observed. This can be considered for a potential application as a more practical thesaurus of based on 3D contents, as opposed to an NL thesaurus.

Reference terms, (e.g., "it", "that", "this"), and verbal omission of an subject, which are open problems in natural language processing (NLP), still remained as problems in our system. As a tentative solution, we manually embedded word references in the GDA tags. A fully automatic process knowing which words to reference will depend on further progress in NLP.

As for the process of transforming dialogues, Interactive e-Hon adds all explanations of locations, people, and other concepts by using ontologiesy, but granular unification of the ontologiesy and user adaptations should be considered from the perspective of which is the best solution for a user's understanding.

6   Conclusion

We have introduced Interactive-e-Hon, a system for facilitating children's understanding of electronic contents by transforming them into a "storybook world". We have conducted media transformation of actual Web contents, and demonstrated the effectiveness of this approach via an experiment using real subjects. We have shown that Interactive e-Hon can generated satisfactory explanations of concepts through both animations and dialogues that can be readily understood by children.

Interactive e-Hon could be widely applied as an assistant to support the understanding of difficult contents or concepts by various kinds of people who with different background knowledge, such as the elderly, people from different regions or cultures, or layman in a difficult field.

As future work, we will consider expanding the databases of animations and words, and applying Interactive e-Hon to several other kinds of contents.

References

1. Johnson-Laird, P. N.: Mental Models, Cambridge: Cambridge University Press. Cambridge, Mass.: Harvard University Press (1983)
2. Norman, D. A.: The Psychology of Everyday Things, Basic Books (1988)
3. Hatano, I.: Intellectual Curiosity, Cyuko Shinsho (in Japanese) (1973)
4. Winograd, T.: Understanding Natural Language, Academic Press (1972)
5. Vere, S., Bickmore, T.: A basic agent. Computational Intelligence, 6:41–60 (1990)
6. Bolt, R. A.: "Put-that-there": Voice and gesture at the graphics interface, International Conference on Computer Graphics and Interactive Techniques archive, Proceedings of the 7th annual conference on Computer graphics and interactive techniques, ACM Press (1980)
7. Badler, N., Phillips, C., Webber, B.: Simulating Humans: Computer Graphics, Animation and Control. Oxford University Press (1993)
8. Cassel, J., Vilhjalmsson, H. H., Bickmore, T.: BEAT: the Behavior Expression Animation Toolkit, Life-Like Characters, Helmet Prendinger and Mitsuru Ishizuka Eds., pp. 163–187, Springer (2004)
9. Tanaka, H., et al.: Animated Agents Capable of Understanding Natural Language and Performing Actions, Life-Like Characters, Helmet Prendinger and Mitsuru Ishizuka Eds., pp. 163–187, Springer, (2004)
10. Marsella, S., Gratch, J., Rickel, J.: Expressive Behaviors for Virtual World, Life-Like Characters, Helmet Prendinger and Mitsuru Ishizuka Eds., pp. 163–187, Springer (2004)

11. Fensel, D., Hendler, J., Liebermann, H., Wahlster, W. (Eds.): Spinning the Semantic Web, MIT Press (2002)
12. Nishida, T., Kinoshita, T., Kitamura, Y., Mase, K.: Agent Technology, Omu Sya (in Japanese) (2002)
13. Rist, T., Andre, E., Baldes, S., Gebhard, P., Klesen, M., Kipp, M., Rist P., Schmitt, M.: A Review of the Development of Embodied Presentation Agent and Their Application Fields, Life-Like Characters, Helmet Prendinger and Mitsuru Ishizuka Eds., pp. 377-404, Springer (2004)
14. Liu, H., Singh, P.: Commonsense reasoning in and over natural language. Proceedings of the 8th International Conference on Knowledge-Based Intelligent Information & Engineering Systems (KES-2004) (2004)

Collage of Video and Sound for Raising the Awareness of Situated Conversations

Yasuyuki Sumi[1,2], Kenji Mase[3,2], Christof Müller[2],
Shoichiro Iwasawa[2], Sadanori Ito[2], Masashi Takahashi[1,2], Ken Kumagai[1,2],
Yusuke Otaka[1,2], Megumu Tsuchikawa[2], Yasuhiro Katagiri[2], and Toyoaki Nishida[1,2]

[1] Graduate School of Infomatics, Kyoto University,
Yoshida-Honmachi, Sakyo-ku, Kyoto 606-8501, Japan
[2] ATR Media Information Science Laboratories,
Seika-cho, Soraku-gun, Kyoto 619-0288, Japan
[3] Information Technology Center, Nagoya University,
Chikusa, Nagoya 464-8601, Japan
sumi@i.kyoto-u.ac.jp
http://www.ii.ist.i.kyoto-u.ac.jp/~sumi

Abstract. This paper describes our attempt to build a communicative medium for capturing and re-experiencing conversations situated in the real space. We first show a system that captures and interprets conversation scenes by ubiquitous sensors. Based on the system, we present three approaches to visualise and facilitate users to access the extracted conversation scenes, i.e., chronological summarisation of videos, spatio-temporal collage of videos, and ambient sound display.

1 Introduction

The spread of the computer networks and media technologies have enabled spatially and temporally distributed people to share knowledge. The knowledge exchanged through the media, however, is basically externalised and verbalised by humans manually. Therefore, the available knowledge tends to be limited to formalised one, not tacit one.

Our daily lives are full with conversations, through which we exchange and share tacit knowledge (awareness, common sense, know-how, nebulous ideas, atmosphere, etc.) with others. The recent advancement of ubiquitous computing and augmented reality technologies are expected to capture our daily conversations and facilitate us to access these.

This paper shows our attempt to build a communicative medium where we can capture and share conversations situated in our daily lives. Throughout this paper, we use the term "conversation" widely to describe various kinds of interactions between people, not only speaking each other but also gazing a particular object together, staying together for a particular purpose, etc.

The first half part of the paper presents a system for capturing human interactions by ubiquious/wearable sensors. The system consists of multiple sensor sets ubiquitously set up around the room as well as wearable ones. The characteristics of our system is that we can obtain multiple viewpoint videos that capture a particular scene. The first goal for building a medium to deal with the captured conversations is to extract conversation scenes with meaningful and tractable size, as quantised conversations [1]. We

L. Bolc et al. (Eds.): IMTCI 2004, LNAI 3490, pp. 185–194, 2005.

show a method to infer interaction semantics, such as "talk with someone", "staying somewhere", "gazing at something", etc., among users and the environment by collaboratively processing data of those who jointly interacted with each other. This can be performed without time-consuming audio and image processing by employing an infrared ID system to determine the position and identity of objects in each video's field of view.

The second part of the paper describes systems that facilitate us to access the extracted conversations. Our approach is "collage" of video and sound fragments associated with the extracted conversations. This paper shows three kinds of "collage" systems as follows.

Video summary: Chronological collage of multiple-viewpoint videos.
Spatio-temporal video collage: Visualisation of conversation scenes in a 3D virtual space.
Ambient sound collage: Acoustic visualisation of past conversations in the real space.

2   Capturing Conversation Scenes by Multiple Sensors

We prototyped a system for recording natural interactions among multiple presenters and visitors in an exhibition room [2]. The prototype was installed and tested in one of the exhibition rooms during our research laboratories' open house.

Our approach is characterised by the integration of many sensors (video cameras, trackers and microphones) ubiquitously set up around the room and wearable sensors (video camera, trackers, microphone, and physiological sensors) to monitor humans as subjects of interactions. Our system incorporates ID tags with an infrared LED (LED tags) and infrared signal tracking device (IR tracker) in order to record position context along with audio/video data. The tracking device is a parallel distributed camera array

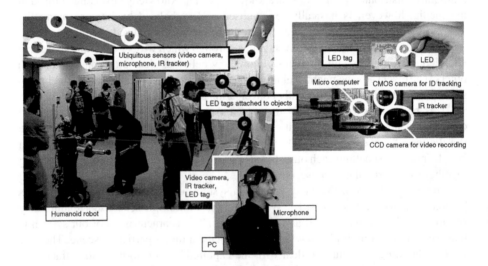

Fig. 1. Setup of the ubiquitous sensor room

where any camera can determine the position and identity of any tag in its field of view. By wearing a tracking camera, a user's gaze can be determined. This approach assumes that gazing can be used as a good index for human interactions [3].

Fig. 1 is a snapshot of the exhibition room set up for recording interactions among visitors and exhibitors. There were five booths in the exhibition room. Each booth had two sets of ubiquitous sensors that include video cameras with IR trackers and microphones. LED tags were attached to possible focal points for social interactions, such as on posters and displays. Each presenter at their booth carried a set of wearable sensors, including a video camera with an IR tracker, a microphone, an LED tag, and physiological sensors (heart rate, skin conductance, and temperature). A visitor could choose to carry the same wearable system as the presenters or just an LED tag, or nothing at all. One booth had a humanoid robot for its demonstration that was also used as an actor to interact with visitors and record the interactions using the same wearable system as the human presenters.

Eighty users participated during the two-day open house providing ~ 300 hours of video data, 380,000 tracker data along with associated biometric data.

3   Segmentation and Interpretion of Scenes

We developed a method to segment interaction scenes from the IR tracker data. We defined interaction primitives, or "events", as significant intervals or moments of activities. For example, a video clip that has a particular object (such as a poster, user, etc.) in it constitutes an event. Since the location of all objects is known from the IR tracker and LED tags, it is easy to determine these events. We then interpret the meaning of events by considering the combination of objects appearing in the events.

Fig. 2 illustrates basic events which we considered.

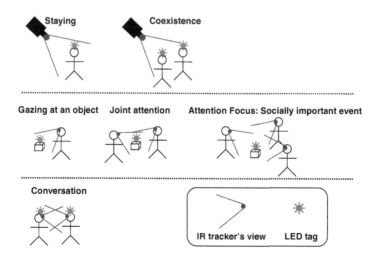

Fig. 2. Interaction primitives

Stay. A fixed IR tracker at a booth captures an LED tag attached to a user: user *stays* at the booth.

Coexist. An single IR tracker camera captures LED tags attached to different users at some moment: users *coexist* in the same area.

Gaze. An IR tracker worn by a user captures an LED tag attached to someone/something: user *gazes* at someone/something.

Attention. An LED tag attached to an object is simultaneously captured by IR trackers worn by two users: users jointly pay *attention* to the object. When many users pay attention to the object, we infer that the object plays a socially important role at that moment.

Facing. Two users' IR trackers detect each others' LED tag: they are facing each other.

4   Video Summary: Chronological Collage of Multiple-Viewpoint Videos

We constructed a system to provide users with a personal summary video at the end of their touring at the exhibition room on the fly. We were able to extract appropriate

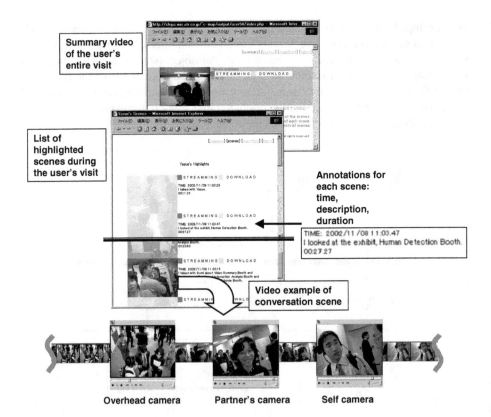

Fig. 3. Automated video summarisation

"scenes" from the viewpoints of individual users by clustering events having spatial and temporal relationships.

Fig. 3 shows an example of video summarisation for a user. The summary page was created by chronologically listing scene videos, which were automatically extracted based on events. We used thumbnails of the scene videos and coordinated their shading based on the videos' duration for quick visual cues. The system provided each scene with annotations, i.e., time, description, and duration. The descriptions were automatically determined according to the interpretation of extracted interactions by using templates, e.g., *I talked with [someone]*; *I was with [someone]*; and *I looked at [something]*.

We also provided summary video for a quick overview of the events the users experienced. To generate the summary video we used a simple format in which at most 15 seconds of each relevant scene were put together chronologically with fading effects between the scenes.

The event clips used to make up a scene were not restricted to only those captured by a single resource (video camera and microphone). For example, for a summary of a conversation "talked with" scene, video clips used were recorded by: the camera worn by a user him/herself, the camera of the conversation partner, and a fixed camera on the ceiling that captured both users. Our system selected which video clips to use by consulting the volume levels of users individual voices. Remember, the worn LED tag is assumed to indicate that the user's face is in the video clip if the associated IR tracker detects it.

5   Building 3D Virtual Space by Spatio-Temporal Video Collage

Our ubiquitous sensor system records huge amount of video data that capture conversation scenes. We are prototyping a system to build a virtual 3D space as a medium for re-experiencing the captured conversations. The important characteristics of our system here is that we have multiple viewpoint videos that capture a particular scene. Suppose that the multiple-viewpoint videos that participate the scene are projected in a virtual 3D space according to the spatial point and direction of the individual video cameras (Fig. 4 (1)). In such a space with spatially mapped multiple-videos, the particular object (a person or exhibit) that collects many attentions at a time is expected to reveal its appearance at the intersection of videos. Conversely, area that does not draw anybody's attention will not be visually rendered at all. We call the method "spatio-temporal (video) collage".

Most of existing attempts to build virtual 3D spaces so far are based on uniform modelling from so-called "the God's view" and then not good for representing alive atmosphere by people residing in the space. On the other hand, a space produced by the spatio-temporal collage method is expected to reveal social attention by participants in the real scenes, although the produced space may be geometrically inconsistent. The vidualised social attention (i.e., intersection of multiple videos) will give a visitor in the 3D virtual space a guidance to walk through (i.e., re-experience) the 3D space.

In order to build the video collage method, we have to tackle the following two issues at least:

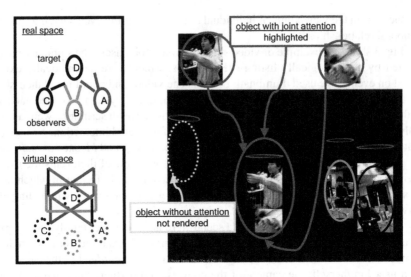

(1) Collage of multiple viewpoint videos   (2) Example snapshot of produced virtual space

Fig. 4. Building 3D virtual space by video collage

1. Observer's information such as the spatial point and direction of cameras are necessary; and
2. If we try to align videos in a strict point temporally and spatially, video resources to render each scene will be insubstantial.

Regarding the first issue, we are prototyping a LPS (Local Positioning System) to track every participant's location and gazing direction by putting the previously mentioned IR tracker on the top of the head of each participant and regularly attaching many LED tags on the ceiling. Regarding the second issue, we are examining a method to increase the visual resources that capture a particular object by extending temporal window.

Fig. 4 (2) shows an example snapshot of a 3D virtual space reproduced by the video collage method. As seen in this example, only three objects that drew attentions of participants in the scene are displayed while four objects were detected in this view by LPS. Such automatic selection naturally reveals viewpoints of participants in the scene and helps a user to re-experience the scene.

6   The Ambient Sound Shower: Sound Collage for Revealing Situated Conversations

The Ambient Sound Shower system [4] shows a user who is touring at an exhibition with ambient sound by earphone, e.g., mixture of conversations by past visitors, in order to intuitively provide him/her with atmosphere of the exhibition site on the fly. The system uses the ubiquious sensors to infer the user's current situation and changes sound modes according to his/her situation.

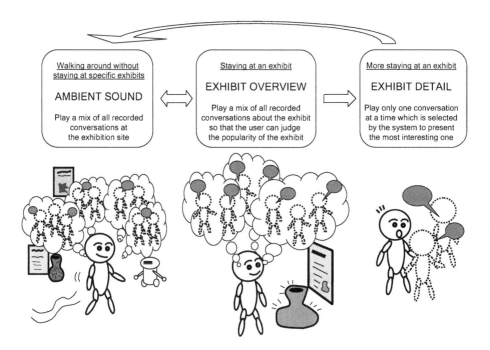

Fig. 5. Usage scenario of the Ambient Sound Shower system

The system automatically changes between three different playback modes as illustrated in Fig. 5. In case the user is at an exhibition which not many people attend at that time the system will first try to establish a stimulating ambient atmosphere by playing back on the user's earphone a mix of all conversations that were held at the exhibits by other participants so far. If the user is then showing interest for a particular exhibit by focussing it the system will switch to playback a mix of all conversations that were held only about (actually, beside) this particular exhibit. The number of conversations the user can hear shows him/her the amount of popularity this exhibit had. If he/she keeps the exhibit in focus the system assumes that he/she is still interested in it and starts the playback of only one conversation at a time. The presented conversation is assumed to be of particular interest for the user. It is selected by taking several context information of the user and his/her environment into account.

The most important part of the system does a matchmaking between the user and the past participants of the conversation by looking at their context history. For detecting the user's current situation and deciding if providing additional information is useful or disturbing the system takes into account the user's context sensed by wearable sensors like a throat microphone or IR tracker. The system infers from the sensory data contextual information like the user's

- conversational status ("is he involved in a conversation?"),
- accompanimental status ("is he accompanied by people?"), and
- interest in particular exhibits ("is he focussing a particular exhibit?").

One of our premises is to avoid the use of automatic speech recognition and natural language understanding systems since the use of them in real environments is still difficult and error prone.

7   Related Works

There have been many works on smart environments for supporting humans in a room by using video cameras set around the room, e.g., the Smart rooms[5], Intelligent room[6], AwareHome[7], Kidsroom[8], and EasyLiving[9]. The shared goal of these works was recognition of human behaviour using computer vision techniques and understanding of the human's intention. On the other hand, our interest is to capture not only an individual human's behaviour but also interactions among multiple humans (networking of their behaviour). We then focus on the understanding and utilisation of human interactions by employing an infrared ID system to simply identify the human's existence.

There also have been works on wearable systems for collecting personal daily activities by recording video data, e.g., [10] and [11]. Their aim was to build an intelligent recording system used by single users. We, however, aim to build a system collaboratively used by multiple users to capture their shared experiences and promote their further creative collaborations. By using such a system, our experiences can be recorded by multiple viewpoints and individual viewpoints will become obvious.

This paper shows a system that automatically generates video summaries for individual users as an application of our interaction corpus. In relation to this system, some systems to extract important scenes of a meeting from its video data were proposed, e.g., [12]. These systems extract scenes according to changes in the physical quantity of video data captured by fixed cameras. On the other hand, our interest is not to detect the changes of visual quantity but to segment human interactions (perhaps derived by the humans' intentions and interests), and then extract scene highlights from a meeting naturally.

A wide range of projects exist which relate to the Ambient Sound Shower system in the area of nomadic information systems, some of them using ubiquitous or wearable sensors. In the HIPS project [13] a hand-held electronic museum guide was developed. The Museum Wearable [14] uses a similar wearable and ubiquitous sensor system to ours. In both projects the presented information is already existing in the way that it is contained and retrieved from a static database. The sensory data is only used to decide which information should be selected or in which way it should be arranged, but it is not captured and used to be presented to other visitors as additional information about the exhibits. In our approach instead we try to enable the experience sharing among the visitors which was also a concept of the C-MAP system described in [15]. With the Ambient Sound Shower visitors and exhibitors can contribute to a dynamic repository of data which is used for providing additional information about exhibits.

With systems like the Audio Aura [16] or the system described by Rekimoto et al. [17] people can attach digital messages to objects which are automatically or manually retrieved and presented if other persons gaze at the object or enter a certain location. The retrieval of the messages is compared to the Ambient Sound Shower system not personalised, which means that all messages attached to one object or location will be presented to the user regardless if they are of interest for him or not.

8   Conclusions

This paper described our attempt to build a communicative medium for capturing and re-experiencing conversations situated in the real space. We first showed a system that captures and interprets conversation scenes by ubiquitous sensors. Based on the system, we presented three approaches to visualise and facilitate users to access the extracted conversation scenes, i.e., chronological summarisation of videos, spatio-temporal collage of videos, and ambient sound display.

Acknowledgements

We thank our colleagues at ATR for their valuable discussion and help on the experiments described in this paper. The research presented here is supported by the National Institute of Information and Communications Technology and Grant-in-Aide for Scientific Research.

References

1. Nishida, T.: Towards intelligent media technology for communicative intelligence. In *Proceedings of International Workshop on Intelligent Media Technology for Communicative Intelligence (IMTCI 2004)*, pages 1–7, September 2004.
2. Sumi, Y., Ito, S., Matsuguchi, T., Mase, K.: Collaborative capturing and interpretation of interactions. In *Pervasive 2004 Workshop on Memory and Sharing of Experiences*, pages 1–7, April 2004. http://www.ii.ist.i.kyoto-u.ac.jp/~sumi/pervasive04
3. Stiefelhagen, R., Yang, J., Waibel, A.: Modeling focus of attention for meeting indexing. In *ACM Multimedia '99*, pages 3–10. ACM, 1999
4. Müller, C., Sumi, Y., Mase, K., Tsuchikawa, M.: Experience sharing by retrieving captured conversations using non-verbal features. In *The First ACM Workshop on Continuous Archival and Retrieval of Personal Experiences (CARPE 2004)*, pages 93–98, 2004
5. Pentland, A.: Smart rooms. *Scientific American*, 274(4):68–76, 1996
6. Brooks, R.A., Coen, M., Dang, D., De Bonet, J., Kramer, J., Lozano-Pérez, T., Mellor, J., Pook, P., Stauffer, C., Stein, L., Torrance, M., Wessler, M.: The intelligent room project. In *Proceedings of the Second International Cognitive Technology Conference (CT'97)*, pages 271–278. IEEE, 1997
7. Kidd, C.D., Orr, R., Abowd, G.D., Atkeson, Ch.G., Essa, I.A., MacIntyre, B., Mynatt, E., Startner, T.E., Newstetter, W.: The aware home: A living laboratory for ubiquitous computing research. In *Proceedings of CoBuild'99 (Springer LNCS1670)*, pages 190–197, 1999
8. Bobick, A.F., Intille, S.S., Davis, J.W., Baird, F., Pinhanez, C.S., Campbell, L.W., Ivanov, Y.A., Schütte, A., Wilson, A.: The KidsRoom: A perceptually-based interactive and immersive story environment. *Presence*, 8(4):369–393, 1999
9. Brumitt, B., Meyers, B., Krumm, J., Kern, A., Shafer, S.: EasyLiving: Technologies for intelligent environments. In *Proceedings of HUC 2000 (Springer LNCS1927)*, pages 12–29, 2000

10. Mann, S.: Humanistic intelligence: WearComp as a new framework for intelligence signal processing. *Proceedings of the IEEE*, 86(11):2123–2125, 1998
11. Kawamura, T., Kono, Y., Kidode, M.: Wearable interfaces for a video diary: Towards memory retrieval, exchange, and transportation. In *The 6th International Symposium on Wearable Computers (ISWC2002)*, pages 31–38. IEEE, 2002
12. Chiu, P., Kapuskar, A., Reitmeier, S., Wilcox, L.: Meeting capture in a media enriched conference room. In *Proceedings of CoBuild'99 (Springer LNCS1670)*, pages 79–88, 1999
13. Benelli, G., Bianchi, A., Marti, P., Not, E., Sennati, D.: HIPS: Hyper-interaction within physical space. In *Proceedings of IEEE International Conference on Multimedia Computing*, 1999
14. Sparacino. The Museum Wearables: Real-time sensor-driven understanding of visitors' interests for personalized visually-augmented museum experiences. In *Proceedings of Museums and the Web*, F., 2002
15. Sumi, Y., Mase, K.: Supporting the awareness of shared interests and experiences in communities. *International Journal of Human-Computer Studies*, 56(1):127–146, 2002
16. Mynatt, E.D., Back, M., Want, R., Baer, M., Ellis, J.B.: Designing audio aura. In *Proceedings of CHI'98*, pages 566–573. ACM, 1998
17. Rekimoto, J., Ayatsuka, Y., Hayashi, K.: Augment-able reality: Situated communication through physical and digital spaces. In *The Second International Symposium on Wearable Computers*, pages 68–75. IEEE, 1998

Dialogue Processing Memory for Incident Solving in Man-Machine Dialogue

Zygmunt Vetulani

Adam Mickiewicz University in Poznań,
Faculty of Mathematics and Computer Science,
ul. Umultowska 87, 61614 Poznań, Poland
vetulani@amu.edu.pl
http://www.amu.edu.pl/~vetulani

Abstract. The present paper aims to analyse some difficult problems in man-machine dialogues and to draft solutions based on the idea of Dialogue Processing Memories. The idea behind the well known technique of translation memories is to economise effort by re-use of previously translated fragments. This could be adapted to other text processing domains, in particular to the field of man-machine dialogue. Simulation of correct human behaviour could be based on memorising the dialogue fragment or, more adequately, the results of its processing. The mechanism of extraction from the memory should be triggered by the same element which had earlier triggered the memorisation mechanism. Each case of making such use of Dialogue Processing Memory may be stored for possible future use with a memory refreshment/oblivion mechanism.

1 Introduction

Obtaining from computer system[1] a reasonable reaction to human command, question or statement often requires more than what may be provided by the three basic layers of analysis: morphological, syntactical and semantic. Problems requiring more then using knowledge and procedures proper to these three layers are usually *difficult*. The present paper aims at analysing a class of difficult problems of that kind and at drafting solutions based on the concept of Dialogue Processing Memories.

2 Difficult Problems: Exceptions

Among typical difficult problems those dealing with exceptions constitute an important class. We will focus on exception handling problems similar to those occurring when trying to understand the following utterance: *Do you know that Hagrid's motorcycle*

---

[1] We consider systems with natural language competence. Our work refers to the question-answering platform POLINT ([2]), without however lowering the general character of our conclusions. POLINT was developed as a system answering natural language questions in Polish and is a test platform for the solutions discussed here. Cf. also the **Implementation** chapter in this paper.

L. Bolc et al. (Eds.): IMTCI 2004, LNAI 3490, pp. 195–204, 2005.

has landed at Privet Drive 4? An uninformed addressee of such an utterance[2] may be surprised or may even reject this sentence as meaningless, as it is well known that motorcycles are not supposed to fly and therefore to land. The following dialogue might ensue.

Example
A: Do you know that Hagrid's motorcycle has landed at Privet Drive 4?
B: Well, but motorcycles do not fly.
A: Yes, but this is the Hagrid's motorcycle. It is magic.
B: O.K., I didn't know.

After such an opening, the dialogue may continue on the ground of the common assumption that Hagrid's motorcycle, as a magic object, is an exception in the class of motorcycles, i.e. it is a flying object and therefore may also land.

The general question arises:

What are the conditions that a computer system with linguistic competence must satisfy in order to be able to perform efficient exception-processing in its dialogue with a human (processing dialogues with words used in a non-standard way)?

In this paper we consider only some aspects of this problem.

3   Analysis of the Example

In the example provided above, two words may cause understanding problems. These are the verb *to land* used as sentence predicate and the noun *motorcycle* used as subject. The typical and sufficiently precise dictionary entry (reflecting the standard intuitions concerning this word) will contain the requirement about subject used with the verb *to land* to be a *flying object*[3]. Moreover, under the same assumption that the dictionary has to reflect the common intuitions about words, the meaning of the term *motorcycle* should exclude, *in principle*, flying objects. Although in many cases, sharp and rigorous distinctions are recommended or even mandatory, it is always possible to use words in a non-conventional way. On the other hand, language concepts often do not have any sharp and unambiguous definitions and systematically allow some fuzziness. We may formalise fuzziness by means of the concept of *"typical representative"* (cf. [4]) addressing the notion of *set of typical features, i.e.* features obligatory for any representative which is to be considered as *typical*. E.g., the *ability to fly* will be considered as a typical feature of the concept *bird*. The notion of *the set of typical representatives* of a given concept increases the flexibility of the inheritance mechanism. The flexibility is obtained by assuming that inheritance for the ISA hierarchy concerns only typical features and applies only to typical representatives of the subclass. E.g., if we consider the *ability to fly* as a typical feature of *flying objects* and *birds* as typical flying objects then

---

[2] E.g., a person not familiar with the Harry Potter's adventures, i.e. someone who does not know that a good-natured giant Hagrid rides a magic flying motorcycle.

[3] We assume that such a category belongs to the considered ontology.

the *ability to fly* will only apply to *typical birds* (so not necessarily to *penguins*)[4]. Saying that the class M is a *class of typical representatives* of the class N means, by definition, that "all typical representatives of M are also typical representatives of N". Using that definition, we can consider *"birds"* as typical representatives of flying objects despite *penguins* can not fly. Let us notice that "being atypical" is not upwardly inherited with respect to the ISA hierarchy, i.e. being *atypical bird* does not imply *being (atypical or typical) flying object* (*penguins* are not). The point is that the concept of "typicalness" is subjective, based on the language experience of the language user and for this reason may be responsible for discourse incidents (misunderstandings).

The example shows that the change of the dialogue participants' knowledge of the world may force reconsideration of interpretation of some linguistic units, as well as of the ontological qualification of some entities. (*Hagrid's motorcycle* is no longer just *a* motorcycle belonging to Hagrid, but appears as a very special, atypical member of the class of motorcycles.) The question is about what should the consequences of dialogue incidents of this kind on the system be (if any). The example shows that detection of atypical individuals may result in modifications to the ontological structure of the world representation the dialogue participant(s) has (have).

Considering the problem discussed above from the language processing perspective may lead to conclusions resulting in modifications of the dictionary. In the case discussed above, the solution of the initial conflict may result in the introduction to the system dictionary of a new compound term ("Hagrid's motorcycle"). It would be categorised as a proper name with an explicit annotation that this term stands for some *atypical* representative of the concept *"motor"* (and with possibly more specific characteristics). There is a question concerning the status and intended durability of such dictionary entries. In particular, it seems necessary to establish (utility-based) criteria to consider the life-time of such dictionary extension. The solution we propose instead of modifying dictionary addresses the understanding mechanism and is inspired directly by the idea of *translation memories*.

4 Dialogue Processing Memory and Its Potential Application

4.1 Incidents

Exceptions handling discussed above in Sections 3 and 4 constitute a special case of the more general concept of dialogue incident processing. By *dialogue incidents* we mean such dialogue situations where the exchange of sentences/questions/answers directly linked to the dialogue objectives (typically shared by dialogue participants) is to be interrupted because of some understanding problems. Consistently, some measures have to be taken by participants in order to solve these problems. These measures usually take form of a sub-dialogue.

---

[4] Cf. the "possible" dialogue, where (B) considers the *motorcycle of Hagrid* to be atypical.

A: *Do you know that Hagrid's motorcycle has landed at Privet Drive 4?*

B: Ho, ho. This must be some atypical motorcycle.

A: Why?

B: Have you ever heard about flying motorcycles?

A: Well, O.K., but in the magic world motorcycles may fly.

It is possible to identify various kinds of incidents. Among them are the following typical cases:

- failure to understand the partner because of the language errors (syntactic, semantic or even pragmatic) resulting from high conversation speed, noisy environment etc.
- ambiguity of the utterance which cannot be solved by the available contextual information,
- misunderstandings resulting from essential gaps in the shared knowledge about the world,
- misunderstandings resulting from significant differences of the cultural background of dialogue participants,
- understanding problems due to the incorrect (insufficient) modelling of the partners' intentions/expectations,
- problems related to the non-typical usage of language (e.g. usage of metaphors).

Dialogue incidents of various kinds are not rare in human-to-human dialogues. Their occurrence in the spontaneous speech is confirmed by a common, every-day language practice of speakers. On the other hand, systematic studies of these phenomena were limited because natural (spontaneous) dialogue corpora are rare and not easily accessible.[5]

Typically, when a dialogue incident occurs, i.e., when the intended exchange is interrupted, the following two processing phases may be distinguished:

- **the lower level processing phase** where the incident is being solved; in this case the processing usually takes the form of controlled sub-dialogue,
- **the higher level processing phase** with no apparent surface form, but where he solution resulting from the lower phase is prepared for a possible re-use in the future.

It is clear from the observation of natural language performance and from the corpus studies that not all dialogue incidents worth higher level processing (as many of them are isolated). Two classes of incidents may be identified:

- repetitive incidents,
- isolated incidents.

It is evident that only this first class merits the two level processing. The problem is in the fact that in the case of many incidents there is no a priori evidence of their isolated character. Two strategies may therefore be considered. The first one consists in trying to identify the formal features of the dialogue incidents permitting correct

---

[5] A partial remedy to this situation consists in designing and performing language experiments in order to acquire necessary corpora. E.g., in our experiments with human-to-human written question-answering dialogues where one of participants was given the task to complete his knowledge about the scene presented at a partially "destroyed" picture, ([1]) we observed 12 cases of I-do-not-understand sub-dialogues in the total of 30 observed medium size dialogues of ca 20 question-answer pairs each. Recently, an experimental platform ENDIACC for dialogue corpora collection was made public. For details cf. www.amu.edu.pl/~zlisi and [5].

categorisation in terms of repetitiveness/non-repetitiveness, whereas the second one –
in applying high level processing in all cases with a strong role of refreshment/oblivion
mechanisms. The choice between these two strategies merits further studies because of
its relevance to processing cost calculations issues.

4.2   Incident Memory

The main idea behind the well known technique of *translation memories* is to
economise effort by the re-use of already translated typical fragments. Our point is
to re-adapt this idea to other text processing domains, in particular to the field of man-
machine dialogue. Note that if the example dialogue were continued and if the participant A asked the question *"Why was the Hagrid's motocycle flying above thick fog?"*
then this new question should not appear surprising to the dialogue participant B. Otherwise he/she would be considered as lacking memory or intelligence. Simulation of
the correct human behaviour (by the participant B being a computer system) may be
based on memorising the dialogue fragment or, more adequately, of the results of its
processing. It is important to observe the following *triggering principle* governing the
use of the memory.

Triggering Principle
*The mechanism of extraction from the memory should be triggered by the same element
which had earlier triggered the memorisation mechanism.*

In the case analysed above, this triggering element is *"Hagrid's motorcycle"*. Its retrieval from the memory of atypical elements/exceptions should result in a *reminder*
that this object is *magic* and *able to fly*, and therefore prompts no semantic conflict with
"flying above thick fog". Each case of making such a use of Dialogue Processing Memory may be stored in the memory for possible further use together with a memory re-
freshment/oblivion mechanism. (The simplest implementation of such mechanism will
consist in deletion of unused items after a given period of time.)

   In the man-machine dialogue situation, the system may "solve" the problem through
a controlled subdialogue consisting in asking the user for explanatory information. The
answer provided by the user (as well as the resulting modifications calculated by the
system) constitutes the *solution* which makes dialogue continuation possible and which
is to be memorised by the system e.g., in some Dialogue Processing Memory. The
overall scheme of using a Dialogue Processing Memory is as follows:

Storing Facts About Atypical Dialogue Incidents in Memory

   - identification of an atypical situation (incident)
   - solution of an atypical situation (incident)
   - solution memorisation under some *key* ("text witness" of the dialogue incident)

Use of Incident Memory (by Machine While Man-Machine Session)

   - identification of the witness of dialogue incident (*key*) in the human utterance
   - extraction of the incident solution (stored under the *key*)
   - application of the incident solution
   - recording of the incident memory usage (for further memory management)

4.3   Some Triggering Problems

Having information about dialogue incidents stored in the processing system (as *inci-dent memory*) the question of when and how to reuse this information is crucial. At least two cases should be considered. One of them is illustrated by the Example of Chapter 2 (*Hagrid's motorcycle*). To have a better feeling of the other case let us first consider the following dialogue fragment.

Example
A: Where is Mary?
B: Which "Mary" – mother or daughter?
A: Daughter.
B: In the garden.

In this dialogue the first question (by A) appears ambiguous to B who is aware of existence of two individuals with the same name ("Mary") and initiates a simple subdi-alogue (just one question-answer pair) to identify the person concerned by the question. The solution consists in finding that, for A, the default identification is Mary=dauhgter, at least in the present situation. What makes difference between these cases is that in the first one the dialogue incident is *dialogue-situation-independent,* contrary to the second case where the dialogue incident occurred in a specific situation (where two people with the same name were involved) and where the incident's results will be limited to this specific situation and perhaps to some related situations (involving the same actors).

In order to make a reasonable usage of the incident memory it is useful to design the triggering mechanism in such a way that it is activated only when necessary. This effect may be obtained by making distinction between *activated* and *non activated* triggering elements (which will give to the set of triggering elements a dynamic character). Only *activated* triggering elements will be taken into account while dialogue processing. A closer analysis of the two cases discussed in this section shows that at least two factors may be taken into account when activating the triggering elements: the *theme* of the discourse and the *dialogue situation*.

Activation presupposes finding the theme and defining the dialogue situation limits. Once the theme of the discourse determined, only those triggering elements which are linked to this *theme* will be *activated* (i.e., "Hagrid's motorcycle" is to be activated when the dialogue is about the Harry Potter's universe). The triggering elements depending on the dialogue situation (as e.g., "Mary" in the example above in this section) are activated as soon as created and maintain active only until the end of this dialogue situation. This means that the life-time of the triggering elements of this kind is limited, i.e. that triggering elements are subject of oblivion mechanisms.

Solutions drafted above require categorisation (annotation) of the triggering ele-ments. Such a categorisation may be effected when the solution is being generated.

5   Implementation

In this section we will present an example of implementation of the scheme presented above on the ground of the system POLINT which was adapted as to be a testing plat-form for the solutions discussed in this paper.

The POLINT system was developed initially as a system answering questions in Polish. The system performs necessary analysis at morphological, syntactic and semantic layers. Morphological analysis fixes the properties of the word forms, syntactic analysis calculates the syntactic structure, in particular providing segmentation into semantically interpretable parts. Finally, the semantic analysis interprets these segments and combines together these partial interpretations into some interpretation of the whole sentence. While processing, words and segments are associated with notions used in the knowledge basis the system operates on. POLINT system uses knowledge about the language stored in the system in form of:

1) dictionary of the type lexicon-grammar[6]

and

2) grammar in form of set of rules (of the form of Horn clauses).

Dictionary entries contain first of all morphological information about words, but also, for predicative words, information about their syntactic and semantic requirements for sentence arguments. The dictionary entries contain also semantic information consisting in associating word forms with corresponding semantic level entities (sets, relations, concepts) represented in a symbolic way. What follows is an (simplified) example of dictionary entry for one of the forms for the word motocykl (motorcycle*)*

s($motocykla$,$motocykl$,common_name,[[m,sing,gen,non_hum],motor]).

This dictionary entry for the word form motocykla, beyond providing relevant morphological information by means of traditional categories (m *for gender:masculine,* sing for *number:singular,* gen for *case:genitive,* non_hum for *semantic_type:non_human*), connects the word motocykl to its counterpart in the *knowledge base* (here the concept represented by the concept identifier motor). Predicative entries (as verbs) are more complex because of syntactic requirements stored in the dictionary items for predicative words. What follows is one of forms for the verb wylądować (to land).

s(0,$wylądować$,$wylądować$,locative_verb,[[m,sing,3,past],to_land_smwhr,
[[m,sing,nom,_],loc]]).

Dictionary description of the word form "wylądował" contains besides the feature values describing its morphological properties (m for *masculine*, sing for *singular*, 3 for *third person,* past for *past tense*) also syntactic requirements with respect to arguments. These are [m,sing,nom,_] for the subject (agent) argument, and loc for *locative* position. This last value means that the complement phrase representing this argument position at the surface level (i.e. in the sentence, as it is written/pronounced) must have the form proper to names of locations. The "_" in [m,sing,nom,_] means that the semantic type is not specified. (Alternatively, it could be specified by means of some items taken from the appropriate ontology, e.g. the item characterising *flying_objects_or_beings.*)

The POLINT system has been modified in order to make it able to support the Dialogue Processing Memory scheme as presented in this paper.

---

[6] What means that an essential part of the grammatical information is being stored in the dictionary.

S:Ask your next question, please!

U:Do you know that Hagrid's motorcycle has landed at Privet Drive 4?

S:How should I understand your question? Is "Hagrid's motorcycle" an exception in the class "motorcycles" which is accepted by the predicate "to_land_somewhere"? Please do answer Yes/No.

U:No

S:The question is not semantically coherent, but I am looking for answer anyway? My answer is: YES! Ask your next question, please!

Fig. 1. Dialogue incident: incoherence between an argument and the predicate. The user did not accept the solution suggested by the system.

Figures 1 to 3 in this section show screens (manually translated from Polish for the convenience of the Reader) of the question-answering sessions initiated with a question from the Example of Section 2. The question is "Do you know that Hagrid's motorcycle has landed at Privet Drive 4?"

Those Readers who are familiar with the Harry Potter story know that the answer to this question is positive. The system (S), however, observes *possible* incoherence of this question because in the standard usage of language by the speaking agent having *standard* knowledge about the world, motorcycles are not supposed to *fly* and therefore to *land*. A reasonable reaction of the system should be trying to solve the "problem" rather then simply refuse the question which does not make sense if interpreted in the *standard* way. This is exactly what the system does. The screen presented at Fig. 1 is about the case where the user refused to accept the modification of the system's knowledge about Hagrid's motorcycle (*The user answers "No" to the suggestion that Hagrid's motorcycle is an exception in the class of motorcycles*). Finally, the system produces the correct answer without modifying its knowledge in any way. The next screen (Fig. 2) represents the immediate continuation of the session where the user asks the system the same question as before, but reacts in a different way to the system suggestion.

At the screen presented at Fig. 2 we see that, now, the user decided to consider Hagrid's motorcycle as exceptional and answered "Yes". Finally, the system's answer to the initial question is YES (as before), but the system's knowledge about the motorcycle is modified, i.e., the dialogue memory will record its exceptional character.

Asking now the same question as before will not invoke any subdialogue and the system will just display the answer "yes", as shown in Fig. 3 (presenting the screen). This time, the dialogue memory effect was that the system did not observe inconsistency between the Hagrid's motorcycle and the idea of lending. This is because the memorised solution consisted in the modification of semantic properties of the argument (Hagrid's motorcycle), now considered compatible with the requirements imposed by the predicate. In this case, the dialogue processing memory generated by the system has the form

S:Ask your next question, please!

U:Do you know that Hagrid's motorcycle has landed at Privet Drive 4?

S:How should I understand your question? Is "Hagrid's motorcycle" an exception in the class "motorcycles" which is accepted by the predicate "to_land_somewhere"? Please do answer Y/N.

U:Yes

S:I am updating the list of dialogue incidents? My answer is: YES! Ask your next question, please!

Fig. 2. Dialogue incident: incoherence between an argument and the predicate. The user accepted the solution suggested by the system (to consider the argument as an exception).

S:Ask your next question, please!

U:Do you know that Hagrid's motorcycle has landed at Privet Drive 4?

S:My answer is: YES! Ask your next question, please!

Fig. 3. Application of Dialogue Memory: the system does not signal inconsistency

of list of "exceptions" declared by the user (in our example the exception is declared when the user answers "yes" to the system, cf. the second of the presented screens).

Let us note that what is considered by the system in order to identify the incident are the properties of entities and predicates specified in the system's knowledge base. On the other hand, in some cases it would be possible to identify the incoherence between arguments and the predicate already at the early level of syntactic analysis. This would be possible if the respective semantic categorisation was done already at the dictionary level, e.g., with the concept "motorcycle" being declared non_human_non_flying_objects and with the concept "lending" requiring some "flying_object_or_being" in the subject position (cf. dictionary entries for "motocykl" and "wylądować" above). Such a solution would require a fine grained dictionary, very difficult to implement and based on extremely complex ontological systems. (Cf. [3] for the concept of *ontological systems*).

6   Conclusions

We claim having shown how the idea of *calculations re-using*, positively verified for translation memories, may be reasonably applied in man-machine dialogue in order to improve dialogue quality (make it more human-human like). Careful analysis of "natural" dialogue scenarios results in solutions feasible within the present day technology. The example analysed in this paper illustrates the class of dialogue situations where the incident solution results in a modification of the cognitive structure of the system (exception recognition). The solution scheme proposed may be considered as a form of machine learning. We claim that the "dialogue-understanding-memory technique" presented above as a tool for exception handling may be generalised in order to approach the extremely complex problem of metaphor understanding.

References

1. Vetulani, Z.: Linguistic problems in the theory of man-machine communication in natural language. A study of consultative question answering dialogues. Empirical approach. Brockmeyer. Bochum (1989)
2. Vetulani, Z.: Understanding Human Language by Computers: Projects in Artificial Intelligence and Language Technology. In: Yosiho Hamamatsu et al. (eds.): Formal Methods and Intelligent Techniques in Control, Decision Making, Multimedia and Robotics. Proceedings of the 2nd International Conference, Polish-Japanese Institute of Information Technology, Warsaw, October (2000) 218-229
3. Vetulani, Z.: Linguistically Motivated Ontological Systems. In: Callaos, N, Lesso, W., Schewe K.-D., Atlam, E. (eds.): Proceedings of the 7th World Multiconference on Systemics, Cybernetics and Informatics, July 27-30, 2003, Orlando, Florida,USA, vol. XII (Information Systems, Technologies and Applications: II), Int. Inst. of Informatics and Systemics (2003) 395-400
4. Vetulani, Z.: Towards a Linguistically Motivated Ontology of Motion: Situation Based Synsets of Motion Verbs. In: Barr, V., Markov, Z. (eds.) Proceedings of the Seventeens International Florida Artificial Intelligence Research Society Conference (FLAIRS-04), AAAI Press, Menlo Park. California (2004) 813-817
5. Vetulani, Z.: An Environment for Dialogue Corpora Collection (ENDIACC), w: M. T. Lino (i inni), Fourth International Conference on Language Resources and Evaluation, Lisbon, Portugal, 24-30.05.2004, (Proceedings). ELRA. Paris (2004) 283-286

Forecasting with a Dynamic Window of Time: The DyFor Genetic Program Model

Neal Wagner[1], Zbigniew Michalewicz[2], Moutaz Khouja[3], and Rob Roy McGregor[4]

[1] Department of Computer Science, University of North Carolina, Charlotte, NC 28223, USA
nwagner@uncc.edu
[2] School of Computer Science, University of Adelaide, Adelaide, SA 5005, Australia,
Institute of Computer Science, Polish Academy of Sciences,
ul. Ordona 21, 01-237 Warsaw, Poland,
and Polish-Japanese Institute of Information Technology,
ul. Koszykowa 86, 02-008 Warsaw, Poland
zbyszek@cs.adelaide.edu.au
[3] Department of Business Information Systems, University of North Carolina,
Charlotte, NC 28223, USA
mjkhouja@email.uncc.edu
[4] Department of Economics, University of North Carolina, Charlotte, NC 28223, USA
rrmcgreg@email.uncc.edu

Abstract. Several studies have applied genetic programming (GP) to the task of forecasting with favourable results. However, these studies, like those applying other techniques, have assumed a static environment, making them unsuitable for many real-world time series which are generated by varying processes. This study investigates the development of a new "dynamic" GP model that is specifically tailored for forecasting in non-static environments. This Dynamic Forecasting Genetic Program (DyFor GP) model incorporates methods to adapt to changing environments automatically as well as retain knowledge learned from previously encountered environments. The DyFor GP model is realised and tested for forecasting efficacy on real-world economic time series, namely the U.S. Gross Domestic Product and Consumer Price Index Inflation. Results show that the DyFor GP model outperforms benchmark models from leading studies for both experiments. These findings affirm the DyFor GP's potential as an adaptive, non-linear model for real-world forecasting applications and suggest further investigations.

1 Introduction

Forecasting is an integral part of everyday life. Businesses, governments, and people alike make, use, and depend on forecasts for a wide variety of concerns. Current methods of time series forecasting require some element of human judgment and are subject to error. When the information to be forecast is well-understood, the error may be within acceptable levels. However, oftentimes the forecasting concern is not well-understood and, thus, methods that require little or no human judgment are desired. Additionally, many forecasting situations are set in environments with continuously shifting conditions. These situations call for methods that can adjust and adapt to the changing surroundings.

L. Bolc et al. (Eds.): IMTCI 2004, LNAI 3490, pp. 205–215, 2005.

The aim of this study is to investigate the development of a new adaptive model that is specifically tailored for forecasting time series produced by non-static environments. The proposed model is based on genetic programming (GP) with additional features that seek to capture such dynamically-changing time series. This Dynamic Forecasting Genetic Program (DyFor GP) model incorporates methods to adapt to changing environments automatically as well as retain knowledge learned from previously encountered environments.

Existing time series forecasting methods generally fall into two groups: classical methods which are based on statistical/mathematical concepts, and modern heuristic methods which are based on emergent algorithms from the field of artificial intelligence. Classical time series forecasting methods can be subdivided into the following categories: exponential smoothing methods, regression methods, autoregressive integrated moving average (ARIMA) methods, threshold methods, and generalised autoregressive conditionally heteroskedastic (GARCH) methods. The first three categories listed above can be considered as linear methods, that is methods that employ a linear functional form for time series modelling, and the last two as non-linear methods.

Most modern heuristic methods which were applied to time series forecasting fall into two major categories: methods based on neural networks (NN), and methods based on evolutionary computation. We can refine the latter category by splitting it further into methods based on genetic algorithms (GA), evolutionary programming (EP), and genetic programming (GP). It is interesting to note that NN, EP, and GP techniques were used to build nonlinear forecasting models, whereas genetic algorithms were primarily used to tune the parameters of some (possibly statistical, linear or nonlinear) forecasting model. All of the methods listed above are motivated by the study of biological processes. NN attempt to solve problems by imitating the mechanism used by the human brain. A NN is a graph-like structure that contains an input layer, zero or more hidden layers, and an output layer. Each layer contains several "neurons" which have weighted connections to neurons of the following layer. A neuron from the input layer holds an input variable. A neuron from the hidden or output layer consists of an "activation" function.

For methods based on evolutionary computation, the process of biological evolution is mimicked in order to solve a problem. After an initial population of potential solutions is created, solutions are ranked based on their "fitness" (i.e., their quality relative to the optimal). New populations are produced by selecting higher-ranking solutions and performing genetic operations of "mating" (crossover) or "mutation" to produce offspring solutions. This process is repeated over many generations until some termination condition is reached. Several applications of NN to forecasting are proffered in [11] while [3,4,5,10] provide examples of evolutionary computation techniques applied to forecasting.

All of the linear forecasting methods listed above assume a functional form which may not be appropriate for many real-world time series. Linear models cannot capture some features that commonly occur in actual data such as asymmetric cycles and occasional outlying observations [8–pp. 433-434]. The non-linear methods above, although capable of characterising such features, assume that the underlying data generating process of the time series is constant. (The linear methods described above also make this assumption.) For actual time series data this assumption is often invalid as shifting environmental conditions may cause the underlying data generating process to change. Additionally, these methods require that the number of historical time series data used for analysis be designated *a priori*. This presents a problem in non-static environments because different segments of the time series may have different underlying data generating processes. For example, a time series representing the daily stock value of a major U.S. airline is likely to have a different underlying process before September 11, 2001 than it does afterwards. If analysed time series data span more than one underlying process, forecasts based on that analysis may be skewed.

Consider the subset of time series data shown in Figure 1. Suppose this represents

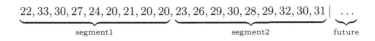

Fig. 1. Time series containing segments with differing underlying processes

the most recent historical data and has been chosen for analysis. Suppose further that the subset consists of two segments each with a different underlying process. The second segment's underlying process represents the current environment and is valid for forecasting future data. The first segment's process represents an older environment that no longer exists. Because both segments are analysed, the forecasting model is distorted unless human judgment is brought to bear. This situation highlights the need for forecasting methods that can automatically determine the correct analysis "window" (i.e., the correct number of historical data to be analysed). This investigation attempts to develop a dynamic forecasting model based on GP that can do just that. Furthermore, this study explores methods that can retain knowledge learned from previously encountered environments.

The rest of this paper is organised as follows: section 2 describes the DyFor GP model, sections 3 and 4 detail experiments involving the DyFor GP model, and section 5 concludes.

2   The DyFor GP Model

An adaptive forecasting model that can handle non-static environments is sought. The desired model would automatically determine the appropriate analysis window (i.e., the number of recent historical data whose underlying data generating process corresponds to current environment). Also, the model should be able to adapt to changing conditions "on-the-fly" (i.e., without the need for halting and restarting the analysis). An additional boon would be the ability to retain useful knowledge from previously encountered environments so that the current setting can be more accurately captured. In this section a discussion of the design of such a model is proffered.

2.1   Natural Adaptation: A Sliding Window of Time

In biological evolution organisms evolve to suit the occurrent conditions of their environment. When conditions shift, successful organisms adapt to the new surroundings.

Over many generations and several environmental shifts, enduring organisms represent highly adaptive solutions that can survive and thrive in a variety of settings. A time series arising from real-world circumstances can be viewed in a similar light. Different segments of the time series may be produced by different underlying data generating processes. Each segment can be thought of as one set of environmental conditions. A successful forecasting model might be seen as an adaptive organism that has evolved through all of the pre-existing environments and gained valuable adaptations (strengths) along the way.

To model this natural adaptation through many environmental settings, a sliding window of time is proposed. For the DyFor GP model, analysis starts at the beginning of the available historical data. Some initial windowsize (number of data observations to analyse) is set and several generations of DyFor GP are run to evolve a population of solutions. Then the data window slides to include the next time series observation. Several generations are run with the new data window and then the window slides again. This process is repeated until all available data have been analysed up to and including the most recent historical data. Figure 2 illustrates this process. In the figure, | marks the

$$22, 33, 30, 27, 24, 20, 21, 20, 20, 23, 26, 29, 30, 28, 29, 32, 30, 31| \ \ldots$$
$$\underbrace{\hspace{7cm}}_{\text{window}-1} \qquad\qquad \underbrace{\quad}_{\text{future}}$$

$$22, 33, 30, 27, 24, 20, 21, 20, 20, 23, 26, 29, 30, 28, 29, 32, 30, 31| \ \ldots$$
$$\underbrace{\hspace{7cm}}_{\text{window}-2} \qquad\qquad \underbrace{\quad}_{\text{future}}$$

$$\bullet$$
$$\bullet$$
$$\bullet$$

$$22, 33, 30, 27, 24, 20, 21, 20, 20, 23, 26, 29, 30, 28, 29, 32, 30, 31 \ | \ \ldots$$
$$\underbrace{\hspace{6cm}}_{\text{window}-i} \qquad \underbrace{\quad}_{\text{future}}$$

Fig. 2. A sliding data analysis window

end of available historical data. The set of several generations run on a single analysis window is referred to as a "dynamic generation." Thus, a single run of the DyFor GP includes several dynamic generations (one for each window slide) on several different consecutive analysis windows.

This sliding window feature allows the DyFor GP to analyse all existing data and take advantage of previously observed patterns. As the window slides through past data, solutions glean useful knowledge making it easier for them to adapt to and predict the current environment.

2.2   Adapting the Analysis Window

As discussed in Section 1, designating the correct size for the analysis window is critical to the success of any forecasting model. Automatic discovery of this windowsize is indispensable when the forecasting concern is not well-understood. With each slide of the window, the DyFor GP adjusts its windowsize dynamically. This is accomplished by using two analysis windows, one a little larger than the other, and noting which produces more accurate forecasts. If the smaller window predicts better, the windowsizes are reduced; if the larger window predicts better, the windowsizes are increased. Thus, at each slide of the analysis window, predictive accuracy is used to determine the direction in which to adjust the windowsize.

Suppose the time series represented by Figure 1 is to be analysed and forecasted using the DyFor GP model. As shown in the figure, this series consists of two segments each with a different underlying process. When the DyFor GP model's two analysis windows are contained inside a single segment (i.e., a stable underlying process is currently in effect), the windowsize is likely to expand because the larger of the two windows contains a greater number of this segment's data and, thus, is likely to better predict future data from this segment. When the DyFor GP model's two analysis windows span both segments (i.e., the underlying process is shifting from an older process to a newer one), the windowsize is likely to contract because the smaller of the two windows contains a smaller number of data from the older segment and, thus, is likely to better predict future data of the newer segment. A detailed discussion of the DyFor GP model's window-adjustment dynamics can be found in [13].

2.3   Retaining and Exploiting Knowledge from Past Environments

A primary objective of time series forecasting is to find a model that accurately represents the current environment and use that model to forecast the future. What if the current environmental conditions resemble those of a prior environment? In such a case, knowledge of this prior environment might be used to capture the current environment with greater speed and/or accuracy than a search that ignores this knowledge. Existing forecasting methods, assuming that the analysis window has been correctly set, do not benefit from knowledge of past environments and, thus, must search for a model of the current environment "from scratch." The sliding window feature (described in Section 2.1) allows the DyFor GP to analyse all historical data and take advantage of knowledge gleaned from previously encountered environments, giving the model search a "head-start." This knowledge comes in the form of adaptations (i.e., solution subtrees) gained by evolution through these previous environments. Past-evolved subtrees are used by the DyFor GP as promising exploration points from which to search for a model that is appropriate for the current environment. In this paper we will refer to such subtrees as "adaptations."

For GP, introns refer to inactive regions of a solution tree, that is solution subtrees which do not affect the fitness [1,2]. Introns allow for retention of past-evolved adaptations through several (possibly non-relevant) environments. When the DyFor GP analyses historical data corresponding to a previous environment, relevant adaptations for that environmant are evolved. These adaptations can then be retained through following environments (even if these environments are dissimilar) by becoming part of intron subtrees. Then, when the DyFor GP model encounters a new environment that is similar to a previous environment, these retained adaptations can be "activated" again by being moved back into active (non-intron) subtrees. Retention and exploitation of past adaptations takes place implicitly as a byproduct of the evolutionary process coupled with the DyFor GP's sliding window of time. For a detailed discussion of this, see [13].

3   Testing the DyFor GP: A Preliminary Experiment

In the previous section the DyFor GP model was presented and its features discussed. The window-adjustment feature of the DyFor GP model is based on intuitions that, although logical, might benefit from some empirical evidence. With this in mind, a preliminary experiment was undertaken. The goal of the preliminary experiment is to test the following DyFor GP window dynamics:

1. windowsize is likely to expand when a time series' underlying data generating process is stable (i.e., when the analysis window is contained inside a single segment) and
2. windowsize is likely to contract when the underlying process shifts (i.e., when the analysis window spans more than one segment).

To allow for these tests, an artificial time series was constructed consisting of three segments, each segment being a small time series generated by a known process. Equation 1 gives the underlying process used to generate the entire time series. Note that this process is a step function defining each of the three segments.

$$f(x) = \begin{cases} \sin(x) + \sqrt{x} & \text{for } 1 \le x \le 20 \text{ (segment 1)}, \\ e^x + 2 & \text{for } 21 \le x \le 40 \text{ (segment 2)}, \\ \sin(x) - \sqrt{x} + 22 & \text{for } 41 \le x \le 60 \text{ (segment 3)}. \end{cases} \tag{1}$$

The time series is constructed using 60 total values, 20 for each segment. Thus, the first 20 values correspond to segment 1 and are generated by evaluating this function for integer values of $x = 1 \ldots 20$, the next 20 values correspond to segment 2 and are generated by evaluating this function for $x = 21 \ldots 40$, and the final 20 values correspond to segment 3 and are generated by evaluating this function for $x = 41 \ldots 60$.

Values of the explanatory variable x are utilised by the DyFor GP as input and outputs generated are one-step-ahead forecasts for $f(x)$. Initial windowsizes for the smaller and larger analysis windows are 4 and 10, respectively and 46 one-step-ahead forecasts are generated that correspond to actual time series values beginning at value #15 and ending at value #60.

Results show that several expansions occurred when the analysis window was focused on segment 1 (time series values 1-20) and when analysis reached time series value #22 the first of several contractions took place. These contractions continued until analysis reached time series value #30 and expansions began again. When the analysis window reached time series value #42, contractions started once again and continued until analysis reached time series value #47, after which only expansions were seen. These expansions/contractions correspond to the three different segments of the time series. Contractions start at time series value #22, only two values after a new underlying process has come into effect. When the analysis window reaches time series value #30, it is entirely contained inside this new segment (segment 2) and expansions begin again. These dynamics are repeated when the analysis window enters and then becomes entirely contained in segment 3 (at time series values #42 and #47, respectively).

These results support the window-adjusting dynamics discussed in section 2. The following section details DyFor GP experiments of a larger scale.

4 Testing the DyFor GP: Full Experiments

The DyFor GP model was implemented and applied to two "real-world" forecasting tasks, forecasting the U.S. Gross Domestic Product (GDP) and the U.S. Consumer Price Index (CPI) Inflation rate.

The GDP is a well-known and widely-used metric that serves as a measure of the nation's economy. A leading contemporary model designed by Kitchen and Monaco [6] forecasts the GDP, a time series with quarterly frequency, using multiple economic indicators that are measured monthly. The idea is to produce a single, one-step-ahead, quarterly GDP forecast by incorporating and analysing the latest monthly indicator values and aggregating their effects.

The real-time forecasting system (RTFS) of Kitchen and Monaco [6] makes use of 30 monthly economic indicators as explanatory variables for the forecasting model. A linear regression model is used to relate an indicator to GDP growth:

$$y_t = \alpha + \beta(L)x_t + e_t, \tag{2}$$

where y_t is the real GDP growth for quarter t at an annualised rate, x_t is an indicator, $\beta(L)$ is a set of coefficients for current and lagged values of the indicator, and e_t is an error term. Each indicator has three separate regression models relating it to GDP growth, one for each (monthly) period of a quarter. When a new month's data for an indicator becomes available, the appropriate regression model is selected and used to produce a forecast for GDP growth that is based only on that indicator. This is repeated for all indicators. Then, all of these single-indicator GDP forecasts are aggregated into one to yield a combined GDP forecast. RTFS generates 1-step-ahead forecasts in a "real-time" fashion, that is each time new data becomes available, the model incorporates this data, updates itself, and produces a new forecast.

The RTFS is used to generate quarterly GDP forecasts when one month, two months, and three months of indicator data are available, respectively. These results are compared to those produced by a linear autoregressive (AR) forecasting model with four lags. Historical data dating back to 1982Q1 is used for analysis and one-step-ahead GDP forecasts are generated for an 8-year range starting with 1995Q1 and ending with 2003Q1. The results of the Kitchen and Monaco study show that the RTFS model outperforms the AR model by a large margin.

The U.S. CPI Inflation rate is a highly-scrutinised economic concern with considerable national impact. The inflation time series has monthly frequency and available historical data exists dating back to 1947. The Philips Curve is a bivariate linear forecasting model that is widely considered as a consistent and accurate predictor of U.S. inflation. Stock and Watson [12] provide a recent study that re-investigates the efficacy of this model, both in its conventional form and in several alternate forms that include various macroeconomic variables. The conventional Philips Curve specification used in their study is meant to forecast inflation over a 12-month period and is given by the following regression model:

$$\pi_{t+h}^h - \pi_t = \phi + \beta(L)u_t + \gamma(L)\Delta\pi_t + e_{t+h}, \tag{3}$$

where $\pi_t^h = \left(\frac{1200}{h}\right) * ln\left(\frac{P_t}{P_{t-h}}\right)$ is the h-period inflation rate ($h = 12$), $\pi_t = (1200) *$ $ln\left(\frac{P_t}{P_{t-h}}\right)$ is the monthly inflation rate, u_t is the unemployment rate, and $\beta(L)$ and $\gamma(L)$ are lag operators specifying 0 to 11 lags. Alternate Philips Curve specifications are constructed by substituting the unemployment rate, u_t, of equation 3 with other macroeconomic variables or indices.

Historical CPI Inflation data dating back to January, 1959 is used for analysis and 12-month horizon forecasts are generated for the period of January, 1970 through September, 1996. Forecasting results are presented for two sub-periods, 1970-1983 and 1984-1996.

The results of the Stock and Watson study show that the Philips Curve in its conventional form outperforms univariate autoregressive models as well as most alternative Philips Curve specifications in which the unemployment rate is replaced by a different economic variable.

4.1   Test Setup

For the GDP experiment, 29 of the 30 economic indicators listed in the Kitchen and Monaco study [6] are utilised as inputs to the DyFor GP model.[1] Outputs are one-step-ahead, quarterly forecasts for the current quarter when only one month of historical data for that quarter is available. Historical GDP data dating back to 1951Q3 is used for analysis and forecasts for 1995Q1 through 2003Q1 are produced.

For the CPI Inflation rate forecasting experiment, the goal is to compare the performance of the conventional Philips Curve specification with that of the DyFor GP model. Therefore, inputs to the DyFor GP model are the same inputs employed by this conventional specification, namely the unemployment rate and past values of the monthly inflation rate. Historical CPI Inflation data dating back to 1950:01 is used for analysis and forecasts for 1970:01 through 1983:12 are produced.

The DyFor GP model requires that a number of parameters be specified before a run. Some of these are general GP parameters commonly found in any GP application. Some of these are special parameters only used by the DyFor GP model. Table 1 gives the general GP parameters and their assigned values while table 2 lists parameters and assigned values that are specific to the DyFor GP model.

The "max. no. of generations" parameter of Table 1 has a slightly different meaning when applied to the DyFor GP model. For DyFor GP it means the maximum number of generations used for one dynamic generation, that is a set of generations run on a single analysis window. Also, the fitness measure used for the CPI Inflation experiment was the mean squared error (MSE) while the mean absolute deviation (MAD) measure was used in the GDP experiment.

In Table 2 parameter "window slide increment" is the number of newer (more recent) historical data to incorporate at each slide of the analysis window. "max windowsize" and "min windowsize" parameters in the table specify the maximum and minimum analysis windowsizes, respectively. The GDP experiment gives values of 80 and 40 which correspond to max/min analysis windowsizes of 20 and 10 years, respectively.

---

[1] One of the indicators, "Business Week Production Index," was not attainable at the time of the experiments.

Table 1. General GP parameter settings

Parameter	Value
crossover rate	0.9
mutation rate	0.1
max. no. of generations	41
termination	max. gens. reached
elitism used?	yes
fitness measure	MSE or MAD
population size	38000 total nodes

Table 2. Specific DyFor GP parameter settings

Parameter	Value (GDP Experiment)	Value (Inflation Experiment)
windowslide increment	1	1
max windowsize	80	240
min windowsize	40	12
start windowsize	54	120
window difference	12	24
window adj. stepsize	1	1

The CPI Inflation experiment gives values of 240 and 12 which correspond to max/min windowsizes of 20 and 1 years, respectively. Parameter "start windowsize" refers to the initial windowsize setting of the smaller of the two windows and parameter "window difference" refers to the size difference between the larger and the smaller window. Parameter "window adj. stepsize" gives the adjustment amount to use when adjusting the size of the windows.

4.2   Results

Competing models of the GDP experiment include the RTFS and AR models of the Kitchen and Monaco study, and the DyFor GP model with parameter specifications listed in Tables 1 and 2. For the CPI Inflation experiment, competing models include the conventional Philips Curve (CPC) specification of equation 3 and the DyFor GP model with parameter specifications as in the GDP experiment. Tables 3 and 4 summarise the results of the GDP and CPI Inflation forecasting experiments, respectively. In the Tables, RMSE is the root mean squared error of forecasts.

Table 3. GDP forecasting results

Forecasting Model	RMSE
RTFS	1.85
AR	2.46
DyFor GP	1.57

Table 4. CPI Inflation forecasting results

Forecasting Model	RMSE
CPC	2.4
DyFor GP	2.3

As seen in Tables 3 and 4 the DyFor GP model outperforms its competitors for both experiments. In the CPI Inflation experiment the margin is small, but for the GDP experiment the margin proves large. This superior performance may be due to the DyFor GP model's ability to capture non-linearities present in the GDP and CPI Inflation time series that are not captured by the competing linear models. The inflation series is considerably more volatile (and, perhaps, noisy) than the GDP series which may make its data generating process more difficult to discover. This may be the reason why the DyFor GP's margin of advantage over competitors is smaller for the inflation experiment as opposed to the GDP experiment.

Other experimental results concerning window behaviour proved interesting as well. In the GDP experiment, the windowsize was initially set at 16.5 years and the best performing runs generally adjusted their windowsize to approximately 14 years. In the Inflation experiment, the windowsize was initially set at 10 years and the best performing runs generally adjusted to approximately 12.5 years.

5   Conclusions and Future Work

In this study the DyFor GP model is developed and tested for forecasting efficacy on two important, real-world economic time series, the U.S. Gross Domestic Product and Consumer Price Index Inflation. Results show that the DyFor GP model outperforms benchmark models from leading studies for both experiments. These findings affirm the DyFor GP's potential as an adaptive, non-linear model for real-world forecasting applications and suggest further investigations. The DyFor GP model presents an attractive forecasting alternative for the following reasons.

1. It is not necessary to specify the functional form of the forecasting model in advance and, thus, a befitting non-linear model, albeit complex, can be automatically discovered.
2. The DyFor GP is an automatically self-adjusting model. Thus, in the presence of a changing environment, it may be able to adapt and predict accurately without human intervention.
3. It can take advantage of a large amount of historical data. Conventional forecasting models require that the number of historical data to be analysed be set a priori. In many cases this means that a large number of historical data is considered to be too old to represent the current data generating process and is, thus, disregarded. This older data, however, may contain information (e.g., patterns) that can be used during analysis to better capture the current process. The DyFor GP model is designed to analyse all historical data, save knowledge of past processes, and exploit this learned knowledge to capture the current process.

4. With greater computing power comes potentially better forecasting performance. The DyFor GP model is essentially a heuristic, fitness-driven random search. As with any random search, when a larger percentage of the search-space is covered, better results can be expected. Greater computational power allows for greater search-space coverage, and DyFor GP forecasting performance can be improved by simply increasing such power. Many other forecasting models cannot be improved in this manner.

Continued development and testing of the DyFor GP model is planned. Future experiments are also planned in which the DyFor GP is applied to other well-known economic time series as well as time series important to other fields of study such as weather-related series, seismic activity, and series arising from biological/medical processes.

All in all, the DyFor GP is an effective model for real-world forecasting applications and may prove to stimulate new advances in the area of time series forecasting.

References

1. Angeline, P.: 'Genetic programming and emergent intelligence.' *Advances in Genetic Programming*, vol. 1 (1994), pp. 75–98
2. Brameier, M., Banzhaf, W.: 'A comparison of linear genetic programming and neural networks in medical data mining.' *IEEE Transactions on Evolutionary Computation*, vol. 5 (2001), pp. 17–26
3. Iba, H., Nikolaev, N., 'Genetic programming polynomial models of financial data series.' *Proceedings of the 2000 Congress of Evolutionary Computation*, vol. 1 (2000), pp. 1459–1466
4. Jeong, B., Jung, H., Park, N.: 'A computerized causal forecasting system using genetic algorithms in supply chain management.' *The Journal of Systems and Software*, vol. 60 (2002), pp. 223–237
5. Kaboudan, M.: 'Forecasting with computer-evolved model specifications: a genetic programming application.' *Computer and Operations Research*, vol. 30 (2003), pp. 1661–1681
6. Kitchen, J., Monaco, R.: 'Real-time forecasting in practice.' *Business Economics: the Journal of the National Association of Business Economists*, vol. 38 (2003), pp. 10–19
7. Koza, J.: *Genetic Programming: On the Programming of Computers by Means of Natural Selection*. MIT Press, 1992
8. Makridakis, S., Wheelwright, S., Hyndman, R.: *Forecasting: methods and applications*. John Wiley and Sons, Inc., 1998
9. Michalewicz, Z.: *Genetic Algorithms + Data Structures = Evolution Programs*. Springer-Verlag, 1992
10. Sathyanarayan, R., Birru, S., Chellapilla, K.: 'Evolving nonlinear time series models using evolutionary programming.' *CECCO 99: Proceedings of the 1999 Congress on Evolutionary Computation*, vol. 1 (1999), pp. 243–253
11. Smith, K., Gupta, J.: *Neural Networks in Business: Techniques and Applications*. Idea Group Pub., 2002
12. Stock, J., Watson, M.: 'Forecasting inflation.' *Journal of Monetary Economics*, vol. 44 (1999), pp. 293–335
13. Wagner, N., Michalewicz, Z., Khouja, M., McGregor, R.: 'Time series forecasting for dynamic environments: the DyFor genetic program model,' *Submitted to IEEE Transactions on Evolutionary Computation*, 2005

A Question Answer System
Using Mails Posted to a Mailing List

Yasuhiko Watanabe, Kazuya Sono, Kazuya Yokomizo, and Yoshihiro Okada

Ryukoku University, Seta, Otsu, Shiga, Japan
watanabe@rins.ryukoku.ac.jp

Abstract. The most serious difficulty in developing a QA system is a lack of knowledge. In this paper, we first discuss three problems of developing a knowledge base by which a QA system answers How-type questions. Then, we propose a method of developing a knowledge base by using mails posted to a mailing list. Next, we describe a QA system which can answer How-type questions based on the knowledge base. Our system finds question mails which are similar to user's question and shows the answers to the user. The similarity between user's question and a question mail is calculated by matching of user's question and a significant sentence in the question mail. Finally, we show that mails posted to a mailing list can be used as a knowledge base by which a QA system answers How-type questions.

1 Introduction

Because of the improvement of NLP, research activities which utilise natural language documents as a knowledge base become popular, such as QA track on TREC [TREC] and NTCIR [NTCIR]. However, these QA systems assumed the user model where the user asks What-type questions and requires just one answer or only a few answers. On the contrary, there are a few QA systems which assumed the user model where the user asks How-type question, in other words, how to do something and how to cope with some problem [Kuro 00] [Kiyota 02]. There are several difficulties in developing a QA system which answers How-type questions, and we focus attention to three problems in this study.

First problem is the difficulty of extracting evidential sentences by which the QA system answers How-type questions. It is not difficult to extract evidential sentences by which the QA system answers What-type questions. For example, question (Q1) is a What-type question and "Naoko Takahashi, a marathon runner, won the gold medal at the Sydney Olympics" is a good evidential sentence for answering question (Q1).

(Q1) Who won the gold medal in women's marathon at the Sydney Olympics?

    (DA1) Naoko Takahashi.

It is possible to extract this evidential sentence from natural language documents by using common content words and phrases because this sentence and question (Q1) have several common content words and phrases. On the contrary, it is difficult to extract evidential sentences for answering How-type questions only by using linguistic cues, such

L. Bolc et al. (Eds.): IMTCI 2004, LNAI 3490, pp. 216–227, 2005.

as common content words and phrases. For example, it is difficult to extract evidential sentences for answering How-type question (Q2) because there may be only a few common content words and phrases between the evidential sentence and question (Q2).

(Q2) How can I cure myself of allergy?
    (DA2) You had better live in a wooden floor.
        (O1) Keep it clean.
        (O2) Your room is always dirty.
    (DA3) Spell the magic word, "chichin-pui!"
        (QR1) I tried, but, no effect.
    (DA4) What is responsible for your disease?
        (QR2) Pollen, maybe.

To solve this problem, [Kuro 00] and [Kiyota 02] proposed methods of collecting knowledge for answering questions from FAQ documents and technical manuals by using the document structure, such as, a dictionary-like structure and if-then format description. However, these kinds of documents require a considerable cost of developing and maintenance. It is important to investigate a method of extracting evidential sentences for answering How-type questions from natural language documents at low cost.

Next problem is wrong information. It is almost inevitable that natural language documents, especially web documents, contain wrong information. For example, (DA3) contains wrong information. As a result, it is important to investigate a method of detecting and correcting wrong information in natural language documents when we develop a knowledge base.

Third problem is imperfect questions. We often ask an imperfect question to others. For example, (Q2) is an imperfect question because there are several causes which are responsible for questioner's allergic disease and information about his allergen is necessary to the proper answers. In this case, the answerer of (DA4) asked the questioner of (Q2) back and made up the imperfect question (Q2). [Kuro 00] pointed out that conversation between an user and the QA system was useful in correcting misspelling and interpreting ambiguous questions. We also think that a QA system should ask the user back when it finds that user's question is imperfect. As a result, it is important to investigate a method of collecting knowledge by which a QA system asks the user back.

To solve these problems, in this paper, we first report a method of developing a knowledge base for a QA system by using mails posted to a mailing list. We have the following advantages when we develop knowledge base by using mails posted to a mailing list:

- It is easy to collect question and answer mails in a specific domain.
- It is possible to extract evidential sentences by which the user can check whether information extracted from the previous mails is true or not. This is because the ML participants often submit mails for correcting wrong information in the previous mails.
- It is possible to collect examples by which the QA system asks the user back for making up user's imperfect questions. This is because, in the ML, the answerer often asks the questioner back for making up the imperfect question.

Then, we describe a QA system: It finds question mails which are similar to user's question and shows the results to the user. The similarity between user's question and a question mail is calculated by matching the user's question and a significant sentence which is extracted from the question mail. Finally, we show that mails posted to a mailing list can be used as the knowledge base by which the QA system answers How-type questions.

2   Mails Posted to a Mailing List

There are mailing lists to which question and answer mails are posted frequently. For example, in Vine Users ML, several kinds of question and answer mails are posted by participants who are interested in Vine Linux [1]. We intended to use these question and answer mails for developing knowledge base for a QA system because

- it is easy to collect question and answer mails in a specific domain,
- it is easy to extract reference relations among mails,
- there is an expectation that information is updated by participants, and
- there is an expectation that wrong information in the previous mails is pointed out and corrected by participants.

However, there is a problem of extracting knowledge from mails posted to a mailing list. As mentioned, it is difficult to extract knowledge for answering How-type questions from natural language documents only by using linguistic cues, such as common content words and phrases. To solve this problem, [Kuro 00] and [Kiyota 02] proposed methods of collecting knowledge from FAQ documents and technical manuals by using the document structure, such as, a dictionary-like structure and if-then format description. However, mails posted to a mailing list, such as Vine Users ML, do not have a firm structure because questions and their answers are described in various ways. Because of no firm structure, it is difficult to extract precise information from mails posted to a mailing list in the same way as [Kuro 00] and [Kiyota 02] did. However, a mail posted to ML generally has a significant sentence. A significant sentence of a question mail has the following features:

1. it often includes nouns and unregistered words which are used in the mail subject.
2. it is often quoted in the answer mails.
3. it often includes the typical expressions, such as
    (a) (*ga / shikasi* (but / however)) + $\cdots$ + *mashita / masen / shouka / imasu* (can / cannot / whether / current situation is) + .
        (ex) *Bluefish de nihongo font ga hyouji deki masen.* (I cannot see Japanese fonts on Bluefish.)
    (b) *komatte / torabutte / goshido / ?* (have trouble / is troubling / tell me / ?)
        (ex) *saikin xstart ga dekinakute komatte imasu* (In these days, I have trouble executing xstart.)
4. it often occurs near the beginning.

---

[1] Vine Linux is a linux distribution with a customized Japanese environment.

Before we discuss the significant sentence in answer mails, we classified answer mails into three types: (1) direct answer (DA) mail, (2) questioner's reply (QR) mail, and (3) the others. Direct answer mails are direct answers to the original question. Questioner's reply mails are questioner's answers to the direct answer mails. Suppose that (Q2) in Section 1 and its answers are question and answer mails posted to a mailing list. In this case, (DA2), (DA3), (DA4) are direct answer mails to (Q2). (QR1) and (QR2) are questioner's reply mails to (DA3) and (DA4), respectively. (O1) and (O2) are the others.

In a direct answer mail, the answerer gives answers to the questioner, such as (DA2) and (DA3). Also, the answerer often asks the questioner back when the question is imperfect, such as (DA4). As a result, significant sentences in direct answer mails can be classified into two types: answer type and question type sentence. They have the following features:

- it often includes the typical expressions, such as,
  - answer type sentence
    * *dekiru / dekinai* (can / cannot)
    * *shita / shimashita / shiteimasu / shiteimasen* (did / have done / doing / did not do)
    * *shitekudasai / surebayoi* (please do / had better)
  - question type sentence
    * *masuka / masenka / desuka* (did you / did not you / do you)
- it is often quoted in the following mails.
- it often occurs after and near to the significant sentence of the question mail if it is quoted.

In a questioner's reply mail, the questioner shows the results, conclusions, and gratitude to the answerers, such as (QR1), and sometimes points out wrong information in a direct answer mail and correct it, such as (QR2). A significant sentence in a questioner's reply has the following features:

- it often includes the typical expressions.
  - *dekita / dekimasen* (could / could not)
  - *arigatou* (thank)
- it often occurs after and near to the significant sentence of the direct answer mail if it is quoted.

Taking account of these features, we think, it is possible to extract significant sentences from question, direct answer, and questioner's reply mails by using surface clues. Furthermore, by using the extracted significant sentences, the system can answer the user's questions or, at least, give a good hint to the user. In the next section, we will explain how to extract significant sentences from mails by using surface clues.

3   Significant Sentence Extraction from Mails Posted to ML

Significant sentences are extracted from question mails, direct answer mails , and questioner's reply mails in the next way.

step 1 extract question mails, direct answer mails, and questioner's reply mails by using reference relations and sender's email address.

step 2 extract sentences from each mail by detecting periods and blank lines.

step 3 check each sentence whether it is quoted in the following mails.

step 4 calculate the significant score of each sentence in a question mail by applying the next four rules. Then, the sentence which has the largest score is selected as the significant sentence in the question mail.

> **rule 4–1:** give 1 point to sentences which include nouns or unregistered words which are used in the mail subject.
>
> **rule 4–2:** a rule for typical expressions. Give points to sentences which include typical expressions below.
>
> > – give 2 point to sentences which include the expression, such as,
> > *ga / shikashi* (but) + · · · + *mashita / masen / shouka / imasu* (can / cannot / whether / current situation is) + .
> > (ex) *install ha buji shuryo suru no desu ga* (The program was installed without accident, <u>but</u>), *X window ga tachiagari <u>masen</u>* (we <u>could not</u> start up X window).
> > or give 1 point to sentences which include the expression below.
> > *mashita / masen / shouka / imasu* (can / cannot / whether / current situation is) + .
> > (ex) *kinput2 ga tsukae <u>masen</u>* (I <u>cannot</u> use kinput2).
> > – give 1 point to sentences which include *komatte, trabutte, goshidou,* or *?* (have trouble / is troubling / tell me / ?).
> > (ex) *HDD ga ninshiki shinaide <u>komatte</u> imasu* (I <u>have trouble</u> accessing HDD). [2]
>
> **rule 4–3:** give 1 point to sentences which are quoted most frequently in the answer mails.
>
> **rule 4–4:** when two or more sentences have the largest score by applying rule 4–1, 4–2, and 4–3, give 1 point to the sentence which is the nearest to the lead.

step 5 calculate the significant score of each sentence in a direct answer mail by applying the next three rules. Then, the sentence which has the largest score is selected as the significant sentence in the direct answer mail.

> **rule 5–1:** a rule for typical expressions. Give 1 point to sentences which include the expressions, such as,
>
> > – · · · + *dekiru / dekinai* (can / cannot) + .
> > – · · · + *shita / shimashita / shiteimasu / shiteimasen* (did / have done / am doing / did not do) + .
> > – · · · + *shite(mite)kudasai / surebayoi* (please do / had better) + .
> > – · · · + *masuka / masenka / desuka* (did you / did not you / do you) + .
>
> **rule 5–2:** give 1 point to sentences which are quoted most frequently in the questioner's reply mails.

---

[2] This sentence includes two typical expressions, *komatte* and *imasu*. As a result, 2 points are given to this sentence by rule 4-2.

Table 1. Results of significant sentence extraction

type	correct extraction	incorrect extraction	total
Q	96	31	127
DA	153	31	184
QR	45	30	75

rule 5–3: when two or more sentences have the largest score by applying rule 5–1 and 5–2, (1) give 1 point to the sentence which is located after and the nearest to the significant sentence in the question mail if it is quoted, or (2) give 1 point to the sentence which is the nearest to the lead.

step 6 calculate the significant score of each sentence in a questioner's reply mail by applying the next two rules. Then, the sentence which has the largest score is selected as the significant sentence in the questioner's reply mail.

rule 6–1: a rule for typical expressions. Give 1 point to sentences which include the expressions, such as,

- $\cdots$ + *dekita / dekimasen* (could / could not) + .
- $\cdots$ + *arigatou* (thank) + .

rule 6–2: when two or more sentences have the largest score by applying rule 6–1, (1) give 1 point to the sentence which is located after and the nearest to the significant sentence in the direct answer mail if it is quoted, or (2) give 1 point to the sentence which is the nearest to the lead.

For evaluating our method, we selected 149 examples of question and answer in Vine Users ML. From these 149 examples, we removed 22 examples because in these 22 cases the senders made no questions and gave some news, notices, and reports to the participants.

First, we examined whether the results of significant sentence extraction were good or not. The results are shown in Table 1. The reasons of the failures were as follows:

- there were many significant sentences which did not include the clue expressions,
- there were many sentences which were not significant sentences but included the clue expressions,
- problems or answers were described in several sentences and one of them was extracted, and
- misspelling.

Next, we examined whether these significant sentences were helpful in choosing and accessing information for solving problems. Our QA system put the significant sentences in reference order, such as,

(Q3) *vedit ha, sonzai shinai file wo hirakou to suru to core wo haki masuka.* (Does vedit terminate when we open a new file?)
   (DA5) *hai, core dump shimasu.* (Yes, it terminates.)
   (DA6) *shourai, GNOME ha install go sugu tsukaeru no desu ka?* (In near future, can I use GNOME just after the installation?)

Then, we examined whether

- there were connections between sentences or not, and
- the user can easily choose and access information for solving problems.

For example, (Q3) and (DA5) have the same topic, however, (DA6) has a different topic. In this case, (DA5) is a good answer to question (Q3). The user can access the document from which (DA5) was extracted and obtain more detailed information. As a result, this case was determined as correct.

In this experiment, 92 cases were determined as correct and 35 cases were failures. The reasons of the failures were as follows:

- wrong significant sentences extracted from question mails (21 cases), and
- wrong significant sentences extracted from direct answer mails (14 cases).

There was no failure which was caused by wrong significant sentence extracted from questioner's reply mails. Failures which were caused by wrong significant sentences extracted from question mails were not serious. This is because there is not much likelihood of matching user's question and wrong significant sentence extracted from question mails. On the other hand, failures which were caused by wrong significant sentences extracted from direct answer mails were serious. In these cases, significant sentences in the question mails were successfully extracted and there is likelihood of matching user's question and the significant sentence extracted from question mails. Therefore, the precision of the significant sentence extraction was emphasised in this task.

We discuss some example sets of significant sentences in detail (Figure 1). Question (Q4) in Figure 1 has two answers, (DA7) and (DA8). (DA7) is a suggestion to the questioner of (Q4) and (DA8) explains answerer's experience. The point to be noticed is (QR3). It guarantees the information quality of (DA7) and lets the user choose and access the answer mail from which (DA7) was extracted.

In example (Q5) and (Q6), the imperfect questions were made up by the significant sentences extracted from the direct answer mails. (Q5) is imperfect question because the questioner did not mention what program he used when he was creating partitions. Then, the answerer of (DA9) asked the questioner of (Q5) back for making up the imperfect question. Finally, (DA9) let the users who used 'diskdruid' choose and access the document from which (DA9) was extracted and let the others choose and access the document from which (DA10) was extracted. (Q6) was also an imperfect question because there was no information about what program the user wanted. The answerer of (DA11) did not ask the questioner of (Q6) back, but (DA11) made up the imperfection of (Q6). In this experiment, we found 25 cases where the imperfect questions were made up by the siginificant sentences extracted from the direct answer mails, and determined these examples as correct.

Example (Q7) is an interesting example. (DA12) which was extracted from a direct answer mail has wrong information. Then, the questioner of (Q7) checked whether the given information was helpful or not and posted (QR4) in order to correct the wrong information in (DA12). In this experiment, we found 4 cases where the questioners posted reply mails in order to correct the wrong information.

(Q4) *sound no settei de komatte imasu.* (I have much trouble in setting sound configuration.)
  (DA7) *mazuha, sndconfig wo jikkou shitemitekudasai.* (First, please try 'sndconfig'.)
    (QR3) *kore de umaku ikimashita.* (I did well.)
  (DA8) *sndconfig de, shiawase ni narimashita.* (I tried 'sndconfig' and became happy.)

(Q5) *partition settei ji ni SCSI disk ga hyouji sarenai node, install deki masen.* (I cannot complete the installation because the SCSI disk was not found when I was creating partitions.)
  (DA9) *e-to, "partition settei ji ni SCSI disk ga hyouji sarenai" toiunoha diskdruid deno hanashi de syouka.* (Hum, did you use 'diskdruid' for creating partitions?)
  (DA10) *typical problems ni kaitearu mondai jya naidesyouka.* (I think this problem is mentioned in 'typical problems'.)

(Q6) *1.0.6 no patch ha ari masuka?* (Is there a patch for version 1.0.6 ?)
  (DA11) *gtk+-1.0.4 wo riyou suru houga ii desyou.* (You had better use gtk+-1.0.4.)

(Q7) *ES1868 no sound card wo tsukatte imasu ga, oto ga ookisugite komatte imasu.* (My trouble is that sound card ES1868 makes a too loud noise.)
  (DA12) *doumo epag300 no mondai no you desu.* (I think it is caused by epag300.)
    (QR4) *epag no mondai deha ari masen.* (epag is not resemble for this trouble.)

(Q8) *ikutsuka mondai ga ari masu ga, kono ken no report ha doko ni okureba iino desuka.* (I have some problems, where do I submit a question?)
  (DA13) *kono ML de kamai masen.* (To this ML.)

(Q9) *kore ha douiu imi desuka.* (What does it mean)
  (DA14) *chan to shitsumon shinaito, dare mo kotae rare masen.* (ask a question properly, or no one answers.)

Fig. 1. Examples of the significant sentence extraction

Example (Q8) and (Q9) are general questions and their answers. These examples show that our method is general and independent of any specific domains. We intend to apply our method to other ML. We may note that (DA14) is impolite and we are afraid that these kinds of answers give the user a disincentive to use our QA system.

4   QA System Using Mails Posted to a Mailing List

4.1   Outline of the QA System

A user can ask a question to the system in a natural language. Then, the system retrieves similar questions from mails posted to a mailing list, and shows the user the significant sentences which were extracted listing the similar question and their answer mails. The system consists of the following modules:

User Interface. Users can access to the system via a WWW browser by using CGI based HTML forms.

QA Processor. It consists of input analyser and similarity calculator.

Input analyser transforms user's question into a dependency structure by using JUMAN[Kuro 98] and KNP[Kuro 94]. Furthermore, it checks whether each content word in user's question is used in the mails posted to Vine Users ML. Similarity calculator calculates the similarity between the user question and a significant sentence in a question mail posted to a mailing list by comparing their content words and dependency trees. The similarity calculation is described in Section 4.2

Knowledge Base. It consists of

- question and answer mails (50846 mails),
- significant sentences (26334 sentences: 8964, 13094, and 4276 sentences were extracted from question, direct answer, and questioner's reply mails, respectively), and
- synonym dictionary (519 words).

4.2   Matching of User Question and Significant Sentence

Matching of the user question and a significant sentence is done by comparing their content words and dependency trees. The similarity is calculated in the following way.

The elements of set T_i $(i = 1 \cdots N)$ are content words in significant sentence S_i which is selected from question mail M_i. The weight of content word t in significant sentence S_i of question mail M_i is:

$$w_{WORD}(t, M_i) = tf(t, S_i) \log \frac{N}{df(t)}$$

where $tf(t, S_i)$ denotes the number of times content word t occurs in significant sentence S_i, N denotes the number of significant sentences, and $df(t)$ denotes the number of significant sentences in which content word t occurs.

The elements of set T'_Q are content words which occur in user's question Q and their synonyms. Then, we introduce the function $f_{WORD}(t, T'_Q)$ which returns 1 when set T_Q contains content word t, otherwise returns 0:

$$f_{WORD}(t, T'_Q) = \begin{cases} 1 \text{ if } t \in T'_Q \\ 0 \text{ otherwise} \end{cases}$$

Therefore, the total weight of content words which occur in user's question Q and significant sentence S_i of question mail M_i, $SCORE_{WORD}(Q, M_i)$, is:

$$SCORE_{WORD}(Q, M_i) = \sum_{t \in T_i} f_{WORD}(t, T'_Q) w_{WORD}(t, M_i)$$

The elements of set L_i are modifier-head relations in significant sentence S_i which is selected from question mail M_i. The weight of modifier-head relation l in set L_i of question mail M_i is:

$$w_{LINK}(l, M_i) = w_{WORD}(modifier(l), M_i) + w_{WORD}(head(l), M_i)$$

where $modifier(l)$ and $head(l)$ denote modifier and head of modifier-head relation l, respectively.

The elements of set L'_Q are modifier-head relations in user's question Q and those in which the modifier and/or head are replaced by their synonyms. Then, we introduce the function $f_{LINK}(l, L'_Q)$ which return 1 when set L'_Q contains modifier-head relation l, otherwise return 0:

$$f_{LINK}(l, L'_Q) = \begin{cases} 1 \text{ if } l \in L'_Q \\ 0 \text{ otherwise} \end{cases}$$

Therefore, the total weight of modifier-head relations which are extracted from user's question Q and significant sentence S_i of question mail M_i, $SCORE_{LINK}(Q, M_i)$, is:

$$SCORE_{LINK}(Q, M_i) = \sum_{l \in L_i} f_{LINK}(l, L'_Q)w_{LINK}(l, M_i)$$

Therefore, the similarity score between user's question Q and significant sentence S_i of question mail M_i, $SCORE(Q, M_i)$, is:

$$SCORE(Q, M_i) = SCORE_{WORD}(Q, M_i) + SCORE_{LINK}(Q, M_i)$$

4.3 Evaluation

For evaluating our method, we developed a knowledge base by using 50846 question mails posted to Vine Users ML. Figure 2 shows 32 questions which were given to the system for the evaluation. These questions were based on question mails posted to Linux Users ML. The result of our method was evaluated

Test 1 by examined first answer
Test 2 by examined first three answers
Test 3 by examined first five answers

The answer of our QA system were the significant sentences which were extracted from one question mail and its direct answer and questioner's reply mails and were put in reference order. The result of our method was compared with the result of full text retrieval. In Figure 3, (a) shows the number of questions which got the correct answer, and (b) shows the number of correct answers.

In Test 1, our system answered question 2, 6, 7, 8, 13, 14, 15, 19, and 24. In contrast, the full text retrieval system answered question 2, 5, 7, 19, and 32. Both system answered question 2, 7 and 19, however, the answers were different. This is because several solutions of a problem are often sent to a mailing list and the systems found different but proper answers. In all the tests, the results of our method were better than those of full text retrieval. Our system answered more questions and found more proper answers than the full text retrieval system did. Furthermore, it is much easier to choose and access information for solving problems by using the answers of our QA system than by using the answers of the full text retrieval system.

Both systems could not answer question 4, "Tell me how to restore HDD partition to its normal condition". However, the full text retrieval systems found an answer in which the way of saving files on a broken HDD partition was mentioned. Interestingly, this answer may satisfy a questioner because, in such cases, our desire is to save files on the broken HDD partition. Our system found the same answer, however, could not

(1) I cannot get IP address again from DHCP server.

(2) I cannot make a sound on Linux.

(3) I have a problem when I start up X Window System.

(4) Tell me how to restore HDD partition to its normal condition.

(5) Where is the configuration file for giving SSI permission to Apache ?

(6) I cannot login into proftpd.

(7) I cannot input kanji characters.

(8) Please tell me how to build a Linux router with two NIC cards.

(9) CGI cannot be executed on Apache 1.39.

(10) The timer gets out of order after the restart.

(11) Please tell me how to show error messages in English.

(12) NFS server does not go.

(13) Please tell me how to use MO drive.

(14) Do you know how to monitor traffic load on networks.

(15) Please tell me how to specify kanji code on Emacs.

(16) I cannot input \ on X Window System.

(17) Please tell me how to extract characters from PDF files.

(18) It takes me a lot of time to login.

(19) I cannot use lpr to print files.

(20) Please tell me how to stop making a backup file on Emacs.

(21) Please tell me how to acquire a screen shot on X window.

(22) Can I boot linux without a rescue disk?

(23) Pcmcia drivers are loaded, but, a network card is not recognized.

(24) I cannot execute PPxP.

(25) I am looking for FTP server in which I can use chmod command.

(26) I do not know how to create a Makefile.

(27) Please tell me how to refuse the specific user login.

(28) When I tried to start Webmin on Vine Linux 2.5, the connection to local-host:10000 was denied.

(29) I have installed a video capture card in my DIY machine, but, I cannot watch TV programs by using xawtv.

(30) I want to convert a Latex document to a Microsoft Word document.

(31) Can you recommend me an application for monitoring resources?

(32) I cannot mount a CD-ROM drive.

Fig. 2. 32 questions which were given to the system for the evaluation

	Test 1		Test 2		Test 3	
	(a)	(b)	(a)	(b)	(a)	(b)
our method	9	9	16	26	17	41
full text retrieval	5	5	5	9	8	15

(a) the number of questions which
is given the correct answer

(b) the number of proper answers

Fig. 3. Results of finding a similar question by matching of user's question and a significant sentence

rank it within first five answers. In this way, it often happens that there are gaps between what a questioner wants to know and the answer, in several aspects, such as concreteness, expression and assumption. To overcome the gaps, it is important to investigate a dialogue system which can communicate with the questioner.

References

[TREC]   TREC (Text REtrieval Conference) : http://trec.nist.gov/
[NTCIR]   NTCIR (NII-NACSIS Test Collection for IR Systems) project:
            http://research.nii.ac.jp/ntcir/index-en.html
[Kuro 00]   Kurohashi and Higasa: Dialogue Helpsystem based on Flexible Matching of User
            Query with Natural Language Knowledge Base, 1st ACL SIGdial Workshop on
            Discourse and Dialogue, (2000)
[Kiyota 02] Kiyota, Kurohashi, and Kido: "Dialog Navigator" A Question Answering System
            based on Large Text Knowledge Base, 19th COLING, (2002)
[Kuro 94]   Kurohashi and Nagano: A syntactic analysis method of laong Japanese sentences
            based on the detection of conjuctive structures, Computational Linguistics, 20
            (4), pp. 507–534, (1994)
[Kuro 98]   Kurohashi and Nagano: JUMAN Manual version 2.6 (in Japanese), Nagao Lab.,
            Kyoto University, (1998)

Towards Extracting Emotions from Music

Alicja A. Wieczorkowska

Polish-Japanese Institute of Information Technology,
ul. Koszykowa 86, 02-008 Warsaw, Poland
alicja@pjwstk.edu.pl

Abstract. In recent years, there has been a tremendous need for the ability to query and process vast quantities of musical data. Automatic content extraction is clearly needed here, relating to various aspects of music. One of desirable options is the ability of identifying musical pieces representing different types of emotions, which music clearly evokes. This paper focuses on scrupulous planning of experiments on automatic recognition of emotions in music. Collecting and labelling of data, extraction of objective features, as well as classification and cross-validation methods are proposed and discussed.

1 Introduction

Music is a subjective quality, related to culture, and can be defined in various ways. For instance, as an artistic form of auditory communication incorporating instrumental or vocal tones in a structured and continuous manner [34], or as the art of combining sounds of voices or instruments to achieve beauty of form and expression of emotion [5].

The experience of music listening can be considered within three levels of human emotion [12]:

- autonomic level,
- denotative (connotative) level, and
- interpretative (critical) level.

The relationship of the listeners and the music is manifold. Music is heard by the listener [14]:

- as sound, therefore, when people listen to music, the constant monitoring of auditory stimuli still works,
- as human utterance, since humans have ability to communicate and detect emotion in vocal utterances,
- in context of knowledge, thoughts and environment, which can contribute to an emotional experience,
- as narrative integrated sounds and utterances

Studies on emotions have been carried out for many centuries, including research on various levels and aspects of music perception. Recent studies focus both on cognitive

L. Bolc et al. (Eds.): IMTCI 2004, LNAI 3490, pp. 228–238, 2005.

and neurophysiological aspects of emotions such as auditory disgust and pleasure responses, intrinsic and expressive emotions, expectation, and personality correlates [12].

Emotions are an inherent part of music and their role cannot be overvalued. Research on this topic is interdisciplinary, relating to music emotion and psychology, philosophy, musicology, and also biology, anthropology, and sociology. Emotions can be communicated via musical structures, and they also affect performance [13].

Data labelling for classification of emotions can be performed using a specified set of adjectives, and a group of a few adjectives may be applied to label a single class. For instance, the following labelling was used in experiments by Li and Ogihara [15]:

- cheerful, gay, happy,
- fanciful, light,
- delicate, graceful,
- dreamy, leisurely,
- longing, pathetic,
- dark, depressing,
- sacred, spiritual,
- dramatic, emphatic,
- agitated, exciting,
- frustrated,
- mysterious, spooky,
- passionate,
- bluesy.

Emotions can be represented in multidimensional space, for instance in 2 dimensions, on activation vs. quality plane. Example of such a space is shown in Figure 1 [17]. Most common representation is based on two dimensions:

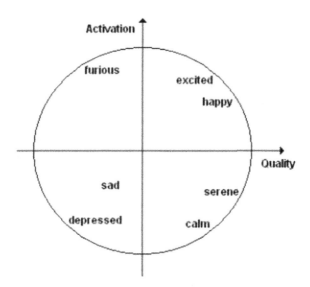

Fig. 1. Emotions represented in Activation vs. Quality space

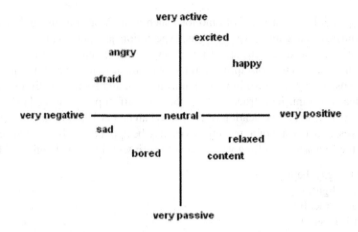

Fig. 2. Examples of emotions in arousal/pleasure plane. Arousal values range from very passive to very active, pleasure values range from very negative to very positive.

– valence, with axis expanding from *happiness* to *sadness*, and
– arousal (activation), ranging from *aroused* to *sleepy*.

Generally, human emotions can be represented in three-dimensional emotional space, with the following axes:

– arousal,
– pleasure (evaluation), and
– power.

Arousal describes the degree of intensity, ranging from passive to active, the pleasure ranges from negative to positive values describing how pleasant is this perception, and the power dimension relates to the sense of control over the emotional state. Examples of emotions in arousal/pleasure plane are shown in Figure 2 [25].

Our goal is to extract parameters from music files that allow labelling music with emotion, along axes described above, or using the appropriate descriptive adjectives.

Research on automatic detection of emotions in music has not been performed until recently. Firstly, automatic extraction of emotions from speech was investigated [17]. Detection of emotions from music data was performed by Li and Ogihara [15], with labelling of classes by means of adjectives. Altogether, thirteen classes were singled out and labelled using one, two, or three adjectives for each class.

2   Music Data Analysis for Extracting Emotions

Although music emotions are very subjective, some impressions are shared by all the audience. We assume that such features as liveliness, sadness or joy are perceived similarly in all cultures. These emotions can be expressed in music even when the music is automatically synthesised from scores, thus generating human-like expressive performances by artificial means [16]. On the other hand, signal parameters based on the time domain, spectrum, and evolution of sound features may be used to extract information on emotions from the recorded expressive performances. Also MIDI files can be used to extract information on emotions that a given piece of music may evoke. Amplitude values or the speed how the key is depressed in the synthesiser may indicate activation and power. Another cue is an absolute and relative length of musical events (notes). KDD methods applied to representative examples of music annotated with emotions can be used to find the correspondence between physical and emotional sound features, and to create a tool for automatic annotation of music files and searching for the desired emotions in music.

3   Features for Description of Audio Data

Various features can be applied to describe properties of audio signal. Most common ones include [20], [21], [24], [27], [30], [31], [33]:

- RMS features, i.e. root mean square of amplitude of the signal,
- zero-crossing rate, i.e. the number of time-domain zero-crossings within an analysis frame,
- loudness, approximated by signal's root mean-square level (in decibels),
- pitch; can be estimated via Fourier spectra (the best method is finding greatest common divisor of frequencies peak amplitudes), or from time domain (using AMDF function, i.e. searching for minimum of average magnitude differences) or via other methods,
- brightness, i.e. centroid of the short-time fourier magnitude spectra,
- harmonicity, which allows distinguishing between harmonic and inharmonic spectra,
- bandwidth, computed as the magnitude weighted average of the differences between the spectral components and the centroid,
- spectral statistical moments,
- spectral flux, comparing magnitude of spectrum of successive frames,
- mel-frequency cepstral coefficients, i.e. coefficient of cepstral analysis in perceptually motivated mel scale,
- linear prediction coefficients, which are used in speech processing as an estimate of the vocal tract, considered as filter altering periodic or noise excitation,
- spectral roll-off, indicating the frequency below which a certain amount of the power spectrum resides; it is calculated by summing up the power spectrum samples until the threshold amount of the total energy is reached

and so on.

One of more significant applications of audio signal processing is speech domain; many features applied to general audio come from speech processing. Automatic recognition of emotion in speech is easier to implement, at least because such emotions are more unequivocal than in case of music. The features used for detecting emotions in speech signal include [6], [25]:

- mean, median, standard deviation, minimum, maximum, and range of voiced pitch signal,

- pitch for the first and last voiced frame,
- slope of pitch contour,
- pitch derivative statistics,
- speaking rate, i.e. average number of syllables per second,
- intervals,
- maximum and minimum pitch position,
- regression coefficients, and mean square error for regression coefficients,
- energy parameters: maximum, maximum and minimum positions, mean, regression coefficients, and mean square error for regression coefficients,
- durational aspects: number and ratio of voiced and unvoiced regions and frames, longest voiced and unvoiced region.

For music signal description, more advanced features can be derived, describing:

- timbral texture,
- rhythmic content,
- pitch content.

4   Automatic Classification of Sound Data

Classification of audio data has already been performed in various research, for instance regarding classification of a type of a signal [1], [28], [29], speech signal classification [8], or musical instrument sound classification [18], [31]. K-nearest neighbours (k-NN) algorithm is most commonly used as classifiers, and also Gaussian mixture model (GMM), and recently also Support Vector Machines (SVM) [4], [19]. In k-NN the class for a tested sample is assigned on the basis of the distances between the vector of parameters for this sample and the majority of k nearest vectors representing known samples. In the Gaussian mixture model classifier, each class probability density function is assumed to consist of a mixture of a specific number of multidimensional Gaussian distributions, whose parameters are estimated using the training set. Gaussian classifier is a typical parametric statistical classifier, assuming a particular form for the class probability density functions. SVM is a classification technique, and it will be explained more descriptively below.

In the simplest case SVM separates a training set of instance-label pairs (x_i, y_i), $i = 1, \ldots, l$, $x_i \in R^n$, $y \in \{1, -1\}$ (binary classification case) with a hyperplane $\langle w, x \rangle + b = 0$, where parameters w and b are subject to the following constraint [9]

$$\min_i |\langle w, x_i \rangle| = 1$$

Binary classification can be easily generalised to any number of classes by discerning any single class from the rest of objects.

The set of vectors is said to be optimally separated by the hyperplane if it is separated without error and the distance between the closest vector to the hyperplane is maximal. Linearly separable classes, learned via SVM algorithm, are presented in Figure 3 [9].

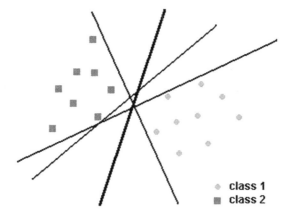

Fig. 3. Separation of 2 linearly separable classes using SVM

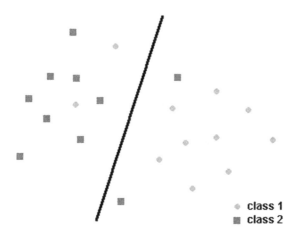

Fig. 4. Separation of 2 classes using SVM when the classes are not linearly separable

Generalised version of SVM classification when the training data are not linearly separable is presented in Figure 4 [9]. Generalised optimal separating hyperplane minimises the following:

$$\min_{w,b,\xi} 0.5 w^T w + C \sum_{i=1}^{l} \xi_i$$

and is subject to the constraint as below:

$$y_i(w^T \phi(x_i) + b) \geq 1 - \xi_i$$

where ξ_i is a measure of misclassification errors (to be minimised), and $C > 0$ is a penalty parameter.

The main idea behind SVM is that training vectors x_i are mapped into a higher dimensional space by the function ϕ. Functions $K(x_i, x_j)$ defined as

$$K(x_i, x_j) \equiv \phi(x_i^T)\phi(x_j)$$

are called kernel functions. Most commonly used kernel functions are listed below [11]:

- linear: $K(x_i, x_j) = x_i^T x_j$,
- polynomial: $K(x_i, x_j) = (\gamma x_i^T x_j + r)^d$, where $\gamma > 0$,
- radial basis function (RBF): $K(x_i, x_j) = \exp(-\gamma||x_i - x_j||^2)$, where $\gamma > 0$,
- sigmoid: $K(x_i, x_j) = \tanh(\gamma x_i^T x_j + r)$,

  where γ, r, and d are kernel parameters.

5   Setup for Experiment of Classifying Emotions in Music

The classifiers mentioned above can be used in the research on automatic detection of emotions in music audio data. Since assignment of emotions to a music piece is a challenging task itself, the research on classifying music excerpts with respect to their emotional contents requires a very careful preparation. Preparing setup of this research is a main topic of this paper.

The first problem involves labelling the data. The emotions elicited by music are very subjective and dependent on cultural context. Additionally, if the data are labelled by a few subjects, the labelling may differ. Therefore, multiple labels can be applied to the same audio sample. One of possible solutions is to work with a single subject, and enforce single labelling, i.e. assignment of each sample into a single class, possibly with a few adjectives labelling the classes. This solution was applied by Li and Ogihara [15]. However, in order to take into account wider range of emotions brought about by music, the experiment should allow multiple experts, and multiple labelling, i.e. assignment of the same sample into multiple classes, if experts decide so. The labelling should be performed within negative-positive vs. active-passive space, with values ranging from -5 to 5 for each axis. Additionally, adjective labels should be available available for subjects preferring such a way of labelling, including the following adjectives:

- Active, Passive,
- Negative, Positive,
- Pleasant, Unpleasant,
- Afraid,
- Agitated,
- Amused,
- Angry,
- Bad,
- Bored,
- Calm,
- Content,

– Disgusted,
– Fearful,
– Good,
– Excited,
– Happy,
– Relaxed,
– Sad.

The next issue to consider is collecting the data. Since a huge amount of audio samples are available in the Internet, collecting of data is the relatively the easiest stage of the experiment. Especially music pieces in MP3 format are abundantly available for a free download, see for instance [10], [22], [23], [26], [32], to mention Polish web sites only. The chunks for labelling should be limited to a few seconds (say 6 s) for a few reasons. Firstly, the mood of the piece of music may change, so the excerpts should be limited to such an extent that the emotions within any given excerpts stay approximately constant. Also, the user will probably check only a short piece of music. Secondly, the analyses will be faster to perform on shorter audio samples. Finally, the use of short samples will not infringe copyright law in any future works with these data. The database big enough should be created, i.e. each class should have at least 2-3 dozens of representant samples. Therefore, a collection of a few hundred excerpts should be gathered.

For feature extraction, short analysing frame should be used, in order to allow extraction of such parameters as pitch, and finally possibly a melody as a sequence of frequency values. 25 ms analyzing frame is suggested, since frame of length about 20-30 ms is commonly used in parameterisation for timbre recognition purposes [2], [3], [7]. In order to observe timbre properties of the analysed pieces of music, the following features should be calculated and placed in the feature vector:

– energy parameters: maximum, minimum, mean, maximum and minimum positions,
– range and standard deviation of pitch of the loudest signal, maximal and minimal pitch position, pitch for the first and last frame, slope of pitch contour, intervals,
– harmonicity, spectral centroid, moments, and flux,
– mel-frequency cepstral coefficients.

As for classification techniques, SVM and k-NN should be used. The audio samples represented by feature vectors and labelled by listeners will be used as the data for training and testing of the classifiers. Validation of results can be performed with division of the data base into 5 randomly chosen parts, and 5 train-and-test experiments should be done. In each experiment, one fifth of the data is removed from the data set and used for testing of the classifier trained of the remaining part of the data. The average of the obtained results describes the accuracy of the classifiers.

The final goal of the experiment described above is to find dependencies between objective sound parameters and subjective, emotional values, assigned by the listeners.

6 Summary

Automatic content extraction may relate to many different types of semantic information related to musical pieces. Some information can be stored as metadata provided by experts, but some has to be computed in an automatic way. Observation of basic features of music signal may aid extraction of information on emotions from the recorded excerpts, allowing identification of the segments of audio containing high level semantic information.

The experiments on automatic detection of emotions in music must take into account all aspects of perceiving emotions in music. Thus, data collection must contain pieces representing various types of emotions. For these data, subjective labelling by subjects must be performed. Feature extraction should allow discernment between particular classes, representing emotions related to the music pieces described by these features. Training of classifiers, i.e. K-NN and SVM should associate subjective emotion labels to the data representing objective, machine-extracted sound features. Cross-validation tests the quality and usefulness of the classifiers and the features as well.

Main difficulty related to automatic detection of emotions in music is subjective perception of emotions in music. Therefore, the first goal of this research is to discover relationships between subjective and objective music description. Tools to be applied include objective sound parameterisation, subjective labelling, and classification tools.

References

1. Burred, J.J., Lerch, A.: "Hierarchical Automatic Audio Signal Classification", J. Audio Eng. Soc., Vol. 52, No. 7/8, 2004, 724–739
2. Batlle, E., Cano, P.: "Automatic Segmentation for Music Classification using Competitive Hidden Markov Models", Proceedings of International Symposium on Music Information Retrieval. Plymouth, MA, 2000. Available at http://www.iua.upf.es/mtg/publications/ismir2000-eloi.pdf
3. Brown, J.C., Houix, O., McAdams, S.: "Feature dependence in the automatic identification of musical woodwind instruments", J. Acoust. Soc. of America 109, 2001, 1064–1072
4. Cano, P., Koppenberger, M., Le Groux, S., Ricard, J., Wack N., Herrera, P.: "Nearest-neighbor generic sound classication with a WordNet-based taxonomy", 116th Audio Engineering Society Convention, May 2004, Berlin, Germany, Convention Paper 6139. Available at http://www.iua.upf.es/mtg/publications/AES116-pcano.pdf
5. Cross, I.: "Music, cognition, culture and evolution", Annals of the New York Academy of Sciences, Vol 930, 2001, pp 28-42. Available at http://www-ext.mus.cam.ac.uk/ ic108/PDF/IRMCNYAS.pdf
6. Dellaert, F., Polzin, T., Waibel, A.: "Recognizing Emotion in Speech", Proc. ICSLP 96 (3), 1996, 1970–1973
7. Eronen, A., Klapuri, A.: "Musical Instrument Recognition Using Cepstral Coefficients and Temporal Features", Proceedings of the IEEE International Conference on Acoustics, Speech and Signal Processing ICASSP 2000, Plymouth, MA, 2000, 753–756
8. Foote, J.: "An overview of audio information retrieval", Multimedia Systems 7 (1), 1999, 307-328. Available at http://www.fxpal.com/people/foote/papers/acm98.pdf
9. Gunn, S.R.: "Support Vector Machines for Classification and Regression", Technical Report, University of Southampton, Faculty of Engineering, Science and Mathematics School of Electronics and Computer Science, May 1998. Available at http://www.ecs.soton.ac.uk/ srg/publications/pdf/SVM.pdf
10. Hip-Hop.pl, Baza MP3, 2004. http://www.hip-hop.pl/mp3/
11. Hsu, C.-W., Chang, C.-C., Lin, C.-J.: "A practical guide to support vector classification". July, 2003, at http://www.csie.ntu.edu.tw/ cjlin/papers/guide/guide.pdf

12. Huron, D., "Sound, music and emotion: An introduction to the experimental research", Seminar presentation, Society for Music Perception and Cognition Conference. Massachusetts Institute of Technology, Cambridge, MA, August 1997. Available at http://dactyl.som.ohio-state.edu/Huron/Publications/huron.emotion.conference.html

13. Juslin, P., Sloboda, J. (eds.): "Music and Emotion: Theory and Research". Series in Affective Science. Oxford University Press 2001

14. Lavy, M.M.: "Emotion and the Experience of Listening to Music. A Framework for Empirical Research". PhD. dissertation, Jesus College, Cambridge, 2001. Available at http://www.scribblin.gs/research/mlavy-thesis-noapp.pdf

15. Li, T., Mitsunori, O.: "Detecting emotion in music". *4th International Conference on Music Information Retrieval ISMIR 2003*, Washington, D.C., and Baltimore, Maryland, October 2003. Available at http://ismir2003.ismir.net/papers/Li.PDF

16. Mantaras, R.L. de, Arcos, J.L.: "AI and Music. From Composition to Expressive Performance", AI Magazine, Fall 2002, 43-58. Available at http://www.iiia.csic.es/ mantaras/AIMag23-03-006.pdf

17. Marasek, K.: private communication, 2004.

18. Peeters, G.: "Automatic classification of large musical instrument databases using hierarchical classifiers with inertia ratio maximization", 115th Audio Engineering Society Convention, 2003, October 1013, New York, NY, USA, Convention Paper 5959.

19. Peeters, G., Rodet, X.: "Hierarchical Gaussian tree with inertia ratio maximization for the classification of large musical instrument databases", Proc. of the 6th Int. Conference on Digital Audio Effects (DAFX-03), London, UK, September 8-11, 2003. Available at http://www.elec.qmul.ac.uk/dafx03/proceedings/pdfs/dafx42.pdf

20. Peeters, G., Rodet, X.: "Automatically selecting signal descriptors for Sound Classification", ICMC 2002 Goteborg (Sweden) September 2002

21. Peltonen, V., Tuomi, J., Klapuri, A., Huopaniemi, J., Sorsa T.: "Computational auditory scene recognition", ICASSP 2002

22. Polski Portal Muzyczny, 2004. http://mp3.com.pl/

23. Rock and Metal, Gery.pl, 2004. http://rockmetal.gery.pl/bazamp3.php

24. Scheirer, E., Slaney, M.: "Construction and Evaluation of a Robust Multifeature Speech/Music Discriminator", Proc. IEEE Int. Conf. on Acoustics, Speech and Signal Processing (ICASSP), 1997. Available at http://www.ee.columbia.edu/ dpwe/e6820/papers/ScheiS97-mussp.pdf

25. Tato, R., Santos, R., Kompe, R., Pardo, J.M.: "Emotional Space Improves Emotion Recognition", *7th International Conference on Spoken Language Processing ICSLP 2002*, Denver, Colorado, September 2002, available at http://lorien.die.upm.es/partners/sony/ICSLP2002.PDF

26. TopLista.pl. Najlepsze strony z muzyka MP3, 2004. http://empetrzy.najlepsze.net/

27. Tzanetakis, G., Cook, P.: "Marsyas: A framework for audio analysis". Organized Sound, 4(3):169175, 2000. Available at http://www-2.cs.cmu.edu/ gtzan/work/pubs/organised00gtzan.pdf

28. Tzanetakis, G., Cook, P.: "Sound Analysis Using MPEG Compressed Audio", IEEE International Conference on Acoustics, Speech and Signal Processing, Istanbul 2000.

29. Tzanetakis, G., Cook, P.: "Musical Genre Classification of Audio Signals", IEEE Transactions on Speech and Audio Processing, Vol. 10, No. 5, July 2002. Available at http://www-2.cs.cmu.edu/ gtzan/work/pubs/tsap02gtzan.pdf

30. Wieczorkowska, A.A., Raś, Z.W.: "Audio Content Description in Sound Databases", In N. Zhong, Y. Yao, J. Liu, and S. Ohsuga (Eds.), "Web Intelligence: Research and Development", LNCS/LNAI 2198, Springer 2001, 175–183

31. Wieczorkowska, A., Wroblewski, J., Slezak, D., Synak, P.: "Application of temporal descriptors to musical instrument sound recognition", Journal of Intelligent Information Systems **21(1)**, Kluwer 2003, 71–93
32. Wirtualna Polska. MP3, 2004. http://mp3.wp.pl/p/strefa/
33. Wold, E., Blum, T., Keslar, D., Wheaton, J.: "Content-Based Classification Search and Retrieval of Audio", IEEE Multimedia May 1999
34. WordIQ Dictionary, 2004, http://www.wordiq.com/dictionary/

Do We Need Automatic Indexing
of Musical Instruments?

Alicja A. Wieczorkowska[2] and Zbigniew W. Raś[1,3]

[1] University of North Carolina, Department of Computer Science,
Charlotte, N.C. 28223, USA
[2] Polish-Japanese Institute of Information Technology,
ul. Koszykowa 86, 02-008 Warsaw, Poland
`alicja@pjwstk.edu.pl`
[3] Polish Academy of Sciences, Institute of Computer Science,
ul. Ordona 21, 01-237 Warsaw, Poland
`ras@uncc.edu`

Abstract. Increasing growth and popularity of multimedia resources available on the Web brought the need to provide new, more advanced tools needed for their search. However, searching through multimedia data is highly non-trivial task that requires content-based indexing of the data. Our research is focused on automatic extraction of information about the sound timbre, and indexing sound data with information about musical instrument(s) playing in a given segment. Our goal is to perform automatic classification of musical instrument sound from real recordings for broad range of sounds, independently on the fundamental frequency of the sound.

1 Sound Data

Automatic sound indexing should allow labelling sound segments with instruments names. Knowledge discovery techniques can be used here for that purpose. First of all, we discover rules that recognise various musical instruments. Next, we can apply these rules, one by one, to unknown sounds. By identifying so called supporting rules, we can point out which instrument is playing or is dominating in a given audio segment, and in what time instants this instrument starts and ends playing.

Generally, identification of musical information can be performed for the following data:

– For audio samples taken from real recordings, representing waveform, and
– For MIDI (Musical Instrument Digital Interface) data.

When we deal with the MIDI files, we have access to highly structured data. We are given information about the pitch (fundamental frequency), effects applied, beginning and end of each note, voices (timbres) used, and about every note that is present in a given time moment. Therefore, the research on MIDI data may concentrate on higher level of musical structure, like key or metrical information.

In the case of recordings, we are dealing with, for each channel we only have access to one-dimensional data, i.e. to single sample representing amplitude of the sound.

L. Bolc et al. (Eds.): IMTCI 2004, LNAI 3490, pp. 239–245, 2005.

Any basic information like pitch (or pitches, if there are more than one sounds), timbre, beginning and end of the sound must be extracted via digital signal processing. There exist many methods of pitch extraction, mostly coming from speech processing. But even extraction of such simple information may produce errors and poses some difficulties. Even for a singular sound, especially octave errors are common, and various errors for border frames, where 2 consequent sounds of different pitch are analysed. Pitch extraction for layered sounds is even more difficult, especially when spectra overlap. Basically, parameters of fundamental frequency trackers are usually adjusted to characteristics of the instrument that is to be tracked, but this cannot be done when we do not know which instrument is playing.

Identification of musical timbre is even more difficult. Timbre is rather subjective quality, defined by ANSI as the attribute of auditory sensation, in terms of which a listener can judge that two sounds, similarly presented and having the same loudness and pitch, are different. Such definition is subjective and not of much use for automatic sound timbre classification. Therefore, musical sounds must be very carefully parameterised to allow automatic timbre recognition. We assume that time domain, spectrum, and evolution of sound features must be taken into account.

2   Basic Parameterisation of Musical Instrument Sounds and Their Classification

Broader research on automatic musical instrument sound classification goes back to last few years. So far, there has been no standard parameterisation used as a classification basis. The sound descriptors used are based on various methods of analysis of time and spectrum domain, with Fourier Transform for spectral analysis being most common. Also, wavelet analysis gains increasing interest for sound and especially for musical sound analysis and representation. Diversity of sound timbres is also used to facilitate data visualisation via sonification, in order to make complex data easier to perceive.

There exist numerous parameterisation methods that have been applied to musical instrument sounds so far, see for instance (Brown, 2001), (Kaminskyj, 2000), and (Wieczorkowska, 1999). In our research, we decided to base our parameterisation on MPEG-7 standard. This standard provides multimedia content description interface (ISO/IEC JTC1/SC29/WG11, 2003), and if this standard gains popularity, the use of MPEG-7 based representation should increase usability of our work.

MPEG-7 provides a universal mechanism for exchanging descriptors of multimedia data. MPEG-7 shall support at least the description of the following types of auditory data: digital audio, analogue audio, MIDI files, model-based audio, and production data (Manjunath, Salembier and Sikora, 2002). The subclasses of auditory data covered by this standard include: sound track (natural audio scene), music, speech, atomic sound effects, symbolic audio representation, and mixing information. In MPEG-7, so-called Multimedia Description Schemes provide the mechanisms, by which we can create ontologies (Sowa, 2000), and dictionaries, in order to describe musical genre as a hierarchical taxonomy or identify a musical instrument from a list of controlled terms. Evolution of spectral sound features in time can be observed in MPEG-7 by means of Hidden Markov Models (HMM). Therefore, indexing a sound in this standard consists of selecting the best fit HMM in a classifier and generating the optimal state sequence (path) for that model. The path describes the evolution of a sound through time using a sequence of integer state indices as representation.

Classifiers used so far in the research on musical instrument sound classification include a wide variety of methods, and the use of HMM is not obligatory in any way. We use MPEG-7 standard as a starting point only, taking sound descriptors as a basis for further processing and research. Low-level descriptors that we use are defined for easy automatic calculation purposes, and they may serve as a basis (for instance AudioSpectrumBasis descriptor) for extraction of new parameters, better suited to instrument classification purposes. High-level descriptors from this standard cannot be extracted automatically, but using low-level descriptors we can calculate new ones, including linear or logical combinations of lower level parameters. Therefore, we decided to choose low-level MPEG-7 descriptors as a research basis, and then search for the classifier.

3   TV-Trees and FS-Trees Used for Content Description Representation of Audio Data

(Wieczorkowska & Ras, 2001) used trees similar to telescopic vector trees (TV-trees) to represent content description of audio data. We briefly summarise the notion we refer to as TV-trees and also the notion of FS-trees. We outline the strategy for constructing TV-trees.

Each audio signal is divided into frames of length four times the fundamental period of the sound. Each frame is represented as a vector consisting of K acoustic descriptors. So, any collection of audio signals can be defined as a set of K-dimensional vectors. This set is represented as $(K \times N)$-matrix where N is the number of frames in all audio signals in our DB. If needed, K can be reduced to a smaller number by using Singular Value Decomposition method [14]. After introducing the notion of a distance (Minkowski's distance is the most popular) between K-dimensional vectors and setting up activity threshold values for all K dimensions, we partition our K-dimensional space into disjoint and dense clusters.

To define descriptor a as an active in a cluster, we require that the span of values of a in that cluster has to be below the activity threshold value. For example, if $\{1, \ldots, 100\}$ is the domain of an attribute and its corresponding activity threshold value is $1/20$, then this attribute is active in a cluster if the distance between values of this attribute for any 2 vectors in that cluster is not greater than 5. Clearly, the activity threshold values are purely subjective and they predefine the notion of a cluster. In spite of the drawback of this subjective definition of a cluster, the freedom to define the domain of an attribute to be active is quite convenient from the application site and welcomed by users. Storage and retrieval of sound files is an example of such an application domain.

Now, we show how to construct TV-tree of order 2 with a goal to represent a set of N points as a collection of clusters associated with leaves of that tree. Initially, the set of N points (initial cluster) is divided into 2 clusters in a such a way that the total number of active dimensions in both clusters is possibly maximised. For each cluster we repeat the same procedure, again maximising the total number of active dimensions in the corresponding sub-clusters. For instance, if $\{[5, 3, 20, 1, 5], [0, 0, 18, 42, 4], [0, 0, 19, 39, 6],$ $[9, 10, 2, 0, 6]\}$ is the initial cluster, $\{1, \ldots, 100\}$ is the domain of each attribute, and the activity threshold value is 1/20, then the following two subclusters will be generated: $\{[0, 0, 18, 42, 4], [0, 0, 19, 39, 6]\}, \{[5, 3, 20, 1, 5], [9, 10, 2, 0, 6]\}$. The initial cluster has only the last dimension active. After split, the first subcluster has 5 dimensions active and second one has the last two dimensions active. We continue this procedure till all subclusters are relatively dense (all points are close to each other with respect to all dimensions). For instance, in the example above, the first subcluster is dense. The underlying structure for this method is a binary tree with nodes storing information about the center of a corresponding cluster, the smallest radius of a sphere containing this cluster, and its list of active dimensions $(d_1, d_2, ..., d_s)$.

The heuristic procedure to construct a binary TV-tree for a collection of audio signals is similar to the strategy used in *Rosetta* or *See5* system for discretising numerical attributes [10], [7]. For m-element domain of an attribute, $m - 1$ splitting points are considered (alternatively, the splitting points can be placed between consecutive dense groups of values of an attribute). Another words, if v_1, v_2 are neighbouring values of the attribute a, then an audio signal with value of a less than or equal to $[v_1 + v_2]/2$ is placed in the left subtree and all other audio signals are placed in the right subtree. When this is done, the total number of active dimensions in both left and right subtree is checked. We repeat this step for each attribute and for its all splitting points mentioned above. A split which gives the maximal number of active dimensions, for both left and right sub-tree, is the winning split and it is used to build two children of the current node. The above procedure is recursively repeated at two children nodes just created.

As we have mentioned earlier, each audio signal is divided into frames of length four times the fundamental period of the sound. In practice, an activity usually spans across several contiguous frames. Thus it makes sense to store data in terms of contiguous sound segments of frames. Frame Segment tree (FS-tree) [14] is a data structure which can be used for compact representation of a sound content.

A frame sequence is a pair $[i, j)$, where $1 \leq i \leq j \leq n$. The interval $[i, j)$ represents the set of all frames between i and j. In other words, $[i, j) = \{k : i \leq k < j\}$. Integer i is the start of the frame sequence $[i, j)$ and j is the end. For example, the frame sequence $[8, 12)$ denotes the set of frames $\{8, 9, 10, 11\}$.

We define a partial ordering $\sqsubseteq$ on the set of all frame sequences as follows: $[i_1, j_1)$ $\sqsubseteq [i_2, j_2)$ iff $i_1 < j_1 \leq i_2 < j_2$. Intuitively, it means that the sequence of frames $[i_1, j_1)$ precedes the sequence of frames $[i_2, j_2)$.

Frame Segment tree (FS-tree) is a binary tree constructed as follows:

– Each node represents a frame sequence $[x, y)$, starting at frame x and including all frames up to, but not including, frame y.

– All leaves are at the same level. The leftmost leaf denotes the interval $[z_1, z_2)$, the second from the left represents the interval $[z_2, z_3)$, the third from the left represents the interval $[z_3, z_4)$, and so on. If N is a node with two children representing the intervals $[p_1, p_2)$, $[p_2, p_3)$, then N represents the interval $[p_1, p_3)$.

– A set of indexes is assigned to each node. Each index is used to denote a single activity or fact associated with the entire frame sequence assigned to that node.

Thus, for example, if a node N represents the frame sequence $[i, j)$, and the activity α occurs in all frames in $[i, j)$, then the label α is assigned to node N.

Now, let us assume that QAS is based both on a TV-tree and an FS-tree and user submitting an audio query to QAS is looking for audio files satisfying certain properties expressed in terms of indexes used in FS-trees. User's audio query contains also a sub-query represented by an incomplete K-dimensional vector a of acoustical descriptors which structure is similar to vectors stored in a TV-tree. For this type of queries, FS-tree is searched first for audio segments satisfying desired properties (index-based search). Next, the TV-tree is searched to identify which segments retrieved from FS-tree have also properties expressed by sub-query a or properties close to them.

Starting from the root, TV-tree is searched recursively checking at each node if:

– its active dimensions cover the complete dimensions of vector a,
– all complete dimensions of vector a, which are active at this node, are close to its center (with respect to l).

If the first condition is satisfied, we stop the search. Otherwise the search is continued.

If both conditions are satisfied, each vector from the cluster associated with that node is checked if it is within the corresponding thresholds values and if so, it is returned as the answer to the query.

TV-tree is a structure originating from textual databases. This structure has been adopted for audio data [14] because segments in audio data are built from frames described by descriptors. The match between descriptors based queries and audio segments does not have to be exact to get successful answer.

4   Hierarchical Classification of Musical Instrument Sounds

The MPEG-7 descriptors extracted for consequent analysing frame are treated as a starting point for further data processing. In order to trace evolution of sound features, we elaborate intermediate descriptors that provide internal representation of sound in our recognition system. These descriptors characterise temporal patterns, specific for particular instruments or instrument groups. The groups may represent instrument family, or articulation (playing technique) applied to the sounds. This is why our system will apply hierarchical classification of musical instrument sounds. The family groups include basically aerophones and chordophones, according to Hornbostel and Sachs classification (Hornbostel and Sachs, 1914). In case of chordophones, we are going to focus on bowed lutes family that includes violin, viola, cello and double bass. The investigated aerophones will include flutes, single reed (clarinet, sax) and double reed (oboe, bassoon) instruments, sometimes called woodwinds, and lip-vibrated, brass instruments, with trumpet, trombone, tuba, and French horn. The articulation applied includes vibrato, pizzicato, and muting.

Hierarchical classification is also one of the means to facilitate correct recognition of musical instrument sounds. Also, obviously classification on the family level yielded better results, as reported in the research performed so far, for instance in (Martin and

Kim, 1998) and (Wieczorkowska, 1999). Another argument for hierarchical classification is that for the user, information about the instrument family or articulation may be sufficient. For example, non-expert user may just look for brass-performed theme, or melody played with sweet vibration, delicate pizzicato motif and so on. Not to mention that some of the users simply may not be familiar with sounds of all instruments, and they may not know how the particular instrument sounds like.

Since we deal with real recordings, the audio data may contain various kinds of sounds, including non-pitched percussive sounds, and in further development of the system, also singing or speech. Therefore, our system should start with classification of type of the signal (speech, music, pitched/non-pitched), performing auditory scene analysis and recognition (Peltonen, Tuomi, Klapuri, Huopaniemi and Sorsa 2002), (Rosenthal and Okuno, 1998), for instance (Wyse and Smoliar, 1998). Then, for pitched musical instrument sounds, the system will proceed with further specification, to get as much information as possible from the audio signal.

5   Conclusion

Automatic indexing of multimedia databases is of great importance, and ISO/IEC decided to provide MPEG-7 standard for multimedia content description. However, this standard does not comprise the extraction of descriptors (nor search algorithms). Therefore, there is a need to elaborate extraction of sound descriptors that would be attached to sound files.

In recent years, there has been a tremendous need for the ability to query and process vast quantities of musical data, which are not easy to describe with mere symbols. Automatic content extraction is clearly needed here and it relates to the ability of identifying the segments of audio in which particular instruments are playing. It also relates to the ability of identifying musical pieces representing different types of emotions, which music clearly evokes, or generating human-like expressive performances. Automatic content extraction may relate to many different types of semantic information related to musical pieces. Some information can be stored as metadata provided by experts, but some has to be computed in an automatic way. We believe that our approach based on KDD techniques should advance research on automatic content extraction, not only on identifying the segments of audio in which particular instruments are playing, but also in identifying the segments of audio containing other, more complex semantic information.

References

1. Brown, J.C., Houix, O., McAdams, S.: "Feature dependence in the automatic identification of musical woodwind instruments", in *J. Acoust. Soc. of America*, 109, 2001, 1064-1072
2. Hornbostel, E.M.V., Sachs, C.: "Systematik der Musikinstrumente. Ein Versuch", in *Zeitschrift fur Ethnologie*, Vol. 46, No. 4-5, 1914, 553-90, available at http: //www.uni-bamberg.de/ppp/ethnomusikologie/HS-Systematik/HS-Systematik
3. ISO/IEC JTC1/SC29/WG11, "MPEG-7 Overview (version 9)", Pattaya, March 2003, available at http://www.chiariglione.org/mpeg/standards/mpeg-7/mpeg-7.htm

4. Kaminskyj, I.: "Multi-feature Musical Instrument Classifier", MikroPolyphonie 6, 2000 (on-line journal at http://farben.latrobe.edu.au/)
5. Manjunath, B.S., Salembier, P., Sikora ,T. (Eds.); "Introduction to MPEG-7. Multimedia Content Description Interface", J. Wiley & Sons, 2002
6. Martin, K.D., Kim, Y.E.: "Musical instrument identification: a pattern-recognition approach", in *Proceedings of 136th Meeting of the Acoustical Society of America*, Norfolk, VA, October, 1998
7. Øhrn, A., Komorowski, J., Skowron, A., Synak, P.: The design and implementation of a knowledge discovery toolkit based on rough sets: The ROSETTA system. In: Polkowski L., Skowron A. (Eds.): *Rough Sets in Knowledge Discovery 1: Methodology and Applications*, number 18 in Studies in Fuzziness and Soft Computing, chapter 19, Physica-Verlag, Heidelberg, Germany (1998) 376–399
8. Opolko, F., Wapnick, J.: "MUMS – McGill University Master Samples", CD's, 1987
9. Peltonen, V., Tuomi, J., Klapuri, A., Huopaniemi, J., Sorsa, T., "Computational Auditory Scene Recognition", *International Conference on Acoustics Speech and Signal Processing ICASSP 2002*, Orlando, Florida, May 2002
10. Quinlan, J.R.: *C4.5: Programs for Machine Learning*, Morgan Kaufmann, San Mateo, California (1993)
11. Rosenthal, D., Okuno, H.G. (Eds.): "Computational Auditory Scene Analysis", *Proceedings of the IJCAI-95 Workshop*, Lawrence Erlbaum Associates, Mahwah, New Jersey, 1998
12. Slezak, D., Synak, P., Wieczorkowska, A., Wroblewski, J.: "KDD-based approach to musical instrument sound recognition", *Foundations of Intelligent Systems*, Proceedings of IS-MIS'02, Lyon, France, LNCS/LNAI, No. 2366, Springer, 2002, 29–37
13. Sowa, J.F.: (2000) Knowledge Representation: Logical, Philosophical, and Computational Foundations, Brooks/Cole Publishing Co., Pacific Grove, CA
14. Subrahmanian, V.S.: *Multimedia Database Systems*. Morgan Kaufmann Publishers, San Francisco, CA (1998)
15. Wieczorkowska, A.: "The recognition efficiency of musical instrument sounds depending on parameterization and type of a classifier", PhD. thesis (in Polish), Technical University of Gdansk, Poland, 1999
16. Wieczorkowska, A., Ras, Z.: "Audio content description in sound databases", in *Web Intelligence: Research and Development, Proceedings of WI'01*, Maebashi City, Japan, LNCS/LNAI 2198, Springer-Verlag, 2001, 175-183
17. Wyse, L., Smoliar, S.W.: "Toward Content-Based Audio Indexing and Retrieval and a New Speaker Discrimination Technique", in Rosenthal D., Okuno H.G. (Eds.): *Computational Auditory Scene Analysis*, Proceedings of the IJCAI-95 Workshop, Lawrence Erlbaum Associates, Mahwah, New Jersey, 1998

Mobile Agents: Preserving Privacy and Anonymity

Aneta Zwierko[1] and Zbigniew Kotulski[1,2]

[1] Warsaw University of Technology, Faculty of Electronics and Information Technology,
Institute of Telecommunications
azwierko@tele.pw.edu.pl
[2] Polish Academy of Sciences, Institute of Fundamental Technological Research
zkotulsk@ippt.gov.pl

Abstract. The mobile agent systems have been well known for years, but recent developments in the mobile technology (mobile phones, middleware) and the artificial intelligence created new research directions. Currently being widely used for the e-commerce and network management are entering into more personal areas of our life, e.g., booking airline tickets, doing shopping, making an appointment at the dentist. Future agents are becoming more like our representatives in the Internet than simple software. To operate efficiently in their new role they need to have the same capabilities as we do, showing their credentials when required and being anonymous when needed. Still they have to fulfill all security requirements for agent systems, including confidentiality, integrity, accountability, and availability. This paper focuses on providing mobile agents with anonymity and privacy. The proposed schemes are based on different cryptographic primitives: the secret sharing scheme and the zero-knowledge proof. The paper also includes a discussion of security of the proposed schemes.

1 Introduction

A software agent is a program that can exercise an individual's or organisation's authority, work autonomously toward a goal, and meet and interact with other agents ([10]). Agents can interact with each other to negotiate contracts and services, participate in auctions or barter. Agents are commonly divided into two types

- stationary agents,
- mobile agents.

The stationary agent resides at a single platform (host), the mobile one can move among different platforms (hosts) at different times.

Agent systems are used for intrusion detection; combined with meta-learning agents create even more powerful tools for detecting security threats in the network environment ([6]). Other fields where agent systems are widely used are management systems for telecommunication networks. The most popular telecommunication management protocol, SNMP (Simple Network Management Protocol), existing for over 20 years, is based on the idea of an agent and a manager. Many similar systems have been proposed in the past and still exist. Mobile agents are also well suited for software distribution and can provide adaptive responses to network events.

L. Bolc et al. (Eds.): IMTCI 2004, LNAI 3490, pp. 246–258, 2005.

Another practical application field for agents systems is the e-commerce where mobile agent-based applications have been proposed and are being developed for a number of diverse business areas like: contract negotiations, service brokering, auctions, and stock trading ([13]). For example, manufacturers can negotiate the delivery of goods and services with suppliers utilising agents. The agents may need to access the supplier's database, transfer money, and negotiate terms of delivery, warranties, and service contracts. Mobile agents representing bidders may meet on an auction house's platform to engage in blind, straight, or Dutch auctions, each employing different strategies and having different financial constraints.

Also producers of the small mobile equipment, such as: cellular phones, personal organisers, car radios, and other consumer electronic devices are introducing more and more functionality into their products, becoming the focus of agent developers. These devices are not continuously on-line and can greatly benefit from a mobile agent's ability to operate autonomously. Agent developers often cite the example of a user launching an agent to make travel, hotel, and dinner reservations by negotiating with other agents, as an illustrative scenario for mobile agent technology.

One of new directions for the development of the agents' systems is a communicative intelligence. The future agents' systems are not only supposed to be communicating or/and interacting with each other but also with real people. They should have the same capabilities as people: to hide their identity when convenient and show their credentials when needed. Preserving privacy and anonymity, so easy in the human environment, is one of the current most significant problems in the agent systems.

Many agent systems are designed to interact with people. Already the research is going on toward agents that will act accordingly to different customs and depending on geographical area where they work; we can imagine an agent being e-teacher, who will differently communicate and work with small child, a school student and an adult. In many other cases such agents, equipped also with some kind of intelligence, will need anonymity, e.g., when working as brokers or insurance agents.

Also many e-commerce systems treat so called trade agents as users' representatives. They can gather and analyse information using artificial intelligence methods (e.g., expert systems), negotiate on behalf of the user and present a set or a subset of negotiation results.

Another research direction is societies of artificial agents and social agents. Social agents are entities that have their own goal and principles. They can interact with one another and exist in a social context. Several types of social agents can be developed: the simplest would be a reactive agent. It just receives a signal from the environment and reacts to it. It has no memory of the past and no goal for the future. The most sophisticated would be the anticipatory agent. It not only has a memory of its past but also has some predictions about the future. It makes decisions basing on these anticipations. Such agents are based on cognitive models of different types.

Such an understanding of the agent systems will widespread with growing use and development of mobile equipment. Also the need for more sophisticated services and systems will be more urgent.

2   Related Work

Many different methods for securing agent systems exist. Here some most popular and interesting are discussed. Note that almost none provide anonymity. However, the systems providing anonymity to different services exist and also are presented in this section.

The most popular methods of securing agent systems are policies. An example of such a concept is the allocation of privileges ([9]). It utilises different types of certificates: the attribute and the policy certificates. To create them an additional Public Key Infrastructure (PKI) is needed. The attribute certificate is bound with an agent: it protects its security relevant information from alteration and assigns privileges to an agent. The second type of certificate is associated with a host and it contains specific policy rules for a given host. This solution does not provide any anonymity or privacy to the agents. Its security is based on the PKI.

Another approach to the agent's security is proposed in [4]. The idea is based on the one-round secure computation and is somehow similar to the concept of the computation with encryption functions, one of the most important methods for protecting agent's integrity. The scheme enables an agent to hide the data computed on one agent platform from all other hosts. The secure computation protocol enables the agent to compute the required data in a way that host cannot learn anything about input, only the output. However, this system does not provide any authorisation or authentication and requires additional communication between the hosts.

In [1] mobile system based on domain architecture is proposed. The system contains centralised authorisation servers, authorisation tokens and authorisation agents. The security of the system is based on PKI. The agents are used to provide authorisation data for any mobile unit, e.g., other agents or mobile hosts.

Another kind of a security scheme for an agent system is evaluated in [11]. It is based on a concept of a master agent (stationary) and slave agents (mobile). The PKI is used to provide security and the system does not offer anonymity to users.

A different proposal of securing an agent system (large-scale and distributed) is outlined in [19]. Its core is the SPKI/SDSI chains of trust and it utilises the certificate delegation infrastructure to provide decentralised authorisation and authentication control. Also the idea of a federation of hosts and a mutual authentication of agent's platforms is used. No anonymity in this system is provided.

Also many similar systems, mostly based on PKI exist; see [3] and [7].

A scheme preserving anonymity is proposed in [5]. The scheme is based on a credential system and offers optional anonymity revocation. Its main idea is based on the oblivious protocols, the encryption circuits and the RSA assumption. However, the possible applications for agent systems are not presented.

Another approach to hide the senders and receivers of messages is presented in [2]. The basic idea was inspired by a public transportation system that naturally hides communication patterns. The "buses" represent messages and each piece of information has its "seat". The buses travel specific, initially chosen routes. Different deterministic and randomised protocols with possible improvements are presented and analysed. However, a possible utilisation for the agent system is not proposed.

One of the systems providing the anonymity during browsing WWW is *Crowds* ([17]). The system hides the action of one user among actions of other users. All users are called *the crowd* and the server issues the request on behalf of its users. The end servers cannot determine which user in reality performed some action.

Some other system providing anonymity, VAST, was described in [14]. Many other anonymity systems were proposed, mostly without any application to agent systems.

3   Security

Providing security is complex and tough for most existing services. It is even more problematic in a distributed environment, such as agents' systems. Most important security requirements are ([10]):

- Confidentiality: any private data stored on a platform or carried by an agent must remain confidential. Mobile agents also need to keep their present location and route confidential.
- Integrity: the agent platform must protect agents from unauthorised modification of their code, state, and data and ensure that only authorised agents or processes carry out any modification of the shared data.
- Accountability: each agent on a given platform must be held accountable for its actions: must be uniquely identified, authenticated, and audited.
- Availability: every agent (local, remote) should be able to access data and services on an agent platform, which responsible to provide them.
- Anonymity: agents' actions and data should be anonymous for hosts and other agents; still accountability should be enabled.

Threats to security generally fall into three main classes: disclosure of information, denial of service, and corruption of information ([10]).

Threats in agent system can be categorized into four groups:

- an agent attacking an agent platform,
- an agent platform attacking an agent,
- an agent attacking another agent on the agent platform,
- other attacks.

The last category covers cases of an agent attacking an agent on another agent platform, and of an agent platform attacking another platform, and also more conventional attacks against the underlying operating system of the agent platform. In this paper we will focus on the threats from an agent's perspective. The possible scenarios of an agent interacting with a malicious host or a group of malicious hosts working together are discussed.

4   Anonymity

The anonymity is very complex and hard to provide in classical services, like browsing web. It is even more complex to provide anonymous agents. Many services require the anonymity to function as in the real world. Many of the e-commerce transactions should be anonymous. If someone is observing actions of an agent, this can be itself a source of a very useful knowledge, even without eavesdropping on agent's data. In many situations privacy and anonymity should be preserved ([12]).

Agents should be able to reveal (or not) their presence to other agents or hosts. For example, an agent shopping for goods and services may wish to do so in privacy. Also during auctions or an initial phase of negotiations agents may want to remain anonymous. In some situations the knowledge that a particular agent is interested in some kind of services can be an advantage for a vendor over its opponents. In addition, an agent may not want to disclose which hosts it has visited before the current one. It may need to keep not only its present location but also the route secret.

However, the anonymity is not always an advantage in agent systems. Every agent has to authenticate itself to other agents or hosts to be able to perform needed actions, e.g. when a financial transaction is to be carried out, the platform may require some form of authentication. Also authentication mechanisms provide accountability for user actions.

An agent's anonymity is also connected with possible security risk. In some cases the security policy of hosts does not accept anonymous agents, or offers different levels of privileges with different anonymity levels. The level of sensitivity of the transaction or data for which agent requests an access may require the agent to offer different degrees of authentication ([17]). Also sometimes the host may not be willing to accept agents that have been on certain platforms, e.g., outside the authority of certain approved security domains. In agent societies where reputation is valued and used as a means to establish trust, other agents through masquerade can harm an agent's reputation. It should be protected by an agent platform.

In this paper we propose two mechanisms of agent's authorisation preserving its anonymity at a certain level.

5   Proposals

This section describes a new idea for the authentication scheme for a mobile agent system that is preserving the agent's anonymity and privacy. Each agent has to authorise itself to the host to be able to perform any action (e.g., buy anything, start negotiations, ask for an offer, etc.). The agent should be anonymous: malicious hosts, even working together, should not be able, basing on an authorisation data, to identify actions performed by each agent. Still, this system should have some management capabilities and auditability: any authorised entity (e.g. manager) should be able to identify actions performed by each agent with every host. So, each pair agent-host should use some different authorisation data, which will be unique, but should not enable any host to differentiate between agents.

First, the utilised cryptographic primitives are briefly introduced: the Merkle's puzzles, concept of the zero-knowledge proofs and the secret sharing scheme. Then, the idea for the new system is presented and details of both proposed solutions are given.

5.1   Cryptographic Primitives

Merkle's Puzzles. Ralph Merkle introduced his concept of cryptographic puzzles in [15]. The goal of this method was to enable secure communication between two parties: A and B, over an insecure channel. The assumptions were that the communication channel could be eavesdropped (by any third party, called E).

Assume that A selected an encryption function F. F is kept by A in secret. A and B agree on a 2nd encryption function, called G:

$$G(plaintext, some\ key) = some\ encrypted\ message.$$

G is publicly known. A will now create N puzzles (denoted as p_i, $0 \leq i \leq N$) in the following way:

$$p_i = G((K, X_i, F(X_i)), R_i),$$

where K is simply a publicly known constant quantity, which remains the same for all messages, X_i are selected by A at random, R_i are the "puzzle" parts, and are also selected at random from the range $(N \cdot (i-1), N \cdot i)$. After creating all puzzles, A sends all of them over an insecure channel to B (they can be observed by E). To solve each puzzle B must guess the R_i. For each message (puzzle), there are N possible values of R_i. If B tries all of them, he is bound to chance upon the right value. This will allow B to recover the message within the puzzle: the triple $(K, X_i, F(X_i))$. B will know that he has correctly decoded the message because the constant part, K, provides enough redundancy to ensure that all messages are not equally likely. Without this provision, B would have no way of knowing which decoded version was correct, for they would all be random bit strings. Once B has decoded the puzzle, he can transmit X_i in clear. $F(X_i)$ can then be used as the encryption key in further communications. B knows $F(X_i)$ because it is in the message. A knows $F(X_i)$ because A knows X_i, which B transmitted in clear, and also knows F, and so can compute $F(X_i)$. E cannot determine $F(X_i)$ because E does not know the F, and so the value of X_i tells E nothing. E's only recourse is to solve all the N puzzles until he encounters the correct puzzle that B solved. So for B it is easy to solve one chosen puzzle, but for E is computationally infeasible to solve all N puzzles.

Zero-Knowledge Proofs. A zero knowledge proof system ([16]) is a protocol, which enables one party to *prove* the possession or knowledge of a "secret"' to another party, without revealing anything about it, in the information-theoretical sense. Such protocols are also known as minimum disclosure proofs. The zero knowledge proof involves two parties: the prover who possesses a secret and wishes to convince the verifier that he indeed has a secret. As mentioned before, the proof is conducted via an interaction between the parties. At the end of the protocol the verifier should be convinced only if the prover knows the secret. If, however, the prover does not know it, the verifier will be sure of it with an overwhelming probability.

The zero-knowledge proof systems are ideal for constructing identification schemes. A direct use of a zero-knowledge proof system allows unilateral authentication of P (Peggy) by V (Victor) and require a large number of iterations, so that verifier knows with an initially assumed probability that prover knows the secret (or has the claimed identity). This can be translated into the requirement that the probability of false acceptance be 2^{-t}, where t is the number of iterations. A zero knowledge identification protocol reveals no information about the secret held by the prover under some reasonable computational assumptions.

Secret Sharing Scheme. A (t, n) threshold secret sharing scheme ([16]) distributes a secret among n participants in such a way that any t of them can recreate the secret. But any $t - 1$ or fewer members gain no information about it. The piece held by a single participant is called a *share* or *shadow* of the secret. A trusted authority, called a dealer, sets up a secret sharing scheme, computes all shares and distributes them to participants via secure channels. The participants hold their shares until some of them decide to combine their shares and recreate the secret. The recovery of the secret is done by the so-called combiner who on behalf of the cooperating group computes the secret. The combiner is successful only if the reconstruction group has at least t members.

Definition 1. *Assume that secrets belong to the set K and shares are from the set S. A (t, n) threshold scheme is a collection of two algorithms. The first algorithm called the dealer*

$$D : K \rightarrow S_1 \times S_2 \times \cdots \times S_n$$

assigns shares to the participants for a random secret $k \in K$. Every participant $P_i \in P$ gets his/her share $s_i \in S_i$. If all share sets S_i are equal we simply say that $s_i \in S$. The second algorithm (the combiner)

$$C : S_{i_1} \times S_{i_2} \times \cdots \times S_{i_j} \rightarrow K$$

takes shares and computes the secret. The combiner recovers the secret only if the number j of different shares is equal to or bigger than t ($j \geq t$). It fails if the number j of shares is smaller than t ($j < t$).

5.2   General Idea

Assume we have a system containing N mobile agents, denoted as a_i, $0 \leq i \leq N$, L hosts, denoted as h_j, $0 \leq j \leq L$ and a manager, denoted as M.

The manager is similar to the trusted third party: he distributes among agents data needed for proper authentication and also distributes among hosts the data needed for validating agents.

Our system is basically built from two pieces: an authentication method, which can be based on a zero-knowledge proof system or a secret sharing scheme and the modified Merkle's puzzles which provide agents with anonymity.

The proposed system has two phases: the initial one and the authentication phase between an agent and a host.

Initial Phase. At the beginning the manager computes the authentication data: AD. The agents will use this to authenticate themselves to hosts. The manager can create different data for different hosts or different security levels; it depends on the specific security requirements of the system. After creation this data is "wrapped" into a puzzle: the manager creates $G((K, AD), R_i)$, where K is a constant, as described in section 5.1 and R_i is a puzzle. The whole set of puzzles P is now distributed among agents: each of them gets its own subset p_i, such that:

$$P = p_1 \cup p_2 \cup \ldots \cup p_N$$

and for each w, q: $w, q \in \{0, \dots, N\}$, $w \neq q$

$$p_w \cap p_q \neq \emptyset \text{ and } p_w \neq p_q.$$

This means that the subsets are not disjunctive: a single authentication data can be used by different agents. But the subset assigned to each agent is unique.

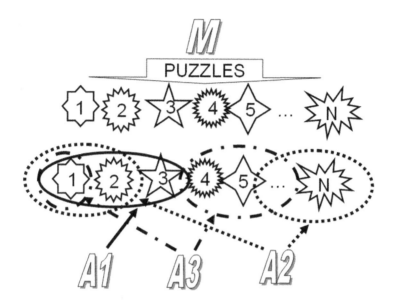

Fig. 1. Initial phase – the puzzles' distribution

Authentication Phase. This takes place when an agent wishes to authenticate itself to a host.

1. An agent sends a randomly selected puzzle to a host.
2. The host solves the puzzle (as described below) and extracts the authentication data.
3. The host checks if the data is proper. He can validate it basing on the information received from the manager. Depending on the underlying authentication method additional steps can be required and the structure of the authentication data and method of validation can differ.
4. If the puzzle (or the extracted authentication data) was previously used within the current host, it asks for another puzzle. If the next verification is successful and the puzzle was not used before, the host provides the agent with required resources or services. If the second puzzle was also already used, agent gets the third chance. If this time the puzzle was also used, the authentication phase fails and has to be started from the beginning.

The Puzzle Generation: Details. As previously stated we utilise Merkle's puzzles (5.1). We propose as G function the DES cipher (or other symmetric cipher) used with a key of approximate length 32 bits. So, the brute-force attack would require approximately 2^{32} computations. The number of puzzles should be of the same order. Using such parameters, a simple brute-force method can be used to solve a single puzzle in a reasonable time and still solving all possible puzzles is computationally hard. Concluding, the puzzles in our system have the following form: $DES((K, AD), R_i)$, where K is a constant and R_i is a key of a symmetric cipher.

5.3   The System Based on the Secret-Sharing Scheme

The first detailed version of our proposal is based on the secret sharing scheme. A brief introduction to secret sharing schemes is in section 1. Our system is utilising the Asmuth and Bloom secure secret sharing scheme ([16]). The secret authentication-message is divided into n-parts: t-1 parts are for host, the rest of them are distributed to agents. The threshold for the secret is t. When an agent comes to a host, it is authorised to perform its actions because it has the t'th part of secret and he can reconstruct it cooperating with the host.

Initial Phase. The manager randomly chooses n prime or co-prime numbers (called public moduli): p_i $(i = 1, \ldots, n, p_0 < p_i < \ldots < p_n)$. They are publicly known. Then, he (playing a role of a dealer in the secret sharing scheme) selects at random an integer s, such that $0 < s < \prod_{i=1}^{t} p_i$. He computes the secret (denoted as k): $k \equiv s$ (mod p_0) and shares: $s_i \equiv s$ (mod p_i). There have to be at least t participants to recreate the secret. The shares for agents and any additional data are wrapped into puzzles: $DES((K, s_i), R_i)$. The $t - 1$ shares are sent to hosts via secure channels. This enables every host to recreate a secret with at least one agent. The manager can create one or more secrets for each host, which later can be used to provide agents with different privileges.

Authentication Phase. The figure below shows general steps of authentication phase in a scheme based on the secret sharing scheme.

$$(1) \text{ Agent } \xrightarrow{puzzle} \text{ Host}$$
(2) Host extracts s_i from the puzzle
(3) Host recreates secret k using his shares and the agent's share
$$(4) \text{ Host } \xrightarrow{\text{is } k \text{ a valid secret}} \text{ Manager}$$

1. When an agent wants to authenticate itself to a host, it sends a puzzle of the form:

$$DES((K, s_i), R_i).$$

Also some other additional data can be included within puzzle (e.g., to which secret this share belongs if the host has more than one).

2. The host solves the puzzle and extracts s_i.
3. All t shares, owned by the host and the agent are used to recreate the secret. The host or the manager can act here as a combiner. The secret can be computed by solving the following system of equations:

$$s_{i_1} \equiv s \pmod{p_{i_1}}$$

$$\vdots$$

$$s_{i_t} \equiv s \pmod{p_{i_t}}.$$

This system has unique solution according to the Chinese Reminder Theorem.

4. After recreating the secret the host has to validate it: he sends it to the manager. Another method of validation is making the secrets public.
5. If the agent's share was previously used, he asks agent for next puzzle as described in the previous section.

The secret can be known to the agent and then be used to provide secure communication between the agent and the host. Alternatively, the host can sent a secret to the agent to authenticate itself.

5.4   The System Based on the Zero-Knowledge Proof

This proposal is not directly based on the zero-knowledge proof, but on the identification system based on zero-knowledge proof. We choose the GQ scheme ([8]) because it is most convenient for our purposes. In this scheme the manager has a pair of RSA-like keys: a public one K_P and a private one k_p. The manager also computes the public modulus $N = p \cdot q$, where p, q are RSA-like primes. For the keys, the following equation is true:

$$K_P \times k_p \equiv 1 \pmod{(p-1) \cdot (q-1)}.$$

The pair (K_P, N) is made public, k_p, p and q are kept secret. The keys can be used for different purposes, not only for our system.

Initial Phase. First the manager computes set of so-called identities, denoted as ID_p, and their equivalents denoted as J_p. It does not matter how J_p is obtained, provided it is obvious for all participants how to obtain J_p from ID_p. The pairs (ID_p, J_p) are public and can be distributed among hosts. The manager wraps the ID_p into the puzzles $(DES((K, ID_p), R_i)$ and computes also secret value for each ID_p:

$$\sigma_p \equiv J_p^{-k_p} \pmod{N}.$$

Each σ_p is distributed with a corresponding puzzle to agents.

Authentication Phase. The diagram below shows general steps of the authentication phase.

(1) Agent $\xrightarrow{puzzle, u}$ Host
(2) Agent $\xleftarrow{b}$ Host
(3) Agent $\xrightarrow{v}$ Host
(4) Host validate v

1. An agent wanting to authorise itself to a host sends him a puzzle with an identity and a challenge. This challenge is a number computed basing on a random value r, $r \in \{1, \ldots, N - 1\}$. It is computed according to:

$$u = r^{K_P} \pmod{N}.$$

2. After receiving the challenge the host chooses a random value $b \in \{1, \ldots, N\}$ and sends it to the agent.

3. Next, the agent computes the v value basing on the number received from the host and on the agent's secret value σ:

$$v \equiv r \times \sigma^b \pmod{N}.$$

4. The host uses information extracted from the puzzle, ID_p to obtain J_p and verifies if v is a proper value. To validate the response from the agent, the host checks if

$$J_p^b \times v_{K_P} \equiv u \pmod{N}.$$

If the equation is true than the agent proved that he knows the proper secret and should gain an access to the specified resources or services.

As in the previous scheme, the manager can compute many identities, which will give agents different kinds of access to hosts. The second phase can be repeated several times to reduce the probability of cheating the host.

6 Security of the Proposed Schemes

The main purpose of the presented schemes is to provide agents with anonymity and still enable them to securely and efficiently authenticate themselves to hosts. Now we will review our proposal from this perspective. We will assume that one or more hosts are malicious, what means they want to identify agent basing on authentication data (e.g., in order to discover his route or to use this data for other purposes). If there is a group of malicious hosts we assume that they are working together sharing any received information.

In the first system, based on a secret sharing scheme, each agent has several shares of the same secret. So, basing on a value of the share, which was sent by the agent in a puzzle, it is impossible to identify the agent that used it, even if it will be used again with this host or any other. Another method for protecting agents anonymity are puzzles: host can easily extract proper information from one puzzle but even for a group of hosts it is infeasible to solve all existing puzzles and identify the agent basing on his unique subset of authentication data.

Also in the system based on the zero-knowledge proof, a host is incapable to retrieve all existing subsets of identities. Even if the agent is using the same identity again, it will probably select other challenge value, so there is no way for host to differ one agent from any other. What differs this scheme from the previous one is that the agent does not have to show the host its secret value to authenticate itself. It can still be kept secret. This is the main advantage of the zero knowledge proof systems.

The necessity of providing the host with a next puzzle if the current one was already used was introduced to prevent the playback attack by the malicious host against an agent. In our system it is infeasible for any host to compute proper authentication data without agent's cooperation. Without the proposed mechanism the host could use the data sent by an agent to masquerade, playing a role of the agent to some other host or to hold the agent responsible for an action that never took place in reality. Another solution of this problem could be utilising timestamps on puzzles.

The authentication systems used in these schemes are well known and secure. There is no need of discussing their security here. Proofs of this can be found in many publications, e.g. [16].

The manager plays in the system a role similar to TTP, so attacks with cooperation of the manager are not discussed in this paper.

To provide agents with full security an additional integrity mechanism should be used. Some are described in [10] and [20].

The proposed schemes enable agents to preserve anonymity and securely authorise themselves to different hosts. They also provide confidentiality of agents route.

7   Conclusions

Recent developments in mobile technology open new fields for applications of mobile agent systems. In future, agents will need to have the same possibilities in the Internet as we have in the real world to act on our behalf. However, preserving anonymity and providing security is still a main issue in many agent systems. In this paper we proposed new authorisation systems, enabling agents to stay anonymous. The presented systems are based on a certain secure secret-sharing scheme and, alternatively, on some zero-knowledge proof. These systems are an effective way of providing the security and the anonymity for mobile agents. The proposed solution is easy to implement in many existing agents' systems, making possible a secure and anonymous communication between agents and other parties.

References

1. Ashley, P., Au, R., Looi, M., Seet, L.T.: Secure Authorisation Agent for Cross-Domain Access Control in a Mobile Computing Environment. ICICS 2001, LNCS 2288, pp. 369–381, Springer 2002
2. Beimel, A., Dolev, S.: Buses for Anonymous Message Delivery, Journal of Cryptology, Volume 16, Number 1, January 2003, 25–39
3. Berkovits, S., Guttman, J.D., Swarup, V.: Authentication for Mobile Agents, in: Mobile Agents and Security, LNCS 1419, pp. 114–136, Springer 1998
4. Cachin, C., Camenisch, J., Kilian, J., Muller, J.: One-Round Secure Computation and Secure Autonomous Agents, Automata, Languages and Programming, pp. 512–523, 2000
5. Camenisch, J., Lysyanskaya, A.: An Efficient System for Non-transferable Anonymous Credentials with Optional Anonymity Revocation, EUROCRYPT 2001, LNCS 2045, pp. 93–118, Springer 2001
6. Chan, P.K., Fan, D.W., Lee, W., Prodromidis, A.L., Stolfo, S.J., Tselepis, S.: Jam: Java agents for meta-learning over distributed databases. In *Proceedings of the 3rd International Conference on Knowledge Discovery and Data Mining*, 1997

7. Corradi, A., Cremonini, M., Montanari, R., Stefanelli, C.: Mobile Agents Integrity for Electronic Commerce Applicatons, *Information Systems* Vol. 24, No. 6, pp. 519–533, 1999

8. Guillou, L., Quisquater, J.-J.: A Practical Zero-knowledge Protocol Fitted to Security Microprocessor Minimizing both Transmission and Memory. Proceedings of Eurocrypt 88, Springer-Verlag Eds, pp. 123–128, 1988.

9. Jansen, W.: Determining Privileges of Mobile Agents, NIST (www.nist.gov)

10. Jansen, W., Karygiannis, T.: NIST Special Publication 800–19 – Mobile Agents Security

11. Chrissikopoulos, V., Katsirelos, G., Kotzanikolaou, P.: Mobile Agents for Secure Electronic Transactions, in N.E. Mastorakis, editor, Recent Advances in Signal Processing and Communications, pp. 363–368. World Scientific Engineering Society, 1999

12. Kulesza, K., Kotulski, Z., Kulesza, K.: On Mobile Agents Anonymity; Formulating Traffic Analysis Problems, in: Advanced Computer Systems, Proceedings of the 10th International Conference, ACS'2003, Miedzyzdroje, October 22th–24th 2003, pp. 15–21.

13. Kulesza, K., Kotulski, Z.: Decision Systems in Distributed Environments: Mobile Agents and Their Role in Modern E-Commerce, in: A.Lapinska, [ed.] Information in 21st Century Society, University of Warmia and Mazury Edition, Olsztyn 2003, pp. 271–282. ISBN 83-89112-60-4.

14. Margasinski, I., Szczypiorski, K.: VAST: Versatile Anonymous System for Web Users. Tenth International Multi-Conference on Advanced Computer Systems ACS'2003, Miedzyzdroje, Poland, October 2003, published as a book chapter by Springer-Verlag, 2004

15. Merkle, R.: Secure Communications over Insecure Channels, in: Communications of the ACM, April 1978 (pp. 294–299).

16. Pieprzyk, J., Hardjono, T., Seberry, J.: Fundamentals of Computer Security, Springer, Berlin 2003

17. Reiter, M. K., Rubin, A. D.: Crowds: Anonymity for Web Transactions, ACM Transactions on Information and System Security, Vol. 1, No. 1, November 1998, pp. 66–92.

18. Reyes, A., Sanchez, E., Barba A.: Routing Management Application Based on Mobile Agents on the INTERNET2. EUNICE 2000, Holland

19. Wangham, M.S., da Silva Fraga, J., Obelheiro, R.R.: A Security Scheme for Mobile Agent Platforms in Large-Scale Systems. CMS 2003, LNCS 2828, pp. 104–116, Springer 2003

20. Zwierko, A., Kotulski, Z.: A new protocol for group authentication providing partial anonymity. NGI 2005 – In Proc of: The First EuroNGI Conference – Traffic Engineering for the Next Generation Internet, 18–20 April 2005, Rome, Italy (accepted)

Author Index

Lecture Notes in Artificial Intelligence (LNAI)

Vol. 3528: P.S. Szczepaniak, J. Kacprzyk, A. Niewiadomski (Eds.), Advances in Web Intelligence. XVII, 513 pages. 2005.

Vol. 3518: T.B. Ho, D. Cheung, H. Liu (Eds.), Advances in Knowledge Discovery and Data Mining. XXI, 864 pages. 2005.

Vol. 3508: P. Bresciani, P. Giorgini, B. Henderson-Sellers, G. Low, M. Winikoff (Eds.), Agent-Oriented Information Systems II. X, 227 pages. 2005.

Vol. 3505: V. Gorodetsky, J. Liu, V. Skormin (Eds.), Autonomous Intelligent Systems: Agents and Data Mining. XIII, 303 pages. 2005.

Vol. 3501: B. Kégl, G. Lapalme (Eds.), Advances in Artificial Intelligence. XV, 458 pages. 2005.

Vol. 3492: P. Blache, E. Stabler, J. Busquets, R. Moot (Eds.), Logical Aspects of Computational Linguistics. X, 363 pages. 2005.

Vol. 3490: L. Bolc, Z. Michalewicz, T. Nishida (Eds.), Intelligent Media Technology for Communicative Intelligence. X, 259 pages. 2005.

Vol. 3488: M.-S. Hacid, N.V. Murray, Z.W. Raś, S. Tsumoto (Eds.), Foundations of Intelligent Systems. XIII, 700 pages. 2005.

Vol. 3487: J. Leite, P. Torroni (Eds.), Computational Logic in Multi-Agent Systems. XII, 281 pages. 2005.

Vol. 3476: J. Leite, A. Omicini, P. Torroni, P. Yolum (Eds.), Declarative Agent Languages and Technologies II. XII, 289 pages. 2005.

Vol. 3464: S.A. Brueckner, G.D.M. Serugendo, A. Karageorgos, R. Nagpal (Eds.), Engineering Self-Organising Systems. XIII, 299 pages. 2005.

Vol. 3452: F. Baader, A. Voronkov (Eds.), Logic for Programming, Artificial Intelligence, and Reasoning. XI, 562 pages. 2005.

Vol. 3451: M.-P. Gleizes, A. Omicini, F. Zambonelli (Eds.), Engineering Societies in the Agents World V. XIII, 349 pages. 2005.

Vol. 3446: T. Ishida, L. Gasser, H. Nakashima (Eds.), Massively Multi-Agent Systems I. XI, 349 pages. 2005.

Vol. 3445: G. Chollet, A. Esposito, M. Faundez-Zanuy, M. Marinaro (Eds.), Nonlinear Speech Modeling and Applications. XIII, 433 pages. 2005.

Vol. 3438: H. Christiansen, P.R. Skadhauge, J. Villadsen (Eds.), Constraint Solving and Language Processing. VIII, 205 pages. 2005.

Vol. 3430: S. Tsumoto, T. Yamaguchi, M. Numao, H. Motoda (Eds.), Active Mining. XII, 349 pages. 2005.

Vol. 3419: B. Faltings, A. Petcu, F. Fages, F. Rossi (Eds.), Constraint Satisfaction and Constraint Logic Programming. X, 217 pages. 2005.

Vol. 3416: M. Böhlen, J. Gamper, W. Polasek, M.A. Wimmer (Eds.), E-Government: Towards Electronic Democracy. XIII, 311 pages. 2005.

Vol. 3415: P. Davidsson, B. Logan, K. Takadama (Eds.), Multi-Agent and Multi-Agent-Based Simulation. X, 265 pages. 2005.

Vol. 3403: B. Ganter, R. Godin (Eds.), Formal Concept Analysis. XI, 419 pages. 2005.

Vol. 3398: D.-K. Baik (Ed.), Systems Modeling and Simulation: Theory and Applications. XIV, 733 pages. 2005.

Vol. 3397: T.G. Kim (Ed.), Artificial Intelligence and Simulation. XV, 711 pages. 2005.

Vol. 3396: R.M. van Eijk, M.-P. Huget, F. Dignum (Eds.), Agent Communication. X, 261 pages. 2005.

Vol. 3394: D. Kudenko, D. Kazakov, E. Alonso (Eds.), Adaptive Agents and Multi-Agent Systems II. VIII, 313 pages. 2005.

Vol. 3392: D. Seipel, M. Hanus, U. Geske, O. Bartenstein (Eds.), Applications of Declarative Programming and Knowledge Management. X, 309 pages. 2005.

Vol. 3374: D. Weyns, H. V.D. Parunak, F. Michel (Eds.), Environments for Multi-Agent Systems. X, 279 pages. 2005.

Vol. 3371: M.W. Barley, N. Kasabov (Eds.), Intelligent Agents and Multi-Agent Systems. X, 329 pages. 2005.

Vol. 3369: V. R. Benjamins, P. Casanovas, J. Breuker, A. Gangemi (Eds.), Law and the Semantic Web. XII, 249 pages. 2005.

Vol. 3366: I. Rahwan, P. Moraitis, C. Reed (Eds.), Argumentation in Multi-Agent Systems. XII, 263 pages. 2005.

Vol. 3359: G. Grieser, Y. Tanaka (Eds.), Intuitive Human Interfaces for Organizing and Accessing Intellectual Assets. XIV, 257 pages. 2005.

Vol. 3346: R.H. Bordini, M. Dastani, J. Dix, A.E.F. Seghrouchni (Eds.), Programming Multi-Agent Systems. XIV, 249 pages. 2005.

Vol. 3345: Y. Cai (Ed.), Ambient Intelligence for Scientific Discovery. XII, 311 pages. 2005.

Vol. 3343: C. Freksa, M. Knauff, B. Krieg-Brückner, B. Nebel, T. Barkowsky (Eds.), Spatial Cognition IV. XIII, 519 pages. 2005.

Vol. 3339: G.I. Webb, X. Yu (Eds.), AI 2004: Advances in Artificial Intelligence. XXII, 1272 pages. 2004.

Vol. 3336: D. Karagiannis, U. Reimer (Eds.), Practical Aspects of Knowledge Management. X, 523 pages. 2004.

Vol. 3327: Y. Shi, W. Xu, Z. Chen (Eds.), Data Mining and Knowledge Management. XIII, 263 pages. 2005.

Vol. 3315: C. Lemaître, C.A. Reyes, J.A. González (Eds.), Advances in Artificial Intelligence – IBERAMIA 2004. XX, 987 pages. 2004.

Vol. 3303: J.A. López, E. Benfenati, W. Dubitzky (Eds.), Knowledge Exploration in Life Science Informatics. X, 249 pages. 2004.

Vol. 3301: G. Kern-Isberner, W. Rödder, F. Kulmann (Eds.), Conditionals, Information, and Inference. XII, 219 pages. 2005.

Vol. 3276: D. Nardi, M. Riedmiller, C. Sammut, J. Santos-Victor (Eds.), RoboCup 2004: Robot Soccer World Cup VIII. XVIII, 678 pages. 2005.

Vol. 3275: P. Perner (Ed.), Advances in Data Mining. VIII, 173 pages. 2004.

Vol. 3265: R.E. Frederking, K.B. Taylor (Eds.), Machine Translation: From Real Users to Research. XI, 392 pages. 2004.

Vol. 3264: G. Paliouras, Y. Sakakibara (Eds.), Grammatical Inference: Algorithms and Applications. XI, 291 pages. 2004.